ARCHITECTURAL MANAGEMENT IN PRACTICE A COMPETITIVE APPROACH

Stephen Emmitt   BA (Hons), Dip Arch, PhD, RIBA

LONGMAN

Addison Wesley Longman
Addison Wesley Longman Limited
Edinburgh Gate, Harlow
Essex CM20 2JE, England
and associated companies throughout the world

Typeset by 32 in 10/12pt ErhardtMT

First published 1999

ISBN 0-582-35696-2

British Library Cataloguing-in-Publication Data
A catalogue entry for this book is available from the British Library

Printed in Malaysia, VVP

ARCHITECTURAL MANAGEMENT IN PRACTICE
A COMPETITIVE APPROACH

CONTENTS

Part 3   ARCHITECTURAL MANAGEMENT IN PRACTICE

LIST OF FIGURES AND TABLES

LIST OF FIGURES

LIST OF TABLES

PREFACE

There are two main drivers behind this book. First, a concern for the quality of the built environment, in particular the challenge of maintaining design quality during the various stages in a building's assembly and use. Second, a concern for those studying subjects associated with the built environment and for those working in the building industry. Both are set against the challenge of building in an information driven, environmentally aware society, with increased competition and the need to provide a better standard of professional service. As such the book is intended to provide both an introduction to the architectural management discipline and a bridge between education and practice.

This book is aimed at building industry professionals who are engaged in providing design-orientated professional services, such as architects, architectural technologists and building surveyors. Although there is an enormous amount of management literature available to the reader there is a paucity of literature which actually addresses issues relating to professional practice management for the built environment. The aim was to write a book that addressed topical management issues within a framework familiar to building industry professionals, accessible to both students and practitioners. The book is also intended to be of interest to clients and other members of the building industry, given its multidisciplinary approach. It is not, however, a 'cook book' of instant solutions to complex challenges: instead the book offers a more holistic approach illustrated with five case studies to show the practical application of some of the theoretical issues.

I should like to acknowledge the help and assistance of many individuals who have been consulted during the preparation of this book. I am particularly grateful to a final year architecture student at the University of Manchester who, at the end of my first guest lecture in architectural management, asked 'will we have to fill in time sheets when we go in to practice?' It led to an interesting debate that highlighted a deeply rooted fear of managerial control among the students; it also, in a round about way, led to this book. I hope it goes some way to addressing those fears.

Stephen Emmitt

CHAPTER 1

INTRODUCTION

Architects, with their systematic and creative problem-solving skills, are well equipped to become effective managers, but paradoxically are notorious for their lack of management ability. The management discipline has not come naturally to the design-orientated profession. It is often seen to be at odds with creative endeavours and often viewed as little more than a specialist interest. The lack of interest in management is difficult to understand, especially when we look at the environment in which the architect works. Building projects are extremely complex, requiring the skills of many individuals from diverse backgrounds who need to be brought together as a well organised team; thus the interaction of sound professional judgement and efficient management systems is essential if a client's goals are to be realised. Modern architects need to be well equipped with design, technological and managerial skills if they are to survive competition from other, more management-orientated, building professionals. That said, and despite clients' demand for the professional management of their concerns, architectural education continues to be concerned first and foremost with 'design'. Such issues related to business and management are largely left to be learned by osmosis in the workplace: an unsatisfactory state of affairs. Restrictions imposed by the professional institution and the lack of management training during education has not equipped architectural firms particularly well for survival in a turbulent and fiercely competitive market; many lack an appropriate management knowledge-base.

Management literature is well developed and provides a comprehensive source of ideas and guidance on formal management systems. However, the principles and techniques applicable to industrial production or mass-consumer markets, based on standardisation, repetitive tasks and products, are inapplicable to the professional firm and may be 'dangerously wrong' (Maister 1993). The majority of professional firms that work in the building industry, such as architects and engineers, are small in size and are faced with managing large numbers of small, extremely complex, bespoke projects, many of which are running concurrently: thus literature about large organisations or large prestigious building projects does not transfer easily to the average professional firm. A further complication is in the very nature of design firms, which could be regarded as unique in the service they provide and one which deserves its own specialist field of knowledge, architectural management.

1

Perhaps because of the lack of interest the literature on practice management and architectural management is sparse by comparison with the vast amount of literature about business management and organisational behaviour.

1.1.1 The field

1962 was a significant year in the history of architectural management: it was the year in which the first study of the architectural profession was published, *The Architect and his Office* (RIBA 1962). Although the publication put down a number of markers for practitioners to follow, many of the issues were largely ignored. Thirty years later the RIBA published a series of reports, the *Strategic Studies*, (RIBA 1992, 1993) that, together with a few independent studies (e.g. Symes *et al.* 1995), echoed the findings of the earlier survey, concluding that the architectural profession must develop management skills if it was to survive. Since 1962 the boundaries in which architectural practices carry out their business have been squeezed, partly because architects have abrogated responsibility for the non-design aspects of a project to others (now their competitors) and partly because the marketplace for professional service firms has become more competitive. It is widely acknowledged that the manner in which buildings are commissioned and procured has changed rapidly over recent years, and will continue to evolve, partly in response to advances in technology and partly in response to increased competition within the building industry. Set against this background many have argued that architectural firms in particular have been slow to react to change, unable or unwilling to acknowledge increased opportunities and greater competition from other, management-orientated, firms within the industry. Indeed, the growth in management-orientated professional service firms has been largely at the expense of the design-orientated architectural firms. It would be reasonable to argue that architectural practices have adopted the dictum 'less is more' a little too literally, and have only recently woken up to the fact that less service usually translates to less business.

During the 1960s there was considerable interest in management from within the architectural profession, fuelled in part by the publication of *The Architect and his Office* and the relatively high profile given to the subject in the architectural press at the time. In 1964 chartered architects Brunton, Baden Hellard and Boobyer published *Management Applied to Architectural Practice* in which the term 'architectural management' was used to refer to both office management and job management. Their publication coincided with the architectural profession's growing interest in management during the 1960s, an era often referred to as the 'decade of management'. Interest in architectural management was abruptly curtailed with the exposure of John Poulson and other corrupt architects during the 1970s, whose business-like approach to architecture had been taken too far. Architects, it appeared, were just as likely to be misled by the lure of quick profits as others associated with building. Instead of learning from these highly publicised mistakes, the response from the majority of the profession was to retreat into professionalism at a time when other players in the market were adopting a thoroughly modern approach to business. Architects were increasingly finding themselves pushed out of the decision-making process. An attempt to redress the balance came in the 1980s in the form of the Alternative Method of Management (AMM), but was not adopted widely because of architects' weak position in the marketplace. It was not until the early 1990s that any momentum for architectural management as a separate discipline developed, which coincided with the RIBA's 'strategic study' and the development of the International Council of Building (CIB)'s 'Architectural Management' working group.

Architectural management, then, is a relatively new field in which scholarly work is limited in quantity but growing in both stature and credibility: a field yet to establish itself. This book attempts to challenge existing beliefs and practices and to provide a number of concepts which may be employed by architectural firms to help them compete in a competitive marketplace. The book looks at the interface of architecture and management from a slightly different perspective, a perspective based on competitive advantage and the pressures of market forces. In particular, it looks at architectural management from the viewpoint of the professional design service firm in which job management and the management of the firm are inextricably linked.

1.1.2　Scope of the study

Management literature is notorious for the jargon it uses to describe new management techniques. Techniques such as benchmarking, economic value analysis, total quality management, and re-engineering are each powerful tools but, with the exception of re-engineering, these tools are used to do what is already being done, only in a different way (Druker 1995). For the designer, it is often difficult to apply these techniques since the management books frequently use examples drawn from big businesses, such as IBM, which bear little resemblance to the professional's more familiar 'small firm' environment. So in an attempt to make this book accessible to the design-orientated professional the jargon has been kept to a minimum and management issues relevant to the small professional service firm form the core of the book. It is not a 'how to' book; instead it offers a holistic approach in which the theoretical issues are outlined and then illustrated by examples drawn from practice. The methods adopted by other authors in the field have ranged from asking practitioners what they do – and using their answers to support their arguments – to participant observation in an architect's office. There is a problem when asking architects to discuss how they carry out their business in that there is a tendency for them to portray themselves as they wish to be seen (Ellis and Cuff 1989), a professional image for public consumption and one that may not necessarily reflect their actual behaviour. A more honest approach is to report what actually happens from inside the office through participant observation, a technique used by Cuff (1991). Both approaches are valid and have been used here; in particular it was felt that the issues raised in this book should be illustrated by a case study based on participant observation. By focusing on one firm, the reasons behind the adoption of architectural management techniques helps to show the time required to carry out such a transformation and the implications of adopting a competitive approach. The firm was a medium-sized architectural practice that had attempted to retain its market share and improve the quality of the finished buildings through the adoption of a number of management innovations. Over a six-year period the firm developed from a traditional architectural office (design-orientated) into an architectural practice that designed, costed, project managed, constructed and maintained buildings, a development made possible through the implementation of architectural management tools and techniques. The firm employed the skills of project managers, construction managers, cost managers, site agents, planning supervisors, architectural technologists and architects within an architectural managed environment (the design-orientated professional service firm) all held together by a very special ingredient: the architect's design vision.

1.1.3   Terms and conventions

Architects, architectural technologists and building surveyors are distinct professional groups, each with its own professional institution and professional identity. As well as offering professional services within the building sector, all three groups have one special feature in common: they all offer varying degrees of design services to their clients. For the purposes of this book, and at the risk of upsetting three professional institutions and their members simultaneously, the term 'architectural firm' is used to cover all design-orientated professional service firms, such as architects, technologists and building surveyors. Their businesses range from solo practitioners, to partnerships, co-operatives, and group practices, all of which may be legally constituted as unlimited, limited or public limited companies. Most of these firms tend to be constituted as partnerships (with associates, partners and principals) and are referred to as 'practices' in the tradition of the professional ethic. More recently there has been a move towards the formation of limited companies (with directors and managing directors), a policy discouraged by the RIBA until relatively recently. The stance adopted for this book is that architectural practices, regardless of size or legal constitution, need to consider themselves first and foremost as businesses if competitive advantage is to be achieved; therefore the term used throughout this book is 'firm' or more specifically 'professional service firm', used to encompass all legal forms of practice.

1.1.4   Readership

This book is aimed at building industry professionals who are engaged in providing design-orientated professional services, such as architects, architectural technologists and building surveyors. Design-orientated professionals are often daunted by the range of management books, all claiming to offer solutions and magic formulae for successful business, but which are largely irrelevant to professional service firms. The aim was to write a book that addressed topical management issues within a framework familiar to building industry professionals that would be accessible to both students and practitioners, but which went beyond issues of professional practice. The book is also intended to be of interest to clients and other members of the building industry, given its multidisciplinary approach.

More specifically, to the professional practitioner, the book provides an accessible overview of topical management issues, many of which, such as project management by architects, have received little coverage in the professional journals. The book is primarily addressed to the small- to medium-sized firms, although the issues discussed will also be of interest to solo practitioners and larger firms. It is written partly out of concern for the architectural profession, but certainly not in defence of it, and through the models presented the need to transform architectural practice into a competitive professional service firm is made clear. To the client, the importance of the client's contribution to building, in particular the importance of the link between the client and the designer, is emphasised throughout this book. Many of the issues confronting architectural firms are of equal concern to clients and the book offers a comprehensive overview of the challenges ahead. To the student, the book provides an introduction to some of the management issues which may be relevant to both academic study and of use in practice. Read alongside other texts, the book will go some way to preparing students to contribute to the challenging environment of architectural practice. Finally, to the researcher, the work reported in the book provides information gathered over many years from within an architectural firm that was undergoing a considerable transformation. Presented as 'warts and all' reports, the case studies provide a rare insight into the professional design firm; it is hoped that it will form the catalyst for further research into the architectural management field.

1.1.5 Agenda

In addition to the Introduction and the Epilogue, the material is presented in four parts for ease of reading. Part 1 forms the background to the book, investigating the development of the architectural management discipline and the professional values of those involved in the building industry. Having set the scene, Part 2 concentrates on the management of the professional service firm, in particular the management of human resources within the firm, the management of information networks and the development of effective business strategies. Part 3 critically examines architectural management in context, in which a number of essential management areas are discussed theoretically and illustrated with examples drawn from practice and the case study firm. Many of the issues highlighted have been overlooked by most architectural practices in the past and some of the barriers to their adoption are addressed. The underlying theme of the book is competitive advantage and the final section, Part 4, looks at the design-orientated (architect led) professional service firm and the challenge of selling its services in an overcrowded, rapidly changing marketplace. More specifically:

Part 1: Chapter 2 describes the history of architectural management during the twentieth century. The paucity of information addressed specifically to the design professional is highlighted, together with important developments in the field. The scope and nature of architectural management within the context of the building industry is addressed in Chapter 3 and the need for an advocate of architectural management is discussed. Chapter 4 looks at the turbulent market in which the professional firm competes, in particular the fragmented nature of the building industry and the roles of the different players who are, in many cases, competing for the same commission.

Part 2: The most important asset of a professional service firm is its staff – more specifically, their knowledge and skills. Chapter 5 investigates issues of leadership, motivation, knowledge acquisition and continuing professional development, before turning to the issue of human asset management, in both the office and the temporary project team. In addition to the management of the knowledge base, the firm also has to manage the rapidly increasing volume of information. Issues of information overload and gatekeeping mechanisms are discussed in relation to the project and the product information networks in Chapter 6, which concludes by exploring the concept of architects as information managers. Although there is no single business strategy to suit all firms, Chapter 7 discusses a number of approaches to the development of an effective business strategy. The issue of fee bidding and the development of new service provision is discussed against the need to balance risk and reward. These issues naturally lead on to a debate about how to achieve competitive advantage, either through specialisation or diversity. The chapter concludes with a look at possible approaches to the management of environmentally responsible ideals and practices.

Part 3: Fundamental to the delivery of a well-designed and well-constructed product is the issue of procurement, client empathy and briefing. Chapter 8 investigates the link between client and architect, and the rise of the independent project manager. Closely linked to the briefing process, it is an area in which the architectural practice must be proficient if it is to maintain contact with the client. The consequences of adopting or ignoring project management are addressed in the case study. Two contrasting approaches to design management are described and compared in Chapter 9; the familiar method of one individual administering a job from inception to completion is contrasted with a sequential model where individuals are responsible for clearly defined segments of individual jobs. A case study is used to illustrate how an architectural practice changed from the traditional model to the sequential model and how it impacted on time, cost and quality control. Chapter 10 deals with issues of quality, from quality control to quality assurance and total quality management. The problems of implementing managerial control over the creative process and more specifically over creative individuals is addressed and then illustrated by the case study which describes the implementation of quality assurance. The management of the construction process is an area from which many architectural practices have withdrawn or have been pushed out by other disciplines, and the importance of the link between design office and building site is discussed in Chapter 11. The case study illustrates how an architectural practice can manage the construction process and reduce the cost of the finished building through effective management. The adoption of such an approach has implications for the quality of the finished product and feedback to the design process. In particular the link back to procurement strategy and client empathy is then discussed as part of the firm's business strategy.

Part 4: Following on from the issues raised through the theoretical debates and the case studies, Chapter 12 puts forward a model of the architect-led professional service firm, the product champion, focusing on staff structure and the multidisciplinary skills base. Such an approach leads on to questions about the traditional office base and the possibilities of networking staff from remote sites. Transformation from a traditional architectural practice to a firm employing architectural management systems, a firm with competitive advantage, is illustrated by the final case study. It is of little use developing a competitive professional service firm if potential clients are unaware of the services on offer; Chapter 13 contests that the challenge for the architect-led practice will be to sell services to clients who may well have a fixed view of what an architectural practice can deliver. Effective business promotion is an essential element of the competitive firm and various strategies are discussed.

Epilogue: Chapter 14 considers some of the main themes emerging from the book and highlights some of the issues likely to confront the architect-led professional service firm in the near future.

Part 1

VALUES AND CONCEPTS

CHAPTER 2

EVOLVING ARCHITECTURAL MANAGEMENT

This chapter starts by investigating the special nature of the architectural firm, the design-orientated professional service firm, before turning to the issue of architects and management. A definition of architectural management is then proposed and the evolution of the architectural management field traced from its early beginnings, through its heyday in the 1960s to the present day.

2.1 THE PROFESSIONAL SERVICE FIRM

The grouping together of professionals to sell their services to clients more effectively than could be achieved by working alone is known as a 'professional service firm' (Maister 1989, 1993). Such groupings of professionals have also been referred to as 'people firms' (Parry 1991) or 'knowledge based organisations' (Winch and Schneider 1993) since their principal asset is the combined skill, knowledge and experience of their staff. More specifically the professional service firm comprises a number of highly skilled individuals who carry out complex work for others, their clients. According to the leading authority in this field, David Maister (1993), there are two special characteristics of the professional service firm: customisation and client contact. Together they demand that a firm attracts and retains highly skilled individuals – its assets are its people. The high degree of customisation causes difficulties in terms of management, especially since situations may be relatively unfamiliar and thus standard management techniques inappropriate. The high degree of client contact, often face-to-face communication, requires very special interpersonal skills for which quality and service have special meanings. Quality and service must also be managed – the theme of this book.

Professional practitioners are first and foremost concerned with satisfying their clients' needs and are notorious for regarding the running of their businesses as a secondary part of their work. As such they are often charged with ineffective management of their business, squandering profits and missing opportunities to expand the firm, leading to lower profits and threatening their firm's long-term

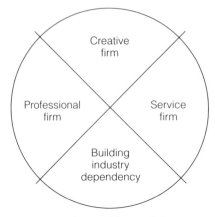

Fig. 2.1   The 'special' characteristics of the architectural firm

viability (Maister 1993). Architectural firms have not escaped from such criticism (e.g. RIBA 1962, 1992), seemingly ill at ease with the concept of business management despite the fact that architecture is both a profession and a business (Sharp 1986, 1991). Architecture is a business and the architectural firm must be managed accordingly. Some authors claim that the task of managing a design firm is different from managing a business because it operates under 'special rules' associated with the creative process (e.g. Coxe 1980). In part this is true. However, it should be recognised that architectural firms have a number of characteristics that set them apart from other types of business organisation (Figure 2.1). According to Winch and Schneider (1993) architectural firms can be distinguished from other knowledge-based organisations because they provide a service, they are regulated by professional bodies, and they are creative. They are also dependent on one particular industry: building (Gutman 1988) – a characteristic frequently taken for granted but one that affects their business the most. Combined, these four characteristics help to distinguish architectural firms from other knowledge-based professional service firms (see Figure 2.1).

2.1.1   Service firms

The majority of architects have been described as working in the building design, information and site-inspection business (Sharp 1991). More specifically, architectural firms are concerned with providing a service to a client which usually results in a product: the finished building. However, the quality of their service, as perceived by the client, is based on the overall experience rather than solely on the finished product (Winch and Schneider 1993). Buildings are expensive products and architectural firms must deliver to their clients as much expertise in the procurement and management of the finished product as in its design. Thus the quality of the service provided during the process that leads to the finished building, the quality of the finished product and the quality of the service provided once the building is in use, are all equally important. The whole service provision must be managed and delivered professionally. To succeed in business requires the same obsession with detail that is needed in the design of buildings – a fastidious approach to every aspect of the firm in pursuit of quality service provision.

2.1.2   Professional firms

Architects, architectural technologists and building surveyors are all regulated by their professional institutions and bound by their respective Code of Conduct. Although the professional institutions were originally set up as a means of protecting their members' interests, some of their professional rules have limited the manner in which their members can trade, for example by restricting the manner in which they may advertise their services. The professional institutions are often perceived by their members as restricting the manner in which they can trade. Registered firms must comply with the relevant professional institution's Code of Conduct, otherwise the firm is free to act in any legal way it chooses (Sharp 1991). Perhaps the biggest criticism of the architectural profession is that it has an insular culture, is too self-referential, and is too protective (RIBA 1993); it is a professional culture characterised by segregated education, outdated values and inappropriate role models. Such claims have been made of other professions and so in the context of this book it is important to recognise that change is likely to be resisted by the institutions. If change is to come about it is more likely to be through the actions of architects in private practice (Lyall 1980).

2.1.3   Creative firms

Architectural firms are commissioned by clients to provide individual design solutions to unique problems; they are primarily concerned with generating and maintaining creativity, an activity that many architects claim they would like to spend more time on in the modern office. Judith Blau (1984) found that architects had a strong identification with work that was creative despite the fact that they worked in highly specialised or very technical areas. Furthermore, 80 per cent wanted more design work (including greater involvement at the initial design stage) and to be able to work more autonomously. But design is only a small part of an architect's job in practice. Much of their time will be spent on issues relating to the construction of the building, legal and financial considerations, the administration of individual jobs and personal time management. When analysed, many of the individual's daily activities are concerned with issues generally referred to as management, yet it has been argued that management is a mystery to many design professionals, unsure whether it refers to business affairs or to bureaucratic control of the firm (Kaderlan 1991). For many in the profession, management is seen as something that has to be done, rather than something that underpins everything carried out in architectural practice. For others the ideas associated with architectural management are often viewed as subversive, seen as something different and separate to design, ideals ingrained in the young architect during architectural education.

2.1.4   Building industry dependency

Architectural firms have a special relationship with one industry: building. This is not a homogeneous industry but is made up of many disparate strands. Building is essentially an industry of assembly. Regardless of the amount of prefabrication off-site there are always factors unique to individual sites, therefore the specific characteristics of each individual contract will vary from one another within the same overall principles (Bennett 1981). Furthermore, buildings are fixed to a particular location which means that materials and labour have to be taken to the site; thus building can never be a manufacturing process. Building is a complex problem because of the many different skills required during the different stages of the product's lifecycle, requiring inputs from different areas at varying times. Managerial controls are specific to individual projects which generate challenges, opportunities and solutions that differ from traditional manufacturing industries, based on repetition and mass-production techniques. As such, firms associated with building are continuously facing change. This is particularly so of the architectural office where both anticipation and response to change will determine the firm's success in the marketplace.

Building industry dependency is further complicated because architectural firms are concerned with issues of design and production, themselves culturally different worlds. These two different worlds are brought together by a temporary bridge in the form of a building project. Issues of conceptual design have been studied by the design methods authors. Issues relating to detailed design have been largely ignored, while issues about the production of the building have been addressed outside the architectural literature. Because architects are concerned with both design and production they are potentially influenced by many other contributors to the building industry, many of whom are simultaneously working with and competing against them. As such the architectural firm cannot isolate itself from the building industry and the adoption of new management concepts by others in the industry will affect the architectural firm to a certain degree.

2.2   ARCHITECTS AND MANAGEMENT

The need to manage both architectural firms and building projects is not new. For those in practice the daily challenge of producing good architecture centres around three core areas, namely design, technology and management; three separate but interdependent areas that rely on clear communication. Since architecture and management are concerned with communication, the two fields are arguably closer than we might at first expect; designers are primarily concerned with communication through visual means and managers primarily through interpersonal communication. Having said that, management is often perceived by architects as time-consuming, inflexible and overly bureaucratic, something that detracts from creativity, something that suppresses rather than generates, hinders rather than helps. The mismatch between managers and professionals, or more specifically the 'creatives', is a common theme: managers are seen to lie outside the architectural culture (Cuff 1991). Good management should support, not interfere with, the creation of good architecture. Although viewed as perfunctory to design, architectural management is certainly an issue that cannot be ignored by the directors of design firms. Nor can it be ignored by individual members of staff within the firm because management should pervade all aspects of the architect's job. Management is a complex area and to become a good manager an individual must develop a wide range of skills and attributes, most of which are not taught in design schools (Kaderlan 1991).

More significantly, design and management demand quite different skills. Problems often arise when an individual attempts to combine the two, often leading to an internal struggle between the chaotic world of design and the restraint of management. To balance the inspirational (eccentric and fragile) world of design with the ordered (sober and robust) world of management is the complex task of the design-orientated professional service firm. Management and design functions need to be both integrated and separated. Space must be found for subtlety and quality of design, delivered professionally to consistently high standards within a managerial framework. The special nature of design and the challenge of managing creative individuals is at the core of architectural management.

As mentioned in the introduction, despite the enormous volume of published material in the management field, literature in the more specialised area of professional service firm management is somewhat sparse by comparison and in very short supply where architectural practice is concerned. There are a number of contributing factors for this. First, directors of architectural firms are reluctant to discuss the business side of their firm since they are concerned that it may help their competitors, from within and outside the profession. Second, the field would appear to be seen as a specialist interest (e.g. Freling 1995) and therefore of little importance compared with other design-related issues. Third, few educational institutions offer courses in architectural management. 'Professional practice' is often seen as the last step to chartered architect status – a right of passage.

2.3   ARCHITECTURAL MANAGEMENT: TOWARDS A DEFINITION

Before discussing architectural management in any detail it is helpful to have a clear understanding of what is meant by the source words architecture and management, since both are open to wide interpretation. There have been many attempts to define architecture – some more successfully than others – but perhaps the most lucid definition was provided by an engineer, Ove Arup, who wrote 'to build wisely, with sensitivity towards human needs and joys, with an ear to the ground and an eye for the hopeful future, that is architecture' (Arup 1970). He went on to conclude 'thus defined, everything is architecture'. For the purposes of this book the word architecture is interpreted widely: it is an art, a science, a business and more importantly a professional service that must be managed. The word management is equally problematic. Management literature can be grouped under three different areas: scientific management, human relations and systems theory. The field has grown rapidly since it originated in 1900 with Frederick W. Taylor's scientific management theory and Henri Fayol's first complete theory of management in 1916 (George 1972). However, it was not until 1955 that Herbert Simon placed emphasis on human behaviour in management. Management is essentially concerned with communication, best illustrated by Gary Kreps' book *Organisational Communication* (1990). More recently managers are being urged to be more creative and architects better managers, as if to reinforce the coming together of two opposite but attractive worlds. Design and management should be seen as having a symbiotic relationship and a bridge between the two worlds can be found in architectural management.

Although the field is, in many respects, still in its infancy, the term architectural management has been in use since the 1960s and has been interpreted in a variety of ways since. Chartered architects Brunton, Baden Hellard and Boobyer (1964:9) provide an early description:

> architectural management falls into two distinct parts, office or practice management and project management. The former provides an overall framework within which many individual projects will be commenced, managed and completed. In principle both parts have the same objectives but the techniques vary and mesh only at certain points.

Once defined, Brunton *et al.* concentrated on the management of the firm (practice management). The separation of the firm's management and individual job management is a common trait in the small amount of literature available and, arguably, potentially misleading since the two mesh constantly (to use Brunton *et al*'s terminology). Management of the firm is concerned with the management of people, premises and finances. Combined, the working environment of the office, the social characteristics of the staff employed and the financial management of the business will create the character, or culture, of the firm; a unique culture that will directly affect the manner in which individual jobs are administered. Management of individual jobs is an equally complex area and one that affects the culture of the firm. The blood that runs through the veins of individual projects also runs through the veins of the firm: architectural management is a symbiotic relationship between the two, and should form an essential component of a firm's culture.

Within the pages of the *International Journal of Architectural Management, Practice and Research* several attempts have been made to describe and define architectural management, from the specific (e.g. Boissevain and Prins 1993) to the holistic (e.g. Nicholson 1995). Writing from the perspective of a Dutch architectural practice over 30 years after Brunton *et al.*, Freling (1995) has provided a most thought-provoking description; for him architectural management 'is only a tool, a sort of ordered way of thinking. More importantly, and I think more interestingly from the view of an architect's firm, is enlarging its knowledge about product, process and communication.'

Whatever the definition, the architectural management discipline is first and foremost concerned with people and communication. For example, the communication of an architectural firm's services (their people skills) to potential clients, the communication of information between people during the design and construction process and the control of these interactions, fall within the architectural management discipline. For the purposes of this book, the term 'architectural management' is used to cover all management functions associated with a competitive professional service firm. For example, project management, design management, construction management and facilities management are all covered by the umbrella of architectural management, areas of specialist interest which are themselves interdependent on quality management and human resource management. In the context of this book, architectural management is best summed up by Freling (1995) who concluded that architectural management 'is a continuous thinking about the position of the architect in the market and the tools he needs for his profession and position'.

2.4   THE DEVELOPMENT OF ARCHITECTURAL MANAGEMENT

As with any historical study, one of the most difficult stages is to find a convenient starting point, and the development of the architectural management discipline is no different in that respect. The history of the architectural profession is well documented (e.g. Kaye 1960; Saint 1983; Powell 1997) in which it is clear that architectural practice was rarely considered as a business until after the Second World War, and even then practitioners appeared concerned about the conflict of business and professional ethics, demonstrating indifference to management. Over the years the small number of books printed tend to fall into two distinct categories. First are the 'how to' books which offer advice on a wide range of issues facing the practitioner. Examples include Hamilton Turner's *Practice and Procedure* (1925), *The Architect in Practice* (Willis and George 1952) and *Architectural Practice and Procedure* (Bennett 1981). Second are the books that have challenged the established patterns of practice through their promotion of architectural practice as a business that must be managed: examples are Wills (1941), Brunton *et al.* (1964), Coxe (1980), Sharp (1986), Kaderlan (1991) and Harrigan and Neel (1996). An early example, *This Business of Architecture* (Wills 1941), argued that the profession should shake off the constraints of outdated ideals and adopt business methods in order to become successful. In a sense this marked a change in attitude and approach to architectural practice although it was the publication of the RIBA's first study of architectural practice in the early 1960s, *The Architect and his Office*, that set the agenda for developments in the architectural management field – a convenient starting point.

2.4.1   The 'decade of management'

Indifference to management among architects began to change and the 1960s became an exciting time for those interested in architectural management. From the late 1950s the RIBA had started to work towards making architects more efficient, driven partly by an economic boom and partly by growing competition from others in the industry. A number of publications and initiatives came out of this period of which the most cited, *The Architect and his Office* (1962), found that practices were too small and management skills lacking, blaming architectural education and architects' failure to co-ordinate design and construction. The RIBA's publication had two, quite opposite, effects. On the one hand it informed everyone of architects' incompetence where costs and organisation were concerned (Lyall 1980), thus providing competitors with ammunition in their fight for control of the building process – they no longer had to suggest architects could not manage since they had said it themselves! On the other hand the report was used as the stimulus to develop management techniques for architectural firms. The initiatives to embrace management by the profession resulted in the formulation and publication of the RIBA's *Plan of Work* (1964), Ronald Green's *The Architect's Guide to Running a Job* (1962) and the RIBA's *Handbook of Architectural Practice and Management* (1964), all of which are still used today (in revised format).

With the profession focused on management came the first book concerned with architectural management, *Management Applied to Architectural Practice* (Brunton *et al.* 1964), discussed above, and *Architecture: A Profession and a Business* (Lapidus 1967). The message, it seemed, was still not getting through, for in 1968 Esher and Llewellyn Davies, writing in the *RIBA Journal*, urged architects to develop management skills to stay in control. If they continued to be complacent they would find themselves at the edge of the decision-making process sooner rather than later. The balance in building was shifting in favour of the contractors.

The period also saw the creation of a new class of architect: the architectural technician. The 1958 Oxford Conference proposed the abolition of pupillage and part-time courses for architects and with it the formal creation of the architectural technician discipline. This essentially created a two-tier system: those responsible for controlling design – architects – and those with practical skills – the architectural technicians. To reinforce the distinction the technicians were given lessons in design appreciation rather than studio-based projects (Crinson and Lubbock 1994:141–42). In 1965 the Society of Architectural and Allied Technicians was formed. This has since evolved into the British Institute of Architectural Technologists (BIAT) whose members now compete with architects for commissions.

2.4.2   A long shadow

It is impossible to write about the developments in architectural management during this period without commenting on John Poulson. An unqualified architect from a small town in Yorkshire, Poulson set up an architectural practice in the 1930s which by the 1960s had grown to the largest in Europe. Infamous for his lack of design skills, he was regarded as a good businessman, although according to Tomkinson and Gillard (1980:12) there was little evidence of any sophisticated business methods. Instead, 'Poulson's method was to promise almost anything to the client together with a totally unreasonable delivery date for his drawings' (while such a technique is common practice now, it was unusual at the time). Poulson was important since he had acted in a totally new way to the architectural profession of the time. He was one of the first to introduce the concept of a 'multidisciplinary' practice, thus controlling every professional service required for building projects (and since adopted by more reputable firms). By 1969 Poulson's empire was in financial trouble and the revelations that followed his bankruptcy and trial exposed corruption throughout the building industry and government (Tomkinson and Gillard 1980). Poulson and the chief architect to Birmingham, Maudsley, were the first of a small number of architects found to be corrupt and sent to gaol during the 1970s.

The fact that architects were as susceptible to commercial pressures as anyone else involved in building both questioned the integrity and rocked the confidence of the architectural profession as a whole (MacEwen 1974; Lyall 1980). To many within the profession, the RIBA's desire for efficient practice through the adoption of modern business and management techniques was to blame. This dealt a serious blow to the development of architectural management, since before his downfall Poulson had been viewed enviously by many within the profession. The response was to retreat to the false security of professionalism. Writing about the period Andrew Saint (1983) concluded that the management-orientated architectural firm had not brought about good buildings. The whole business cast a long shadow over the development of the architectural management field.

2.4.3   A failed attempt

From the early 1970s there was a shift from public authorities to the private sector which, combined with increased competition from general contractors offering design-and-build services, further undermined existing roles and relationships. The 1980s saw markets becoming fragile and traditional boundaries in many business sectors being challenged and redefined. The abolition of professional fee scales and a more relaxed stance on advertising came about because of competitive forces both from inside and outside the profession. Although competition between architects was becoming fiercer, it was nothing compared with the competition from players outside the profession.

While the Code of Conduct prevents (theoretically) one architect from stealing the work of another, there was nothing to stop those from outside the profession from doing just that: something the architectural profession was slow to realise. For example the quantity surveyors in the UK were quick to replace the architect as lead consultant and then reinvent themselves as the client's representative through the project manager role, championing value for money, in many cases at the expense of design, and at the same time relegating architects to the role of consultant. Clients also started to perceive architects as lacking in the management skills necessary to execute increasingly complex building projects which, combined with increased competition from the 'management' professionals, posed a further threat.

During the 1980s an attempt was made by architects to redress the balance with a proposal for an Alternative Method of Management (AMM) where the main contractor was excluded from the building process and the architect became responsible for design and the management of the sub-contractors. AMM recognised the importance of sub-contractors and proposed that the construction management role be delegated to the architectural firm. Despite its potential advantages AMM failed to catch on because of the already weak position of architects compared with contractors and also because of the internal conflict between the freedom of design and the constraints of contract management that could not be resolved satisfactorily (Ball 1988). The period also saw the publication of the influential *Managing Architectural and Engineering Practice* by Weld Coxe (1980), and Derek Sharp's book *The Business of Architectural Practice* (1986) firmly put the cards on the table when he stated that the architectural office should be run as a profitable undertaking – not a popular view in all sectors of the profession.

2.4.4   A return to architectural management

As the excesses of the 1980s gave way to the insecurities of the 1990s, interest in architectural management increased once again, fuelled partly by concern for the future of the architectural profession and partly through demands for a better service from clients set against increased competition. Growing insecurities within the architectural profession were confirmed when the RIBA launched their wide-ranging strategic study. This resulted in a number of publications and workshops, not to mention debate within the architectural press. The first of the publications claimed to be the most detailed examination of the architectural profession since the publication of *The Architect and his Office* some 30 years earlier. It was in fact a number of papers that sought to address the challenges facing the profession and once again the more negative aspects of the study made the headlines.

During this period the University of Nottingham developed postgraduate courses in architectural management at masters and doctoral level, first offered in 1979–80 (Nicholson 1995). The first conference dedicated to the subject of architectural management was held at the University of Nottingham in 1992. A number of topical issues were addressed in the conference proceedings, although for the first publication to use the title *Architectural Management* (Nicholson 1992) it was a little surprising that there was no attempt to define the subject area, nor were there any references back to the earlier work of Brunton *et al.* (1964). The conference led to the formation of an International Council of Building (CIB) working group, 'W96 Architectural Management'. Drawn from a wide range of disciplines from different countries, CIB W96 continues to meet twice yearly and to publish the proceedings of their conferences via *The International Journal of Architectural Management, Practice and Research*. The conferences provide an opportunity to present case studies and engage in theoretical debate while the proceedings provide the foundations upon which to build new constructs. The architectural management working group was set up to promote architectural management to practising architects – and it could be argued that the working group has failed in this respect since the proceedings are printed in small numbers and are very much a collectors item. This is a shame since the proceedings comprise an interesting collection of theoretical debate and case studies drawn from practice from around the world. However, the publication does little to advance a common understanding of the field since there is little evidence to suggest any consistent models, terminology or concepts within this growing body of literature.

A study of architectural practice by Symes *et al.* (1995) *Architects and their Practices: A changing profession*, based on analysis of an extensive postal questionnaire, tends to reinforce the view that much work needs to be done in the management field. *Reflections on Architectural Practices in the Nineties* (Saunders 1996) identifies similar challenges facing architectural firms on the other side of the Atlantic. In the spring of 1996 the *Journal of Architectural and Planning Research* published a special edition dedicated to 'management and architecture', in which it highlighted the lack of scholarly work in the field, although the contributors were unaware of the small but important contribution of CIB's Architectural Management working group referred to above.

It is only more recently, then, that the practice of architecture has been viewed as a service to changing demands. According to Powell (1997) the marginalisation of architectural practice has arisen because demand has changed and the response has lagged. The challenge for architects is to demonstrate that effective design and responsiveness to demand may be sustained simultaneously, demonstrated through the professional management of both their firm and its projects. Architectural management is vital to the competitiveness and market viability of the design-orientated professional service firm and is clearly more than a specialist interest, given the challenge ahead.

CHAPTER 3

IN SEARCH OF AN ADVOCATE

The scope and nature of architectural management within the context of the building industry and within the current educational framework is addressed in this chapter. The main principles of architectural management are discussed and the need for an advocate of architectural management is proposed. The chapter looks at architectural education, the changing nature of architectural practice and the introduction of the new architectural technology degree, especially the implications for both educationalists and practitioners.

3.1   CONTEXT

Buildings are extremely complex products. A complexity has arisen not just from the vast number of different components that are assembled to make a bespoke product, but also from the manner in which they are procured. As technology has advanced and buildings have become more sophisticated, the number of individual players involved in building procurement has increased. The building industry has witnessed the growth of specialist disciplines such as project management, construction management, facilities management and value engineering, to name but a few. Design of the built environment is no longer the preserve of the architect, but is carried out by a variety of different professionals, all taking decisions at different levels, and in many cases competing with each other for the same market share. These specialist disciplines have started to claim areas of work, once the domain of the architect. This was highlighted by Smith and Morris (1992:63) in phase one of the Strategic Study where a graphic representation noted the areas of the design process already lost or under threat to other players in the industry. The only areas seen to be safe havens were (1) planning approval, (2) scheme design and proposals and (3) production information (drawings and specifications). Interestingly, the areas lost all require more management than design input. It could be argued that the areas lost to competitors are the direct result of leaving architectural management to be learned in the office, a consequence of the professional institutions' inability to tackle the management agenda during education.

To the academic, the constant jostling for position and the creation of new professional disciplines is fascinating, both to observe and in terms of the potential for new course provision. Academe has responded (or contributed) to this fragmentation of traditional roles with the development of degree courses in new disciplines such as architectural technology, construction management and project management which have encroached on what was always considered to be the architect's territory. Increased fragmentation has also led to the formation and growth of new professional bodies, associations and societies that are first and foremost concerned with protecting the interests of their members and the promotion of their discipline, often at the expense of others. To the practitioner, the constant jostling for position has been viewed both as a threat and as an opportunity to develop new expertise and seize a larger percentage of market share. But to the members of society who have to interact with the end result of the building project it has become more difficult for their views to be considered, despite a greater opportunity to participate in the process.

3.2   EDUCATION AND PRACTICE

Writing on the subject of architectural management Taylor (1956) noted that architectural students often asked why they had not been taught the business side of architecture. It is certainly a question that I asked when entering architectural practice; indeed, it is a question that many still ask. At the time, Taylor (1956:2) conceded that he had no answer as to why it was neglected, but he noted that,

> A Head of a school would no doubt reply that this is not laid down in the curriculum 'nor have we the time; we are here to teach architecture'. The administrative side of an architect's business is as important as his ability to design. There is no point in being an excellent designer if you have no clients.

It is tempting to see the gulf between architectural education and architectural practice as a recent phenomenon. This is misleading, because the separation of management from design goes back to the turn of the century when, in 1904, a clear decision was taken by the RIBA Board of Architectural Education to leave practice issues outside the curriculum, to be studied in the architect's office (Crinson and Lubbock 1994:189). This trend has continued for almost a century, during which time the gulf has widened because of changes both in the building industry and the way in which architects carry out their business. In his advice to architects about to enter the profession Turner (1950:12) suggested that, despite years spent in an architectural school, they still had a lot to learn and a vast amount of knowledge to gain. Perhaps in the 1950s life was a little less competitive and the rate of change a little less frantic. However, Turner's advice would still be appropriate today, because schools of architecture continue to teach design at the expense of management, despite considerable changes within the building industry and changes to the architect's role. It is not surprising, therefore, that on entering the building industry, albeit under the umbrella of architectural practice, students are always shocked at the amount of time they are expected to spend on important aspects of the job, loosely described as management, for which they have received little or no training. Their ability to design is unquestionable: after all, it is the one skill that the architect has over and above that of his or her competitors. In *The Architect and his Office* (RIBA 1962) there were calls for a greater emphasis on architectural management in architectural education which were repeated 30 years later in the RIBA's wide-ranging *Strategic Study of the Profession*: calls that have largely been ignored. Recent research into the changing nature of the architectural profession (Symes *et al.*, 1995:184) highlighted the gulf between what is delivered in architectural education and what is expected from practice. They concluded,

> Good architectural design continues to be needed, everywhere. But the profession must develop the management skills needed to help it seize these opportunities. To do this rapidly it will need considerably more sophisticated education institutions than it can currently rely on.

3.3   THE PROMOTION OF ARCHITECTURAL MANAGEMENT

The somewhat tiresome argument between the providers of architectural education and the consumers of their products, the practitioners, is never far from the surface. On the one hand the educationalists are often found defending their ground while the practitioners constantly complain that architectural students are lacking in the skills required for modern architectural practice. It has been suggested that this has always been the case and that the expectations of practice and those of students differs considerably (Carolin 1992). To the architect in practice, management and design are an integral part of an architect's job which have to be considered at the same time, not as separate issues. This is particularly important given the recent introduction of the health and safety regulations (CDM) and where quality management systems are employed. The established practice of separating the two during education and essentially ignoring management issues is an outmoded model, clearly at odds with the business of architecture in a competitive world. However, there would appear to be little initiative for the promotion of architectural management to practitioners, and there is certainly anecdotal evidence of resistance to a management-led form of practice. The often quoted stereotype is that if a practice is good at design, it will be less adequate at management and delivery, while if the practice is market-orientated, with a good reputation for delivery, it must therefore be less good at design. In the concluding paragraph of Eric Schneider's paper 'Segmenting a diverse profession' he wrote (1992:133),

> For a long time 'management' to architects has tended to mean office administration – something carried out by an individual with a lower status. It has also been something of a dirty word, in some ways the antithesis of professionalism. For success in architectural practice in the 1990s, this will need to change.

The concept of management as a dirty word is evident within the architectural profession where an architect, skilled in architectural management, is often referred to as a 'marchitect'. The term 'marchitect' comes from the title of a very comprehensive and well-intended guide to marketing for architectural practices produced by the Royal Incorporation of Architects in Scotland (1990). Unfortunately the term was coined in the 1990s by architects and used in a derisory fashion, a professional insult bestowed on commercially orientated firms and individuals. For those who have been branded a marchitect by fellow professionals this is a compliment: a term used to describe an architect who, unlike his or her contemporaries, is also capable of competing in the business world. An architect with competitive advantage.

Clearly there needs to be a change in attitude and behaviour within the professional institution if such constructs are to be promoted to the profession as a whole, but Everett M. Rogers (1995) has shown that getting a new idea adopted is never easy. Since architects must be aware of an innovation – be it a new idea, product or method – before they can consider its adoption, the communication of information about management innovations to the potential adopter is critical to their adoption. The most commonly adopted promotion strategy is the provision of information to individuals and groups through two communication channels, namely mass media (journals, leaflets, guides) and interpersonal channels (face-to-face communication) (Rogers 1995). The exposure of an individual to repeated stimulus (message) may be sufficient to enhance their attitude towards the message. However, diffusion research has shown that only a small proportion of information is noticed by the recipient, because of their level of attentiveness and need for the information at the time of exposure: a condition known as selective exposure. The challenge for the professional institution (assuming it wishes to promote architectural management) then is to present information in such a way that it will be noticed and be relevant to busy practitioners.

Information is more likely to be accepted if it is delivered by someone who knows about and is sympathetic to the audience. This is where the institution (fellow architects) is in a stronger position than, say, management consultants (non-architects) speaking at a continuing professional development (CPD) event. People need to have some basis for judging the credibility of information; therefore the greater the prestige of the communicator, the greater the likelihood that the message will be received and change will come about. Thus the more famous members of the profession would be the most likely change agents. However, they usually become famous for their design abilities, not their business acumen. In addition to these potential agents of change, peer pressure and local opinion leaders within the social system are seen as influential in bringing about a change in behaviour. Perhaps it is a little harder to become a good marchitect than the design-centred architects would concede given that there are few icons of architectural management that others can learn from. So how does an architect find out about new ideas and trends in architectural management? A number of possibilities are discussed briefly below.

3.3.1 Peer group learning

The traditional method has been to rely on peer group learning within the office where the senior partner disseminates his or her wealth of knowledge and experience to less senior members of the firm as they rise from architect, to associate, and eventually to partner or director. No doubt this method of passing on management skills, acquired from the field of battle rather than the training ground, was adequate when the speed of change was much slower and the threat of competition less prevalent. In today's competitive marketplace this strategy is suspect because there will be a tendency to perpetuate practises that worked in the past, but which may no longer be viable. Furthermore, how do practitioners develop and refine their management skills other than from painful experience?

3.3.2   Continuing professional development

Continuing professional development (CPD) offers one route to learning more about architectural management, and could be seen as a crucial source of knowledge for architectural firms to keep abreast with change. Firms must be able to attract and retain excellent staff as well as being able to update those whose skills have become outdated. This may involve learning about new materials and construction techniques or being aware of new legislation that affects building. More importantly, there is a need for CPD in the area of architectural management since architectural students receive relatively little training in how to manage professional firms, how to obtain commissions or how to identify and fight competition. A variety of agencies offer CPD courses, from the solo practitioners who organise their own meetings, to events promoted by the building product manufacturers, to the formalised events organised by the RIBA regional offices. None of these agencies have formulated a deliberate strategy for change among the profession. Furthermore, their programmes tend to be reactive rather than proactive, concentrating on disparate subjects with a variety of individuals attending different events for different reasons. Since it is easy to meet individual CPD obligations from other, design-orientated sources, interest in, or the need to attend, such events must be there in the first place. It has been proposed that CPD could form an 'agent of change' (Emmitt and Neary 1995) although paradoxically this too needs a champion for it to be effective.

3.3.3   Architectural journals

Architectural journals are important because they provide a window on the world for many busy practitioners. But this window is also a filter because they tend to be preoccupied with architectural fashion and provide little advice on issues relating to architectural management. For example, there has been particularly poor coverage of important topics such as project management by architects (Emmitt 1995). The *RIBA Journal* is issued monthly to all members of the RIBA and is the main vehicle through which the professional institution is able to communicate with its members. From the outset, the institute's journal carried a wide selection of material and covered issues related to architectural management. However, more recently the journal has become more commercially orientated with a decline in the amount of space given over to management issues (relegated to a separate section called 'Practice'). Management apparently does not sell. Similar trends can be seen in the two main weekly publications aimed at the architectural profession, the *Architects' Journal* and *Building Design*.

3.3.4 Conference proceedings

Research has shown that dissemination of conference proceedings to those who need them – the practitioners – is poor (Bardin *et al.* 1993). Despite the recent proliferation of published conference proceedings and the growth of specialist journals (as academics aim to meet their research targets) few practitioners are aware of their existence. If they were, many may well question their content's relevance to someone in practice. The efforts of the CIB's working group Architectural Management was documented in Chapter 2. However, it should be noted that their output, *The International Journal of Architectural Management, Practice and Research*, is published twice-yearly, but in very small quantities, again largely acquired by academics not the practitioners who are the focus of its endeavours. Despite the efforts of CIB W96 Architectural Management more needs to be done to bring these proceedings to the attention of busy practitioners who, it could be argued, have the most to gain from reading them. At present the AM literature is difficult to access, having something close to cult status with a hard core following at the conferences. This may change in the future as more and more research becomes available on the world wide web and, theoretically, is easier to access.

3.3.5 Society for the Advancement of Architectural Management (SAAM)

Set up in 1993 to help support CIB's Architectural Management working group the SAAM has a small following. However, as this book goes to press there are moves to promote the architectural management discipline through this society.

3.3.6 The professional institutions

Perhaps the need to promote change was not felt strongly enough at the RIBA or among its members in the past. Indeed, Saint (1983) noted that fear of the open marketplace would lead to protectionism by architects rather than a commercial approach. Clearly there has been a change in emphasis at the RIBA with the implementation of the Strategic Study. The study recommended change and the RIBA has responded with a series of road-shows (although attended by a very small proportion of the profession) and articles in the architectural press in an attempt to disseminate this information. However, more needs to be done to bring about a change in attitude and approach. The British Institute of Architectural Technologists (BIAT) are going further than the RIBA by promoting the discipline through some of their newly launched architectural technology degrees.

3.3.7   Books

With the exception of the books referred to in Chapter 1, architectural management has not been particularly well covered in book format. There are the 'how to do it' books, ranging from managing the practice to setting up quality management systems. While extremely useful in themselves, they do not address some of the fundamental underlying issues. Because of the lack of good literature aimed specifically at architects, it is necessary to look outside the architectural literature for good management material. The problem here is that it is difficult to tell which are the good, indifferent or poor sources of knowledge from the extensive number of publications which are available, especially when we have no reference point from which to analyse them. Furthermore, management literature is fickle: today's miracle cure is often tomorrow's bad medicine. It is particularly difficult, therefore, for the professional designer to rise above the level of amateur manager.

3.3.8   Undergraduate and postgraduate education

Within the architectural management literature it is easy to find criticisms of architectural education and calls for a refocusing of the architect's core skills. For example Wyatt (1995) suggested a restructuring of the architectural discipline to meet the demands of sustainable product design. So perhaps the natural conclusion would be to broaden or refocus the education of architects. However, there is another route. The introduction of the architectural technology degree in the United Kingdom and Northern Ireland, championed by the British Institute of Architectural Technologists (BIAT) is a significant development in architectural education since these degrees are being structured to cover a wide range of architectural issues, to include management, technology and design. Architectural schools are vocational in nature: they are primarily concerned with teaching *design* at the expense of management. The architectural technologist, on the other hand, will be very well qualified in management issues and in particular the management of the design process, one of the areas advocated by Symes *et al.* (1995:180) as a possible specialist area for architects. There is clearly going to be a lot of competition for similar areas of work. In particular, the areas identified by Smith and Morris (1992) as safe havens for architects may soon be threatened by the graduate architectural technologist. As such it has been argued (Emmitt 1996b) that while on the one hand such a development may constitute a further threat to architects, architectural technologists and their professional body BIAT may well emerge as a natural vehicle through which the architectural management discipline may be promoted.

3.4   IN SEARCH OF AN ADVOCATE

Architectural management should be integral to architects' education part of their culture, and training. So why not teach the fundamentals, the foundations for lifelong learning in architectural management, from the first year of the degree course? Management concepts such as quality assurance and project management can, without too much difficulty, be introduced to the design studio as an underlying structure to the design projects with additional supporting lectures and seminars; management issues should be seen as an integral part of the design process, not a chore that has to be done in practice. It will, however, require a change in the type of person who teaches in the design studio, with a mixture of design-centred architects and management-centred ones. Whether the traditional schools of architecture will move further towards abstract design issues or will be forced back to a more technically based degree with a management core remains to be seen.

We could argue that the schools of architecture have a duty to teach aspects of architectural management in the studio to enhance the excellence in design tuition. Education could and should be the leading advocate for architectural management. Students are full of energy and ideas and are a positive benefit to any architectural practice; they should be capable of challenging the established practices and beliefs in management as well as in design. Architectural practices would then be in a position to develop in the manner suggested by the Strategic Study rather than continuing to perpetuate the familiar (and outdated) modes of practice. It is then, and only then, that the architectural profession as a whole will be better equipped to compete with other players in the industry.

Anecdotal evidence suggests that a small number of practices are leading the way for the rest of the profession, through their adoption of architectural management, but their success as a business is rarely promoted within the architectural press (not consistent with professional values and behaviour). Thus the less well-informed practices continue to operate using outdated methods of marketing their practice, unsure of how to reposition themselves in the changing marketplace for architectural services. If a few architectural practices have responded to the changing marketplace, there should be no reason why the remainder of the profession cannot follow. These individual practices have responded on their own initiative and have altered their attitudes and adjusted their behaviour in response to change; they have not waited for direction from their professional body. The challenge, however, will be to bring about a change in ingrained values and beliefs within the remainder, that is the majority, of the profession, for which an advocate of architectural management is required.

CHAPTER 4

A TURBULENT ENVIRONMENT

This chapter looks at the turbulent market in which the professional firm operates, in particular the fragmented nature of the building industry and the roles of the different players who are, in many cases, competing for the same commission. Many of these issues are recurring themes in building. However, an investigation of the marketplace for services and the players competing in it helps to identify some of the issues facing the competitive firm. The chapter concludes by looking at the main challenges facing the architectural firm and suggests that the battle is as much from within the firm as from outside it.

4.1   RECURRING THEMES

'There's blood on the street, and some of it's mine' was a claim made by a director of an architectural firm in the early 1990s, who had seen a prosperous firm with more than 100 staff be reduced to a total staff of five in the space of six months: as Derek Sharp (1991) points out, architecture is indeed a volatile business. Volatile because it is inextricably linked to the building industry which is notorious for its dramatic swings in fortune from boom to slump to boom, often with short transitional periods between the two extremes. For example, the dizzy heights of the late 1980s when architectural firms were extremely busy was followed very quickly by a severe economic recession in the early 1990s, from which it has taken the building industry some time to recover. Architectural workload and construction output are both linked and dependent on the economic fortunes of the country in which they operate (Ball 1988; Sharp 1991; Harvey and Ashworth 1993). The problem for businesses is that economic growth and recession is not easy to predict. In addition to the global and national economies there also exist local economies, physical areas of a country or market segments, that may well exhibit different trends to those on the macro level. Certain market segments, such as food retail, remained buoyant during the 1990s while housing has been subdued. The successful firms are those best able to market their services to the most profitable (or potentially the most profitable) market sector or region.

Although architectural firms often have advance warning of swings in the economy (be it on the macro or micro level), reflected in an increase or decrease in enquiries from clients, there is little they can do, other than to be prepared to adapt to the changed economic circumstances. The effect of economic fluctuation is reflected in the number of staff a firm employs, with firms increasing their size in a boom and decreasing staffing levels in a slump. The most difficult period in many respects is the transitional period, when staff are being dismissed or employed, because of the problems of reorganisation and the challenge of maintaining a quality service throughout. Clearly an attempt should be made to minimise any adverse economic effects in the structure and service provision of the firm. This is easier stated than done since clients will still be demanding quality service, often at reduced fee levels, in a downturn and will want the service to be delivered much faster in a boom. But prevailing economic conditions are not the only concern for the professional service firm: fragmentation, leadership, competition and procurement routes all influence its competitiveness.

4.1.1 Fragmentation

Boundaries are familiar to architects: they define inside from outside, private from public, soft from hard, professionals from amateurs. The prospect of disturbance to boundaries is often seen as a threat to identity, rather than as an opportunity. Fragmentation in the building industry is nothing new. However, the recent trend has been for an increase in complexity of building procurement and further growth in the number of individual consultants engaged on any project. These specialists such as project managers, construction managers, facilities managers and value managers are often in competition with one another for the same market share. Indeed, the balance has shifted away from an integrated team to one made up of competing individuals representing different interests.

Fragmentation has led to the formation and growth of new professional bodies, associations and societies which are first and foremost concerned with protecting the interests of their members and the promotion of independent roles. The fragmentation or 'unbundling' of the traditional service is consistent with the competitive advantage model proposed by Porter (1985), but while this may provide good business opportunities for some of these individual disciplines it does not necessarily bode well for the built environment. What appears to have been lost in the hustle and bustle of this busy marketplace is the fact that the building procurement process was, and still could be, a very simple process. But what of the client, the building user and the environment? While all the individual players would argue that they, and they alone, are essential to the successful delivery of the finished product, none of them have stood back and faced the most difficult question. What have they, the intermediaries, contributed to the quality of the finished product over and above that achieved by a simpler procurement route? Furthermore, can clients really get independent advice and single point responsibility from a design-orientated professional service firm? Is such advice any different to, say, that offered by a contractor-led design-and-build firm?

4.1.2   Leadership

To say that different members of the project team may have different values is, perhaps, to state the obvious. But it needs highlighting because it is these differences in values which go some way to creating barriers to communication flow, both within the firm and within the temporary project team, and to fuelling the ever present argument over who should lead, i.e. manage, the temporary project team. Leadership is an emotive topic and something worth fighting for, for a number of reasons. For some authors it is the interrelationship of a client's needs and the restrictions of the site that 'ensures' the position of building team leader to the architect (Bennett 1981), but recent trends have seen the leadership role pass to other management-orientated professions, for example independent project managers. It is an area some architects seem happy to concede. Leadership is important, first and foremost, because it is the most active link with the building sponsor, an important link if business opportunities are to be maximised. Leadership is also important from a sustainable viewpoint, since it is little use advocating and designing for an environmentally responsible manner if other people within the temporary project team have the power to override decisions. We must be pragmatic when it comes to sustainability: social and economic factors are far more important than technical issues. For example:

- How can design quality be transferred to the finished building without losing any of its special characteristics if designers are not involved in the decision-making process?
- Is it possible to adopt sustainable principles when others may have different concerns?
- Does the professional design firm really want to rely on other professionals for work? It is a dangerous business policy to rely on others (who may well be competing with the design firm) for work. Whoever has the client's ear is in a very powerful position in terms of dictating procurement decisions and thus designing the temporary project culture.

4.1.3   Competition

The building industry is experiencing a new era of competition. Competition has always existed between traditional adversaries and latterly a number of new entrants to the market has increased the heat. The biggest change has been the breakdown of barriers to previously protected markets. Firms are aggressively seeking work outside of, and in addition to, their traditional client base. It is a trend that is radically reshaping other industries, for example the provision of banking services by large high street retail stores and out-of-town supermarkets in the UK has challenged the established banks. The result of removing the barriers is that firms can no longer be confident about their market share because competition can come from any direction at any time. As such it is increasingly difficult for firms to establish competitive advantage without constantly monitoring and responding to changes in the marketplace. Perhaps it is worth remembering that the ultimate aim of competition is to eliminate the competition.

Architectural firms face a paradox. Traditional markets are changing, either shrinking or becoming very competitive, while rising client demands for quality services, the abolition of fee scales and the additional uncertainty of fee bidding are creating additional demands on firms. In many cases these pressures have resulted in reduced profit margins and have forced firms to improve the management of their business in order to survive. Some have responded by concentrating on their core competence, design, and abrogated responsibility for project management to their competitors. Others have expanded their core competences and offer a wide range of management-orientated services in direct competition to other providers in the market.

Although architects are renowned for their creativity and willingness to innovate in design, there is little evidence of the profession reaching out to embrace new management techniques. For example, architects have been slow to adopt quality assurance. What has emerged in recent years is the ability of the chartered surveyors and the chartered builders, members of the RICS and CIOB respectively, to reinvent their role within the building industry: that is, their ability to adopt management innovations to their commercial benefit, an approach promoted by the aggressive stance of their professional institutions. These professionals have led the way by providing parts of the full service to clients, by marketing their services in a new way. They are the innovators within the building industry in terms of responding to client needs and offering a more targeted approach, while architects have acted in a manner associated with 'laggards' (Emmitt and Neary 1995).

In marketing literature the traditional architectural service would be referred to as a 'bundled' service, in that it offers the client a number of services in one package or bundle. One of the problems with offering a bundled service is that all clients are offered the same service regardless of their individual needs. Porter (1985) notes that unbundling within an industry is triggered or accelerated by a competitive marketplace, or by an economic downturn. Increased diversity of clients' needs and changing procurement methods have resulted in additional pressures. The chartered surveyors and chartered builders are very good at marketing services as separate packages, which have been 'chipped off' the complete service traditionally provided by architects. Their ability to sell unbundled services such as project management and facilities management, for example, is consistent with the views of Porter (1985) and their success has led to an increased pressure for others, i.e. architects, to respond by unbundling their own services.

4.1.4 Procurement routes

Within this competitive marketplace it is widely accepted that the architect's role has moved from traditional team leader to one of designer and with it the loss of contact with and influence on the client. This trend is further reinforced by the rapid growth of procurement routes and hybrid contractual techniques such as novation, with a decline in the use of traditional contracts. The increasing commercialism of clients in all sectors and their use of different procurement routes, such as design and build, has shifted the designer's contractual position of project leader to one of consultant, with a resultant decline in influence over the

development process. In most cases these new procurement routes have further
undermined the architect/client relationship, with many architectural firms finding
themselves working as consultants to new team leaders.

4.2 MARKETPLACE FOR SERVICES

The business of architecture is being conducted in an increasingly competitive
marketplace, but many architectural firms have tended to concentrate on offering
design-orientated services, while their competitors have seized the opportunities
offered by management innovations such as project management. These firms are
successfully attacking an established industry leader – architectural firms – without
the use of radical technological innovation. Their biggest weapon is management, a
weapon rarely stocked in the architectural firm's arsenal. Architectural firms are in
danger of becoming so marginalised that they can no longer provide the services
required by today's clients. In management literature, especially that concerned
with strategic innovation, there is evidence to prove that the vast majority of
attackers fail and the established market leaders defend their market share for long
periods. So why are architectural firms losing their market share to the
management-orientated firms? Quite simply because the majority have made little
attempt to defend their position from the attackers, abrogating responsibility for the
management aspects of the job to their competitors, and also because the attackers
have changed the rules of the game through strategic innovation.

It is widely accepted that the decline in both the status and responsibilities of
architects continues unabated. This has come about partly because the architectural
profession has abrogated responsibility for specialist design work to competing
professionals (e.g. Cole and Cooper 1988; Gutman 1988), and partly because of
architects' lack of control over finance, delivery and quality of service (Schneider
and Davies 1995). This has resulted in the failure to respond quickly or
competently to client demand (Powell 1997). With a few exceptions, the profession
has resisted the potential for providing innovative services to its clients, despite the
recommendations contained in the RIBA's wide-ranging Strategic Study. Architects
have remained content with their role while other professional groups, such as the
quantity surveyors, have pursued new outlets for their burgeoning membership
(Powell 1997). Opportunities have been seized and exploited by architects'
competitors, at the expense of the traditional architectural practice. Allinson (1993)
noted that architects have brought the situation on themselves by their failure to
adapt their architectural values and the way in which they practise as economic
conditions have changed. Some of the reasons for the profession's resistance to
change were tentatively proposed by Powell:

1. Avoidance of new, untried or extended services to limit professional risk (fuelled
   by adversarialism and litigiousness).
2. A restrained response has helped to maintain professional unity.
3. A restrained response has helped to maintain core design skills by avoiding

dilution with new service provision, reinforced by the RIBA (1992) which urged architects to concentrate on their central role as designers and to strengthen the delivery of their design services.

4.3 THE RISE OF THE MANAGERS

The competitive nature of the industry and the marketplace for services is best looked at through the players in the market. Clearly the client is the enabler. The other players can be grouped under the 'design-orientated professionals' and 'management-orientated' professionals. The design-orientated professionals, to whom this book is addressed, comprise architects, architectural technologists and building surveyors. The management-orientated professionals comprise construction managers, facility managers, project managers and quantity surveyors. Further competition comes from planners who do not fit easily into either category and also from sub-contractors who design and manufacture.

There are three separate but overlapping areas of management which are relevant to the building industry. First, those concepts potentially relevant to all members of the building industry, such as re-engineering and benchmarking, which are essentially tools to enhance business while the adoption of total quality management and formal partnering have the potential to affect all those involved in building. Second, an area unique to the architectural profession, design management, but it is not the exclusive domain of the architectural firm. Third, those management areas claimed to be the domain of architectural firms' competitors, such as project management, construction management, value management and buildability. These are areas which architectural firms' competitors have claimed as their domain. These management disciplines are important because they pose both a threat and an opportunity to architectural firms and are discussed briefly below.

4.3.1 Project management

This is perhaps one of the most emotive areas for architects to discuss since as a profession they have always seen themselves as project managers. Project management is a well-defined discipline and one that may sit comfortably within the architectural firm's portfolio of service provision. Project managers have established themselves as the link between the client and the rest of the team on large projects, making the briefing process their domain on medium and even small projects; they have become the guardian of the client's aims and objectives. Although this has been promoted as a good thing for the industry, it has serious consequences from the architectural firm's point of view. The independent role has broken the link between client and designer, with instructions passing through an intermediary, a gatekeeper; thus architectural firms have become disengaged. The disengaged will also become isolated from the client, resulting in a further loss of work. It is also a service offered by other players in the industry and one of the main areas of competition to architects' traditional service provision (discussed more fully in Chapter 8).

4.3.2 Construction management

The term 'construction management', for most architects at least, tends to be associated with the management of the construction project during the contract period. However, the field of construction management continues to grow and the term has come to represent a management field which encompasses value management, constructability, benchmarking, re-engineering, total quality management and partnering (McGeorge and Palmer 1997). Clearly there are overlaps with the architectural management literature, so for the purposes of this book the term 'construction management' will be taken to refer to the contract phase of the building project. Although traditionally the domain of the main contractor, in an attempt to improve the quality of the finished building a small number of architectural practices have adopted construction management during the 1990s and charged a fee for their services (discussed in further detail in Chapter 11).

4.3.3 Facilities management

There is a tendency to look at the parts, rather than the whole social system in which buildings are conceived, built, refurbished and eventually dismantled. It has been argued that a total build approach can come through the facilities management discipline (Haugen 1994). Facilities management is a relatively new discipline which covers all aspects of property maintenance, space planning and support services to allow buildings to support and enhance business activities. Many of the concepts, such as generic management, communication, risk, value and quality management are common to the architectural management discipline.

4.3.4 Value management

Critics of value management claim that this activity is little more than cost-cutting, with little evidence of value and even less of any management. Based on a study of 17 value-management exercises in the UK, Simister and Green (1997) concluded that for a value-management exercise to be successful the project team needs to be committed to participation. Clear objectives need to be set, the participants need authority to implement the outcome of the value management exercise and time is required for collection of all the relevant information. From this book's perspective, the main issue is about who should lead the value-management exercise. Although McGeorge and Palmer (1997:29) favour the use of an external facilitator and claim that the members of design team are unlikely to have the skills required to facilitate the exercise, the study by Simister and Green (1997) included three architects in their sample of 17. It is likely that the exercise will be carried out by those willing to take it on as a business venture, whatever their background. From an architectural firm's perspective, the value-management exercise has parallels with the design audit under a quality management system. Who better to carry out the exercise than the architectural firm with project management expertise?

4.3.5   Health and Safety management

As a result of the change to health and safety legislation in the UK a further player has emerged: the 'planning supervisor'. While the emphasis on improving safety is applauded, it has had the effect of creating yet another role, that of the planning supervisors. In contrast to their belligerent stance on project management by architects, the RIBA has made a real attempt to communicate the benefits of adopting this role to the architectural profession. Although, strangely, the firms in the best position to undertake this role are the firms with project management experience.

4.4   THE CHALLENGE AHEAD

It is important to look at some of the challenges facing the professional service firm in the future. Architectural businesses are undergoing (rapid) transformation in response to external forces in order to stay competitive and in business. Change has always been present, but it has become more frantic and the consequences of inadequate response much greater, if not fatal, for architectural firms. Architecture has always borrowed language from other disciplines. Deconstruction is a recent example, but it has been slow to adopt new developments from the management discipline, such as re-engineering. In management literature there are a number of recurring themes which are seen as drivers for a new business to remain competitive and to compete in a rapidly changing environment. Although terms vary slightly depending on the author, these are discussed here from the perspective of an architectural firm.

First, and perhaps most importantly, the issue of quality. As quality expectations continue to rise, professional service firms are experiencing greater demands from clients for improved service quality. Quality is broadly interpreted to cover consistency and reliability as well as continuous improvement through employee motivation and participation, known as total quality management. For the architectural firm life is tough because it will be judged not just on the quality of its service provision but also on the quality of the finished product, the building. While the control and improvement of service provision is largely in the hands of the service firm, the quality of the finished building is more challenging since it is contributed to by a wide range of professionals and built by a general contractor who sub-contracts work to others who in turn sub-sub-contract work. Hence it is very difficult for architectural firms to maintain the quality of the product.

Second, is the relative performance of the firm, judged against its own criteria and those of its competitors, usually known as benchmarking and closely related to quality issues. Third, is the issue of responsiveness of the firm to external pressures. More than ever before, architectural firms need to react rapidly to changing market conditions, competitive threats and client demands. Globalisation, with the removal of access barriers and free trade, brings with it threats to the home market as well as opportunities for the more adventurous. Furthermore, the time from project inception to practical completion and commissioning is constantly being reduced, thus putting additional pressure on all those concerned with the building process. External pressures are also present in trends such as outsourcing which provides new opportunities as large organisations disband their 'in-house' departments to seek more cost-effective and better quality service providers elsewhere. Other management innovations such as partnering, where firms form joint ventures to pursue new business opportunities, must also be responded to.

Fourth, is the issue of social and environmental responsibility. Concern for the built environment and the interaction of people and buildings has always been of considerable interest and concern to architects. However, with the recent trend towards 'signature architecture' and abrogating responsibility for decision-making to others (to whom time and money are paramount concerns) architects are losing their power to influence decisions within the sustainable agenda. There is a growing acceptance in business that firms must act responsibly in their relationship with people outside and inside the firm. Customers and suppliers are starting – or at least claiming – to adopt environmentally responsible practices and are looking for consultants with tangible environmental credentials. More specifically, the concept of managing for sustainability has been and will continue to be explored within the architectural management literature. An environmentally responsible, rather than altruistic, approach to business and building is required, an approach that should underlie all of the firm's activities.

Last, but certainly not least, is the issue of new technologies, both advances in materials technologies and in information technology. In particular, information technology and expert knowledge systems provide the opportunity for more efficient working practices, but they also offer the competitors easier access to design typologies, once the domain of architects, and as such constitute a threat to the core business.

All these interdependent themes have been and are being explored as separate disciplines, each with its own area of interest. As such the individual themes are explored further within this book in terms of their contribution to the architectural management field. Clearly there is no single business strategy to suit all situations, but firms must recognise that they need to take a stance and decide which strategy they are going to pursue because they are more likely to fail if they get caught in the middle. For some firms, competitive advantage will be achieved through concentrating primarily on their core skill, design: the design-only practices where management and technology are abrogated to others. For others, competitive advantage will be achieved through diversity. Whatever strategies are adopted to anticipate and meet market forces, the firm's success will be dependent on the consistency of the service provided to its clients, an area dependent on the skills of its members. The manner in which the firm and the individual jobs are managed are tied up with the firm's culture and the characteristics of its most valuable asset, its members, whose ability to adapt as the firm adapts will be critical to its success. As such, the biggest battle facing the design-orientated professional service firm is likely to come from within. These issues are addressed in Parts 2 and 3.

Part 2

ASSETS AND STRATEGIES

CHAPTER 5

PEOPLE AND TEAMS

The most important asset of a professional service firm is its staff; more specifically their knowledge and skills. Their recruitment, motivation and skills development through continuing professional development (CPD) is vital to the firm's ongoing competitiveness. This chapter investigates issues of leadership, motivation, knowledge acquisition and continuing professional development, before turning to the issue of human asset management and self-managing teams.

5.1   PEOPLE FIRMS

Managing the firm as a profitable business – that is managing individual jobs effectively and profitably – is an essential component of the architectural firm; the management of staff and the running of the business are very closely linked in professional service firms. An essential requirement is that the management intentions of the directors should be clear and effectively communicated to the employees. The objectives of the firm, the range of services it offers and the purpose of its managerial controls need to be clearly defined, then (and some would argue only then) communicated to all those participating in the firm.

Effective management of the firm should be concerned with both the organisational structure of the firm and the motivation of its members. The organisational structure of the firm is concerned with the control of its members' activities, through job descriptions and bureaucratic rules. Once a firm has its goals set and documented, it is on the way to being managed, since with set goals the day-to-day management becomes much clearer (Coxe 1980). However, management literature has conceded that individuals exercise free will, despite the existence of managerial controls, and they may choose not to comply with the constraints placed on them. This is especially true of individuals who see themselves as creative, such as designers, who appear to take pleasure in 'bending the rules' or resisting managerial controls such as quality assurance. As such it is important to provide a stimulating environment which will encourage people to work creatively and communicate easily with one another within its managerial framework. Human beings are much more difficult to control than technologies and tools; thus management of the firm must be concerned with the motivation of its members (Kreps 1990), its most important asset. Before looking at the firm's principal asset it is useful to understand the different types of people firm, usually described by typology and organisational configuration.

5.1.1   Firm typologies

Three types of firm have been identified (Coxe *et al.* 1987; Kaderlan 1991), namely, strong delivery, strong service and strong idea firms.

1. The strong delivery firm is organised for efficiency, relies on standard design solutions, has a formal structure and a relatively stable working environment. This firm tends to specialise in a few building/project types. According to Kaderlan (1991), by reducing client involvement and standardising the production process the firm has little need to change very often.
2. The strong service firm is organised for service and tailors its services to the needs of clients, has a flexible structure and a highly complex internal environment. Standardisation is less possible and there is greater client involvement in the project. Since they deal with a variety of both client and project types they must have flexible management systems to allow them to adapt.
3. The strong idea firm is organised for innovation and seeks to provide innovative solutions to unique problems, has a flexible informal structure and a highly changeable environment. Standard solutions are rarely considered because clients employ the firm for a unique project. The firm organised around the 'star architect' is a good example of this, notorious for its lack of management systems. The stereotypical creative genius working in an office that is beyond management is typical of the strong idea firm, and an image a little to convenient to hide behind.

The division of firms into three distinct types is common and rarely questioned. It is easy to find firms that fit these categories. However, it should be noted that one single firm may change its typology over time, for whatever reason, or may operate within at least two of these categories simultaneously. For example, many firms claim they are able to offer strong delivery as well as strong service and also with a strong idea, thus claiming a foot in **all three** camps.

5.1.2   Organisational configurations

In addition to the type of firm, the type of organisational control, usually reflective of the principal's personality (Coxe 1980) needs to be considered. Kaderlan (1991), drawing on the work of Henry Mintzberg (1989), has highlighted the four fundamental organisational configurations of firms: namely, entrepreneurial, bureaucratic, professional and innovative organisations.

1. The entrepreneurial firm is run by a single director and since 70 per cent of all practices are constituted of five professionals or fewer this is not surprising. The

organisational structure is very simple and all decisions are made by the director. Because of its size, the firm is capable of being very flexible/adaptable, but its size prevents it from dealing with much complexity.

2. The bureaucratic organisation is very organised, highly formalised, described as 'machine-like' and hence disliked by designers. Mention the word 'management' to an architect and an image of a bureaucratic firm comes to mind. It is regarded as stifling creativity, more suited to a stable environment and inflexible.
3. The professional organisation comprises a number of professionals, all directors, sharing the same office and staff, but principally working independently of one another, sometimes known as a co-operative partnership agreement. Sensitive management is required if problems of co-ordination are to be avoided. Since the directors all work independently, albeit within a common framework, problems of consistency in the process and the product are inevitable, whilst staff may find it difficult to adapt to different directors' working methods.
4. The innovative organisation is based on expertise. It has the most flexible structure, is responsive to change and does not use standard solutions. This is regarded as inefficient and demanding on the members of the firm. Essentially they are set up for single projects and since they are innovative, established or formalised patterns of behaviour are not used.

Again it should be remembered that firms may change over time, and it is not uncommon for the innovative or entrepreneurial firm to become bureaucratic or vice versa.

5.1.3 Evolution of the firm

Most design firms will pass through a number of distinct evolutionary phases over time; from inception to survival and then to success, predictable stages, often resulting from the firm's growth rather than from any specific business strategy (Kaderlan 1991). Inception covers the stage when a firm is first formed, either by design or necessity, when the challenge is to get enough clients and projects to be financially viable; the main concern is staying in business. Second comes the survival stage, where the firm has enough work to stay in business, staff numbers will have expanded and the pressure to be more successful will increase. Third comes success: the firm has proved itself in the marketplace and has grown in size and complexity. The possibility of failure will exist throughout a firm's life, regardless of its developmental stage. Thus some firms never make it past the inception stage, others may get stuck in the survival stage and never reach the third, successful, stage.

5.1.4 Shaking and trembling

Firms have also been described as growing from birth, through adolescence to middle age, old age and eventual death: a neat, but naïve model. Firms are constantly adjusting their size and focus to meet external pressures, often reinventing themselves through adversity, growing and shrinking throughout their existence. As such it would be misleading to write about firms as if they were stable organisations with well-established networks; with architectural firms classified by size it would be an easy mistake to make. Firms are collections of individuals working with one another to achieve their goals and, more importantly, to survive and prosper. Weick (1979) has claimed that such social systems are seldom stable, are usually quite hectic and adaptive. For any firm to be competitive a balance has to be achieved between stability and adaptability. This is particularly so in a design office, a dynamic environment that is rarely ordered, coherent or static. Within any design office there is constant friction and a balance needs to be maintained between creative and destructive forces. The confrontation that is the essence of good design needs careful management in order not to shake itself apart. In this context 'management' could be seen as a loose glue that helps to keep things together; something that allows for a gentle shaking and trembling.

5.2 ASSETS

Staff are an important asset; they account for some 50 to 60 per cent of the cost of running an architectural business (Kaderlan 1991) and must be deployed effectively to ensure profitability. The individual knowledge, skill and experience of the staff combine to give the firm its special characteristics and culture, and they will affect the quality of service provided. It is often said that a professional service firm's most distinctive characteristic is that it only has the assets or knowledge of its staff with which to trade. As such they are particularly difficult to value financially. While this may be true of very small firms and some poorly managed firms, such a statement is misleading since a well-managed professional service firm has three types of intellectual capital (Caulkin 1997): human, system and customer (client).

1. *Human capital:* This comprises the knowledge and talents that reside in the human brain: it walks into the office in the morning and out again in the evening. This asset is not owned by the firm, it is rented (via salaries) and must be managed accordingly.
2. *System capital:* It is easier to manage than human capital: this is the know-how contained in a firm's processes and documented past projects. The more a firm can incorporate knowledge into their systems, theoretically, the less their reliance on human capital. Well-designed and managed quality management systems are a good example of system capital.
3. *Customer (client) capital:* This describes the value of a firm's relationship with its clients. It is shared knowledge and not owned.

Since the firm is constantly adjusting its shape to compete and stay competitive, the skills of the staff will inevitably have to change, possibly through CPD activities or changes in staffing. A firm is only as good as the collective efforts of its members; thus the assembly, motivation and development of this principal asset is crucial to a firm's success in the marketplace. This is particularly true of the knowledge-based firm where the proper selection, training and development of staff is essential if a high quality service is to be delivered. Staff selection and the constant updating of a firm's members is a principal function of the firm's directors; it is vital to the development of a firm's culture but often neglected (Coxe 1980).

5.2.1 Culture of the firm

Every firm is unique. Its character is drawn from the unique individuals that make up its workforce and the organisational structures that exist to control and manage its collective talents. Figure 5.1 provides a simplified view of the firm's culture, manifest in the interaction of the firm's members – directors, professionals and support staff – and those positioned outside the firm – clients, consultants and suppliers.

The culture of the firm will influence its members' judgements and the manner in which they communicate. Furthermore, the perceptions of the firm's past, present and future will influence the development of the firm's cultural climate (Kreps 1990). Four key elements of firm culture have been described by Deal and Kennedy (1982) as values, heroes, rites and rituals, and cultural communication networks. Peters and Waterman (1982) identified eight important cultural themes in their survey of more than 60 'excellent business organisations'. Excellent organisations, according to Peters and Waterman, have a bias towards action and

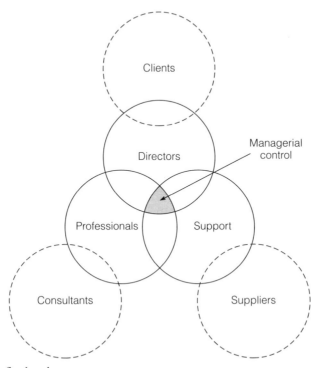

Fig. 5.1 The firm's culture

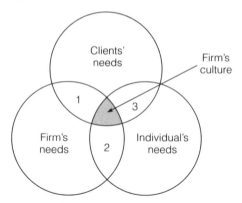

Fig. 5.2 Factors contributing to the firm's culture
    1. Client contact with the firm via secretaries/receptionists, etc.
    2. Professional's relationship with the firm.
    3. Client contact with individual professionals within the firm.

are close to their clients: they emphasise entrepreneurship, productivity through people and have a hands-on approach to management. Furthermore excellent organisations stick to what they are good at, have simple, lean staffing levels based on small work groups to improve communication, and demonstrate 'loose and tight properties' simultaneously. This final point is especially important for architectural firms since the management structure should be loose enough to allow for creativity but tight enough to deliver a consistent service.

    The culture that exists within the firm is important since some cultures may help to promote the firm's growth while others may work to the firm's detriment (Kreps 1990). The way in which staff are treated in an architectural practice is related to its structure, personality and the managerial ability of the directors. There is plenty of anecdotal evidence claiming that staff are treated badly in some firms (long hours with little reward). One famous example was a director of a very large architectural office whose catchphrase was 'I told you not to think, draw!'. The office, not surprisingly, had a problem with staff morale and staff turnover was a major concern. The firm's culture is expressed in Figure 5.2 where the three main contributing factors, clients' needs, the firm's needs, and the individual's needs, are shown. The manner in which all three areas interact, or rather the manner in which they communicate with one another, will influence the firm's culture. As such culture is manifest through communication.

5.2.2 Motivation and rewards

Personal motivation is a complex area, but one well covered in management literature. Motivation theory, based on the fulfilment of individual needs, is well developed (e.g. Maslow 1954; Hertzberg 1966). Gary Kreps (1990:155) provides a useful definition, '*Motivation* is the degree to which an individual is personally committed to expending effort in the accomplishment of a specified activity or goal', and the manager who is able to motivate and reward staff fairly is well on the way to establishing a firm with competitive advantage. For example, a good designer may need little motivation when designing, but may need encouragement when dealing with a part of the job, such as contract administration, which is seen as non-creative and therefore less interesting. Productivity and quality are related to the degree in which the professional is 'engaged' and committed. It is closely linked to delegation (Maister 1993) and the firm's managers must understand what motivates the individuals in their firm.

Two important factors central to motivation are known as intrinsic rewards and extrinsic rewards, both of which need to be balanced through effective management. Intrinsic rewards are based on the fulfilment of individual beliefs and values and are rather illusory. Described as 'higher-order motivational needs' by Hertzberg (1966) intrinsic rewards include personal career advancement, achievement, recognition, achievement and enjoyment. Extrinsic rewards are more obvious since they are based on economic rewards, described by Hertzberg as 'basic hygiene needs' and encompassing salary, job security, working conditions and status. Rewards to professionals are expressed in a variety of ways. A good salary, benefits, bonuses and profit-sharing are important, but so is status within the firm, recognition of a job well done and recognition by fellow professionals (Blau 1984; Cuff 1991). Financial rewards are most effective when related to excellent service; thus a bonus paid based on project profitability is particularly effective in reinforcing teamwork and efficiency (Kaderlan 1991).

Closely associated with personal motivation and reward is the issue of expectations, both on behalf of employees and the directors of the firm. The directors' expectations of the staff must be both realistic and set at a level capable of motivating the team; more importantly it must be communicated to the employees, perhaps through regular feedback and support. Similarly the staff's expectations of their managers and the firm's directors is important. In many professional offices with problems of staff morale and motivation there is a clear mismatch between the directors' expectations and those of its staff, usually a direct result of the two groups failing to communicate.

5.2.3 Performance review and evaluation

Linked to the issue of motivation and reward is the staff performance review or staff appraisal. The performance review and evaluation should be conducted as a formal interview between the employee and manager. The interview should be carried out with employees at least once a year before the annual review of salaries and should consider the following points both from the employee's and the manager's perspective:

1. *Quality of work:* Has it met expectations? What are the individual's strengths and weaknesses?
2. *Contribution to teamwork and office morale:* How has the individual influenced the team? Has he or she motivated or demotivated the team/office?

3. *Contribution to the profitability of the firm:* Has the individual brought new business to the firm or suggested cost-saving ideas?
4. *Staff development:* What new skills has the individual acquired since the previous review? Have CPD activities been met? (see below)
5. *Staff grievances:* What are the problems? How can they be resolved to mutual satisfaction?

Again, regardless of firm size, adequate time should be set aside for this activity, a record kept of what was agreed, and a commitment by directors and staff to try and meet their obligations. This needs to be an open, honest exchange of views on a one-to-one basis; done properly it will benefit both the firm and the individual. A note of warning is also needed here because staff reviews are often perceived (and sometimes used) as a tool to reinforce hierarchical systems; they can be self-defeating if not handled with a degree of sensitivity and common sense. The staff performance interview provides an excellent opportunity for vertical communication (Kreps 1990) and should be carried out before an evaluation of the firm's current 'health', discussed in Chapter 7. Feedback through regular 'quality circles' and project-specific reviews is also important but should be kept separate from the individual staff review. It may be appropriate to undertake a project-specific performance review either at the completion of a job or at a stage during its lifecycle. This is in addition to individual staff reviews and a natural development/extension of the design review (discussed later).

5.3   TRAINING AND DEVELOPMENT

The professional development of staff during their working career, their expansion of knowledge and acquisition of new skills may go some way towards keeping staff happy while at the same time helping the firm to maintain a competitive edge through its collective development. As qualified and trained professionals it is no longer possible to rest on the laurels of professionalism. Professionals must stay up-to-date with the rapidly increasing and changing body of knowledge. Expertise based solely on experience is no longer adequate; no practitioner can rely on existing knowledge without constantly validating it against current information (Lohmann 1993). Knowledge and practice become obsolete, often faster than we would like to acknowledge, and to stay in business it is inevitable that some form of planned professional development, geared towards the development of the individual and the firm, must form part of our daily activities. The use of the words 'planned professional development' is deliberate since the needs of the individual and those of the firm must clearly be identified *before* continual professional development programmes are instigated. In part the areas for enhancement and improvement may be identified by the firm's management, for example during a staff appraisal, and in part identified by the professionals themselves, through the use of reflective practice.

5.3.1   Continual professional development

At the heart of professional development is the individual's attitude to work and life, an attitude that promotes a responsible and creative approach which is underwritten by personal and professional integrity. For many professionals the boundaries between work and life are blurred. It is one of the characteristics of professionalism, and the growth of an individual is determined by the manner in which life and work skills are harnessed. The true professional recognises that professional development is never complete: there is always something new to learn, a new situation to experience and respond to. The concept of continual professional development (CPD), or lifelong learning, is not new to professionals. The RIBA's interest started in 1962, although it was not until January 1993 that the institution made participation a duty of membership. Qualified architects are obliged to undertake a minimum of 35 hours CPD activity a year, draw up a Personal Development Plan and to keep a record of the activities undertaken. At the time, the RIBA did not offer any incentive or deterrent to members who chose to follow or ignore such advice, although early in 1998 the institution announced that it was to 'get tough' with those who did not participate.

There are two strongly held views about CPD in the architectural profession, or rather about the imposition of a formal responsibility for carrying it out (Emmitt and Neary 1995). At one extreme some architects believe that, as professionals, part of their competence comes from the fact that they continue to develop and enhance their knowledge and skills throughout their professional life and they do not need their professional institution to police this activity. At the opposite end of the scale some architects believe there is a need for their professional institution to act in a much stronger way and monitor CPD. These two views seem consistent with the motivation theories expressed by McGregor (1960), and relate to the basic difference between individuals who are self-motivated and eager to develop to their full potential, or individuals inclined to carry out the least effort necessary to survive. Plainly these two approaches indicate extremes of view and are as much a product of management styles as they are of individual motivation. Clearly the topic is emotive to professionals. However, to measure CPD activity entirely through the number of hours committed or through attendance at recognised events is to miss the point.

The concept of lifelong learning, or more appropriately continuing professional development, has implications for individual members of the firm and for the firm as a whole. From a firm's viewpoint it is essential to stay up-to-date. CPD offers one route to this goal and, in the context of this book, provides a vehicle to strengthen the business acumen of the firm. Furthermore, it has been argued that CPD can act as an agent of change by introducing new managerial techniques to practitioners (Emmitt and Neary 1995). Regardless of the differing requirements of different professional institutions, individual firms must establish their own policies to maintain a fair system for all employees. A carefully designed and adequately resourced staff development programme will not only help to keep existing employees motivated but will also help to attract new staff (Kaderlan 1991). The better the knowledge of individual staff, the better the collective knowledge of the firm and the better it is able to compete.

So CPD may be one of the keys to gaining and retaining competitive advantage through the constant updating of the firm's collective skills. But there is a catch. Both time and money must be allocated and fairly distributed for education, training and staff development. The boom or bust nature of the building industry makes it difficult to plan staff time and allocate projected finances. In a boom the money may be available but time may be in short supply as the firm struggles to meet the growing workload; in a downturn the time may be available but the finances are often not available to pay for attendance at conferences and seminars. Furthermore, in a climate where fee levels and profit margins are low, can architectural firms afford to spend money on staff development? Can individual architects afford to fund their CPD themselves from low salaries? It is the classic catch 22 situation. It will cost money to effect a programme of change, but failure to invest will lead to a further loss of the architect's credibility and responsibilities.

5.3.2   Reflective practice

Professional development has often been left to the individual, self-directed and not always directly associated with the development of the firm in which they practise. The move to more formally instigated CPD programmes has, to a certain extent, shifted the responsibility in the direction of the firm. However, if professional development is to benefit the firm and the individual it should be based on both the practitioner's and the firm's experience, based on reflective learning. Donald Schon's (1983) idea of the reflective practitioner was a way of demonstrating the professional's use of knowledge. The professional has at his or her command a repertoire of strategies and techniques that provide the capacity to think creatively in context; that is to reflect during the event, rather than after, and is an integral part of professional practice.

That said, it is widely accepted that although we learn from experience, more experience does not guarantee more learning. Learning from experience tends to be most effective when the experiences are painful or novel in some way, but learning from our mistakes is not a good policy (nor is it consistent with the total quality management ethos) if we wish to stay in business. Furthermore, the opportunity to learn from novel experiences may diminish as time passes. Thus reflective practice after the event is important because the individual will reflect on his or her actions, which may have been rather ordinary and uneventful, rather than waiting to learn from experience. The reflective practitioner has the opportunity to reflect on procedures and habits taken for granted, but which may be open to improvement when analysed. A number of tools to assist with reflective practice range from keeping a reflective journal to organised discussion groups with peers (quality circles). Reflection on practice is an essential component of professional development; the better the management of an individual's direction, the better equipped the firm is to respond to change.

5.4   COMINGS AND GOINGS

Firms are not stable environments. Over their lifetime they experience many changes in size, direction and personnel. Some of these changes may form part of a firm's strategic plan, others may not have been anticipated. Staff join and leave for a variety of reasons and some attempt must be made to manage these comings and goings over the short term and strategically. The workforce is more mobile than ever before and a source of personal knowledge leaves with departing employees and enters with every new member of the office. Staff turnover will affect the knowledge base of the firm.

5.4.1   Staff turnover

Staff turnover is usually seen as a problem rather than an opportunity by the directors of firms. Apart from the loss of a valued employee, taking valuable knowledge with them (usually to a competitor), suitable replacements need to be found. The vacancy may need to be advertised and time invested by the firm to filter the applicants, interview and select someone appropriate. That done, the new member of the office must then be quickly integrated into the firm's culture. It is a costly and stressful process and one that may result in the firm having to adapt to the change, especially in the smaller firms. The competitiveness of the firm *will* be affected by staff changes and the process must be managed accordingly. In a boom period staff may move, simply to increase their salary and promotion prospects, while in an economic recession staff are more likely to stay put (unless made redundant), partly because there are fewer opportunities to move and partly because of fears over job security. Staff turnover can be controlled through good management, motivation, reward, training and communication between the firm's members. High staff turnover is a good indicator of a poorly managed firm.

   Although most staff changes are initiated by individual members of staff there are occasions when managers need to make changes for the good of the firm: to make people redundant or dismiss them. All members of the firm, whatever their responsibilities, must accept that firms change over time. Some staff may find that, for a variety of reasons, they no longer fit within the team; some may leave on their own accord and find more suitable employment; others may have to be dismissed. Milton Friedman (1962) has argued that management's only real social responsibility is to pursue their firm's economic self-interest. While this may be true of some architectural firms, others are often driven by a larger responsibility for their staff, tending to put off difficult decisions because of their concern for the well-being of their employees. Although this is admirable, it is often done at the expense of the firm. A firm is only as strong as its weakest member of staff. It is unfair to others in the firm to carry ineffective staff, often leading to problems of motivation, and always leading to a reduction in the firm's competitive potential; they must be dismissed (Sharp 1991). A tough but fair and open policy is required within the spirit of a country's prevailing employment legislation.

Although it was argued earlier that CPD may help to keep employees, the flow of staff from one architectural firm to another should be seen in a positive light. Staff movement provides the opportunity for individuals to gain new experiences and develop their careers while at the same time bringing new knowledge to the firm. Changes in staff provide an opportunity for firms to redefine roles and take on individuals with knowledge more appropriate to the future direction of the firm. It may prevent the firm from becoming stale and losing its competitive edge. Furthermore, the greater a firm's investment in system capital such as quality management and expert knowledge systems the less the impact of changes in staff. So a modest staff turnover may well benefit the competitive firm, but the job function of the incoming member of staff needs to be carefully considered against the firm's strategic plan before the job is advertised.

5.4.2   Recruitment

Recruitment policy links back to the development and growth of the firm, whether it is the appointment of new staff because of business expansion or the replacement of staff who have decided to move on. Firms compete for staff in the same way as they compete for clients and the firm's reputation as a place to work and for the quality of the service provided will affect the type of employee it attracts (Kaderlan 1991; Maister 1993). It is an area to be borne in mind during all the firm's marketing activities.

Staff should be hired with a view to the future growth of the firm as well as to its current needs and aspirations: new staff with new skills can help the firm change and develop positively. Since staff are the lifeblood of any professional service firm, their recruitment should be taken extremely seriously. Before any recruitment campaign starts, the firm's directors must agree on the qualities they are looking for and, just as importantly, discuss the issue with the existing employees. After all, it is they who are going to interact with the new staff on a daily basis. New staff can be seen as a threat by established employees, therefore it is essential to keep everyone informed to limit any negative feelings. A good manager will discuss the issue with existing staff *before* the vacancy is described and advertised.

What type of person is really needed? In a rapidly changing business environment an individual's ability to adapt to changing situations is an essential requirement. Second is the individual's potential contribution to the overall team performance, and third is the individual's technical ability, such as design skills. Do all members of staff need to be highly skilled designers who also have technical and managerial skills? Advertising for staff should also be carefully considered because advertisements are often looked at by potential clients as well as potential employees and should be carefully linked to the firm's marketing strategy.

5.4.3   A flexible workforce

Temporary workers are an important part of many firms' business plans since they give a considerable degree of flexibility, allowing the firm to respond more effectively to changing demands for their services. Temporary staff are contracted in when (and only when) required to cope with additional demand for a firm's services and/or to provide skills not available in-house: a valuable but disposable resource. The use of temporary staff has the advantage of flexibility and the supply of specialist knowledge otherwise unavailable to the firm. But there are also disadvantages. Lack of consistency can lead to ineffective communication within the team and may well unbalance it, even when an effective quality management system is in place. Temporary workers lack firm-specific knowledge – they will not know the firm's operating practices – and as such will require a greater degree of managerial control than permanent employees.

5.4.4 Integration of new staff

The smooth integration of new employees into the existing system is essential if the firm is to function effectively, a process described as their 'cultural socialisation' (Kreps 1990; Kaderlan 1991). New employees will bring expectations and experiences to the firm that will be evaluated against its actual experience, which will in turn lead to an adaption to the firm's cultural norms. The newcomer's ability to adapt quickly to the firm's culture is important for the continuity of the cohesive firm and is vital to continued success in the market. The new staff member will spend a lot of energy getting used to how things are done in their new firm, how jobs are administered and how they fit into the existing social structure within the office, a challenging and stressful time for the newcomer and also for the firm's existing members. New employees need to feel part of the firm quickly. A lack of relevant information and guidance can mean that a new member of the team fails to identify with the job quickly and can have a negative effect on the firm's performance. Interpersonal communication between new and existing staff is an important tool for introducing new members into the firm's cultural norms – formally through job instruction and informally through the telling of stories and legends (Kreps 1990).

The effectiveness of the new member of staff can be improved by dedicating time to the integration process from day one of his or her employment: that is the familiarisation of both formal and social controls. It is no use sitting a new employee at a desk with a copy of the office manual to read or, just as bad, giving him or her a lot of urgent work to be completed by the end of the week. The first few weeks or so should be seen as a training period, not just for the new employee but also for the existing staff. Time must be allocated so that all the firm can be involved in this integration process. It is just as important not to alienate the existing staff as it is the newcomer. Be open and clear about responsibilities and the role of team members. New members of the firm should be helped to grow into their role. One technique which transfers well to smaller firms is to use the staff review system from the first week. The new staff member is asked to assess their own skills against the skills needed and to agree three objectives they hope to achieve in their first three months (usually the probationary period). At the end of the three-month period a staff evaluation is conducted.

Since few architectural firms are large enough to justify the employment of personnel managers, this is a job to be carried out by one of the firm's more experienced staff members, perhaps the quality manager. This role is additional to an individual's existing commitments and time must be made available for it, an investment which will quickly be repaid. If new members of staff are integrated quickly and smoothly they perform better sooner, a benefit to both the firm and the employee in terms of job satisfaction. Even if they move to another firm after two years they will have been an integral productive part of the team during that time.

5.5   TEAMS

The importance of group and team development is well documented in management literature and new developments in teamworking strategies have become an important theme in management literature (Druker 1995; Hartley 1997). Architecture, the making of buildings, is a team effort, requiring the input of a variety of individuals both from inside the firm and outside it. Within the firm groups of individuals can be brought together as self-managing teams with great effectiveness. However, the temporary project team, unique to each project, has a far more complex interaction of formally constituted teams and less formal groups which makes it particularly difficult to manage.

In many small-to-medium-size practices, job architects take a project from inception to completion with additional input coming from persons outside the office. Thus individual projects tend to be a personal crusade rather than a 'team' effort in the true sense of the word. On larger projects small teams may be set up within the office to deal with specific stages of a project and then disbanded or reallocated once the task is complete. Such groups will be either project-specific or task-specific (e.g. the design group). The manager's role is primarily to co-ordinate, facilitate and motivate. Control should be firmly in the hands of the professionals. Thus the challenge for the design manager or project manager is to manage these groups of individuals so that they can grow into cohesive, essentially self-autonomous teams. Good managers need to work constantly to transform a group of people, with varying skills and interests, into a focused team and then work hard to sustain the energy and commitment, often in a climate of inadequate resources and tight deadlines. Management literature has been advocating the benefits of working in self-managing teams (SMTs) for some time.

5.5.1   Self-managing teams

The concept of the self-managing team is not new, but it has been slow to gain acceptance. The self-managing team should comprise a number of people with complementary skills who are committed to a common goal. To be effective they must both possess and develop the right mix of complementary skills (ie. design, technical and managerial) while at the same time having operational autonomy to be able to constantly evaluate and evolve as they learn from their collective experience.

Like any important decision, self-managing teams need careful consideration before they are set up and then guidance through their team leader once they are operational. Team-building is critical since it determines the effectiveness of SMTs and the style of leadership needs careful consideration; training may be necessary for the team leader if the team is to maximise its potential. It is widely accepted that the teams should have no more than ten members if they are to be effective (Katzenbach and Smith 1993). The sequential design model (see Chapter 9) provides an ideal opportunity for the use of self-managing teams. They also provide a greater degree of consistency, since the start and the end of projects – the most difficult phases to manage – are easier to handle because of the collective knowledge of the SMT. Feedback, so often neglected, may be accommodated much more easily.

Self-managing teams are important because they are enablers of information-sharing and knowledge creation. The team culture encourages information-sharing and knowledge generation is continually enhanced. This is an important construct both within the professional office and within the project team. Within the office the link between self-managing teams is potentially the weak link and needs careful management to ensure that work within separate teams is disseminated throughout the firm where necessary. The greater the integration of teams the greater the potential for the firm to learn from its collective experience. Within the temporary project team, however, the link between teams (if they exist) is more problematic (see Chapter 8). Continuous improvement will only come about through continuous learning – a process that must be managed.

5.5.2   The management of continuous learning

The concept of lifelong learning was discussed above. The concept behind the SMT has synergy with the total quality ethos. The issue of learning is important both for the individual and for the collective learning, and thus the development of the firm. To a certain extent, especially in smaller firms, the problem of knowledge loss through an employee leaving the firm may constitute a major problem if there is no system in place to incorporate individual knowledge into systems, procedures and expert knowledge systems.

It is important to see the firm developing: not so much in terms of size, more in terms of its ability to compete in the marketplace through a managed programme of experiential learning. Individuals can learn about themselves and their environment through reflection on past action, represented by Kolb's (1984) cycle of experiential learning and Schon's (1983) 'reflective practitioner'. The cyclical view of learning comprises four stages: (1) experience, (2) understanding, (3) planning, and (4) action. Observing and reflecting on experience can lead to a new understanding which allows for new strategies for action, leading on to another evaluative cycle of reflection and learning, represented as a spiral in Figure 5.3.

It is important for the firm that such reflective practice is shared with other staff. The total quality approach based on feedback and the use of quality circles to discuss such issues is a good example. Knowledge generated through the use of

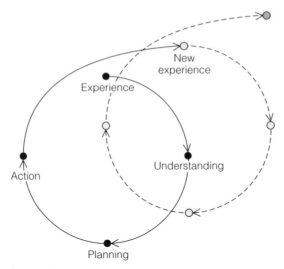

Fig. 5.3   The learning spiral

reflective action and quality circles should be incorporated into some form of knowledge base which is easily accessible, both to existing and new staff. It is through shared experience that the firm may be in a better position to compete.

People are a firm's most important asset and the argument for their continuing improvement through CPD and the use of self-managing teams has been made. However, it is of little use having the structure to generate knowledge if it cannot be managed effectively. Such a strategy will be dependent on the effective utilisation of information technologies and expert knowledge systems. It will also be dependent on the manager's ability to plan staff time so that they have an opportunity to reflect, both individually and within the team. Thus issues of communication, information management, knowledge acquisition, storage and retrieval deserve special attention.

CHAPTER 6

INFORMATION NETWORKS

In addition to the management of the knowledge base, the firm also has to manage the rapidly increasing volume of information. The link between effective management and effective communication in building is addressed, which leads on to issues of information overload and gatekeeping mechanisms. These are discussed in relation to both the project and the product information networks. The chapter concludes by exploring the concept of architectural firms as information managers.

6.1 COMMUNICATION AND BUILDING

The building industry has a poor reputation for the manner in which its individuals communicate with one another. Studies in the 1960s (e.g. Higgin and Jessop 1965) drew attention to the lack of effective communication and also commented on the gulf between the designers and the producers, a situation that has not improved over the years (Rougvie 1995). A recently published paper by the Cabinet Office on sustainable living and working (*RIBA Journal* 1997) expressed concern about the fragmented approach of the building process. It suggested there were missed opportunities about the adoption of ecologically sound ideas and technologies resulting from professionals' inability to work as a team. Perhaps we should not be surprised by this, given the enormity of the task facing anyone charged with managing building projects. Relationships in this non-homogeneous, volatile industry are often adversarial in nature and convoluted because of the procurement routes used, resulting in complex – and arguably ineffective – communication routes. As discussed earlier, the response to problems in the building industry has been to add further complexity in the form of new management disciplines. Unfortunately these new intermediaries add a further strata, or another link to the chain through which information will pass, thus adding the potential for greater complexity and misuse of information.

6.1.1 Communication in building

The building process relies on a vast quantity of information to enable a project to be built, maintained, reused and eventually recycled. Building projects require information in the form of drawings, specifications, schedules, calculations and written instructions. Not only do they have different purposes, but they are usually prepared by individuals from different backgrounds, such as architects, engineers, sub-contractors and specialist suppliers, often using different terms and graphical representation. Thus verbal communication between two or more individuals is often concerned with resolving queries about the interpretation of the information provided.

Drawings are used to transmit the designer's intent to the contractor. However, it is widely accepted that the format and intent of the drawing is far more apparent to the originator than it is to the receiver. As such it is not uncommon for the receiver to request clarification or even misread the originator's intentions, sometimes with costly consequences if it happens on site. The effect is magnified when several drawings from different originators are being referred to at the same time. It is rare, even with the use of electronically generated drawing systems, for architects, structural engineers, electrical and mechanical engineers to use the same symbols and terminology, thus co-ordination is a challenge for the user and especially the co-ordinator, the project manager, whatever their background happens to be. The generation of drawings within the originating office is a process that relies on the use of information and knowledge, much of which will not be included in the finished drawing. Such information must be managed within the office and the quality of the resultant documents checked and controlled before it is issued. In a much cited study of a young architect at work in the design office (Broadbent 1988:205–6) his actions were concerned with communication in the following ways:

Drawing and associated activities	33.4%
Discussion/verbal communication	31.1%
Miscellaneous	12.1%
Thinking	9.5%
Information seeking	7.6%
Letters/written communication	6.3%

Although it was accepted that more senior architects would spend their time differently, the study helped to emphasise the role of communication. Building is about information transfer, exchange and use. In recent years the communication field has been claimed by the information technology (IT) advocates who have suggested that communication will be improved through effective use of information technology. Information technology can improve communication but its development must take into account the social complexity in which information is exchanged. The problem is not so much with the speed of delivery, but more in the quality of the information delivered and the managerial structure of the communication networks. There is a danger in concentrating entirely on IT and not the value of the information transmitted. From inception to use, reuse and disposal, people are involved. The manner in which they communicate (or fail to communicate), has a considerable impact. As such it is necessary to look at the whole process, rather than the parts, if communication and information-processing is to be improved (Paterson 1977). Thus communication and information are inextricably linked and need to be addressed as integral, not separate issues.

6.2 COMMUNICATION

Although the roots of communication theory go back to the mechanistic Sender-Message-Channel-Receiver model, in which information is transmitted from sender to receiver (implying control over the process in which the power rests with the sender of the message), the model has been adapted to recognise that communication is a two-way process. More recent work has moved to a shared perception model in which each person is a 'participant', rather than a 'sender' or 'receiver' (Rogers 1986). One of the more robust definitions is provided by Rogers and Kincaid who define communication as 'a process in which the participants create and share information with one another in order to reach mutual understanding' (Rogers and Kincaid 1981:63). From this definition it follows that 'information' is exchanged in the communication process. Communication (and the absence of communication) is used by individuals and organisations to achieve a number of objectives. First, communication channels are used to inform, transmitting information from sender to receiver. Second, communication channels are used to both establish and maintain relationships. Third, communication may be used as a tool to influence individuals' behaviour. Thus communication forms the link between human behaviour and management – management through communication (Roodman and Roodman 1973).

6.2.1 Organisational communication

Organisational communication is based on four levels of human communication (Kreps 1990):

- *Intrapersonal communication:* Enables an individual to process information.
- *Interpersonal communication:* Enables individuals to establish and maintain relationships.
- *Small-group communication:* Enables members of work groups to co-ordinate activities.
- *Multigroup communication:* Enables different work groups to co-ordinate their efforts.

Interpersonal communication is important because it is at this level in the communication hierarchy that relationships are established and through which individuals co-orient their behaviours towards common goals. Hence interpersonal communication is crucial to co-orientation and the ability to organise (Kreps 1990) and fundamental to effective communication within small groups (e.g. within the office) and multigroups (e.g. within the temporary project team). Groups will develop a structure over time based on (1) power, status and authority, (2) individual roles within the group, and (3) the degree to which individuals like or dislike each other; structure and communication are irretrievably interlinked (Hartley 1997). Communication studies have identified the importance of network structures (discussed later) and the role of individuals within networks who may act as gatekeepers to the flow of information.

6.2.2 The gatekeeping construct

For communication to be effective the message must first be received and then understood by the receiver. But barriers to communication, in the form of cultural and/or physical dissonance, do exist and must be recognised and accommodated within any communication process. In particular the importance of individuals as potential barriers or gatekeepers must be understood. The two-way communication model is rarely appropriate in building since communication often takes place via at least one intermediary, such as the client-project manager-architect. Thus communication is via a third party or a 'gatekeeper', illustrated in Figure 6.1.

'Gatekeeping' is a term used to describe the behaviour of an individual who withholds or alters information as it passes him or her, the gatekeeper, into the social system over which they have a certain amount of control. It is concerned with the selection, creation and control of messages. Simplistic models are concerned with the behaviour of individuals, but the complexity of the process requires consideration of many other factors, including the organisational level gatekeeping decisions and social system influences such as culture. The gatekeeping construct was first proposed by Kurt Lewin (1947) and translated into the first and highly influential research project by David Manning White (1950) who looked at the gatekeeping decisions made by a wire editor on a small newspaper. He found that the wire editor (whom he called 'Mr. Gates') made 'highly subjective' decisions when rejecting or accepting news stories. Drawing on both Lewin's and White's research, Westley and MacLean (1957) proposed a gatekeeping model, in which the gatekeeper is also an encoder, that has been used by other researchers. The gatekeeper can select messages transmitted from the sender and pass on to the receiver those messages that the gatekeeper feels are appropriate to the receiver's needs. Messages can be withheld or transformed before passing them on; thus the receiver will receive different messages to those sent (see Figure 6.1).

Gatekeeping research has largely concentrated on the mass media field with special emphasis on the selection of news items by editorial staff, although the construct has been extended by Pamela Shoemaker (1991) and applied to the architects' office (Emmitt 1994, 1997a). An attempt has been made to show the process in diagrammatic form from the perspective of an individual working within an architectural office (see Figure 6.2). Information in the form of messages exerts forces on the individual from both inside and outside the firm. Messages may be deliberately directed at the firm (e.g building product manufacturers advertising literature) or exert force simply by being present within the firm's milieu (e.g social pressures to design for a sustainable future). Some may enter the firm; others may be ignored or rejected. From the individual's perspective, messages may not be received simply because they have not passed through the organisational gates. Furthermore, some messages may come directly to the individual, others through the organisation gatekeeper (a modified message) while information generated from within the firm will also exert pressures on the individual.

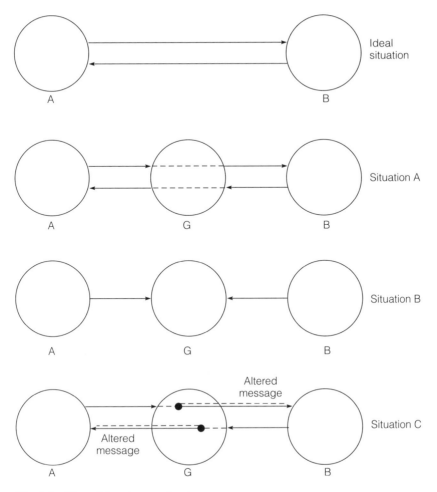

Fig. 6.1 The gatekeeping construct
A & B = participants in the information exchange, G = gatekeeper.
Ideal situation Information can be exchanged without interference from a third party, a gatekeeper.
Situation A Gatekeeper is present in the communication chain, but does not alter the message, simply passes it on; the best situation, but unlikely.
Situation B Gatekeeper exerts maximum influence on communication, messages are not passed on; the worst situation.
Situation C Gatekeeper controls the situation to his or her advantage by altering the messages as they are passed on. The most likely situation.

Once the individual's behaviour is appreciated it is possible to look at gatekeepers' control of information flow within a network. Gatekeepers are important since they act as a physical gate through which information has to pass; they are in a powerful position, conveying messages from one person to another or withholding all, or part, of the message. Gatekeepers can help other members of the

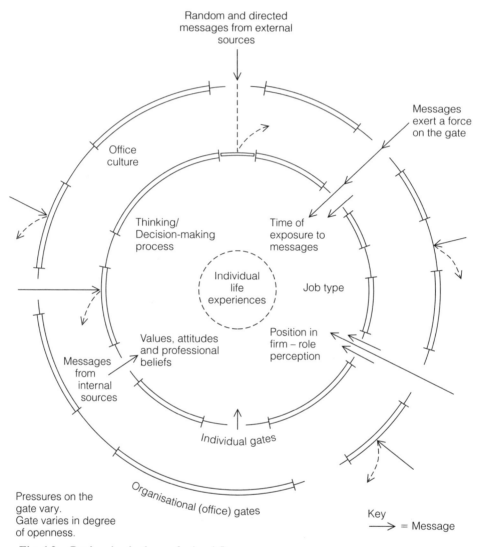

Fig. 6.2 Gatekeeping in the professional firm

network to avoid information overload by allowing through only what they feel is important information. It is the gatekeeper who decides what is important to send on and what is important to withhold, so there is always the danger that information may be withheld that should have been passed on simply because the gatekeeper has made an incorrect decision. It is important to recognise that all members of a network operate as gatekeepers, operating their gates on different levels depending on their position or perceived position within the network. The importance of the gatekeeping construct within the project management environment has been made (Emmitt 1995) and is addressed later. It is only when the gatekeeping construct is appreciated that it is possible to look at information and knowledge management.

6.3 INFORMATION

Earlier it was stated that information was exchanged in the communication process. Information is a means of communicating with people who do not know one another and who have little personal basis for mutual understanding (Porter-Theodore 1994). Information technology is a tool to store, organise and deliver information quickly from one destination to another. However we should not limit our discussion to speed and quantity, but rather we should emphasise on the value of the information transmitted and the problem of information overload.

6.3.1 The value of information

Information is data in a usable form: it allows people to make decisions and take action (Daniels 1994). Data has a cost and information value. The cost of researching, analysing, using, storing and transmitting is relatively easy to quantify compared with the value of the information to the user. But information only has value if it is accurate, timely and properly used by the receiver (Daniels 1994). More specifically, the value of information depends on the people who are going to use it, the circumstances in which they use it and *their* perception of its value to them at any particular time. Meeting the criteria of accuracy, timeliness and appropriate use is, and will continue to be, a major challenge for information managers. More specifically:

- Information must be useful and relevant to the intended audience.
- The message should be simple. Information that is complicated is more likely to fail.

6.3.2 Information overload

Another problem facing both individuals and managers of a firm is the vast quantity of information available to the potential user. The amount of information available to a firm has increased to such an extent that some form of specialised management structure and technology is required to store, process and retrieve relevant information to avoid a state of information overload. Information overload occurs when an individual or organisation receives more information than it can handle; thus some has to be rejected or ignored. It is tempting to view information overload as a new phenomenon, but it has been a cause for concern among professionals for some time. For example in *The Principles of Architectural Design* published in 1907, Marks suggested practitioners should look at the trade catalogues left by travellers (travelling salesmen) on a weekly basis and then dispose of them after reading: an early example of managing the volume – if not quality – of information.

The volume of information attempting to enter the architectural office has grown significantly since Marks' advice. As such there is a need to manage it if information overload is to be avoided. Research into how architectural firms attempt to manage trade information as it comes into the office (Emmitt 1997b) found that there were a series of complex managerial controls in place, with managers acting as gates through which information had to pass before it reached the specifier in the office. Through a series of structured interviews with the directors of architectural firms, the research concluded that the reason for controlling the information coming into the office was not just associated with controlling information overload, but was a managed process to try to limit the firm's exposure to risk, with gates operating at organisational and individual levels.

With the advent of cheap publishing and more recently digital information the problem of managing the information received in the office has mushroomed. This is a particular problem for the 'information rich' (Rogers 1986): professionals such as engineers and architects, who both need to stay up-to-date with current developments and need to keep the information base at a manageable level. Evidence tends to suggest that professionals are failing in this regard, since according to the Building Research Establishment one of the causes of defects in

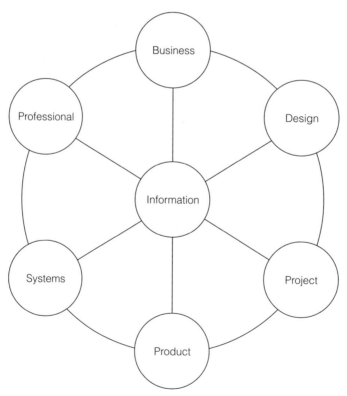

Fig. 6.3 Information drivers

Table 6.1 Information drivers

1. Business information	2. Design information	3. Project information
external source:	*external source:*	*external source:*
market segment	trade literature	client
competitors	professional journals	consultants
collaborators	design typologies	contractors
(consultants,	legal (e.g. planning	statutory
contractors)	and building	user groups
internal source:	regulations)	*internal source:*
staff records	health and safety	design typologies
financial records	*internal source*:	planning and
individual projects	'standard' details	monitoring
mission statement	design typologies	
marketing literature	design guides	
equipment and		
materials		
4. Product (user) information	5. Systems and management controls	6. Professional institution
external source:	*external source:*	*external source:*
feedback from	consultants'	code of conduct
building (faults)	management	professional journals
feedback from client	systems	*internal source:*
internal source:	*internal source:*	code of conduct
analysis to assist	plan of work	professional indemnity
future jobs	office manual	insurance
	quality management	

buildings is the inability to use available information. The information is out there, but inability to use it may be related more to information overload and the inability of the professional to gather, assimilate and consider all pertinent information. Much of the information coming into the office is from an external source, although the office will produce information internally which also needs managing. It is worth considering the different types of information required by a professional design firm: see Figure 6.3. The different types of information can be broken down further as shown in Table 6.1, which makes no attempt to be an exhaustive listing. Much of this information is available, and becoming increasingly more available, to the design firm's competitors. For example, design typologies and standard details are often used by participants in building who have little need for the services of a professional designer. Housing developers and design-and-build are examples where professional design firm input is rarely sought, except perhaps for challenging sites. Specialist areas (with specific informational requirements) are permission for development (closely linked to design quality), project management, repair and maintenance. As such IT represents a further threat to the design professional since it makes access to standard solutions much easier and quicker, often for little financial outlay.

6.3.3   Information audits

A firm capable of managing information overload will have a certain degree of
competitive advantage over its competitors since it should be capable of responding
quicker. Christie (1981) has argued that the value of information should be
accurately assessed, through the use of regular audits, to 'weed out' unnecessary
documentation, since there is no point in storing or transmitting valueless
information because it costs money to store and access. The challenge is to be able
to distinguish between information that is useful and that which may be
superfluous. Filters and delimiters are required as part of a management policy and
ideally part of a quality management system. But for many managers the thought of
throwing away or deleting information goes against their better instincts; what if
there is a problem and we need to check our files? This is a particular problem for
professionals dealing with work to existing buildings, where access to old
regulations, codes and building product information will be necessary.

6.3.4   IT and management roles

Digital information is all-pervasive. Managers and staff at all levels in a firm need to
be comfortable with IT, an essential tool. There is a tendency to say: here is the
technology – what do we do with it? rather than carefully investigating a firm's
requirements and then, and only then, deciding how it can help. Most literature
concerned with information technology is flawed because it has failed to address the
deeper and much more complex issue of human communication. Information
technology is nothing more than a tool which, if utilised well, can certainly improve
communication. If utilised badly it merely transmits a large quantity of unwanted
information leading to information overload, a state to be avoided. IT is also
expensive, not so much in terms of the cost of hardware and software, but in the
maintenance, up-dating and management of information systems. That said, digital
management information systems provide effective tools for managers to make
informed decisions. Whether or not a specialist information manager is required
will depend to a certain extent on the system employed and the volume of
information being processed. It should be remembered that any information
systems (regardless of cost and pedigree) are social systems whose success or failure
is linked to the dynamics of the organisation. This point was demonstrated in the
report of a case study of a firm's executive information system (McBride 1997)
where failure of an electronic system was found to be linked to social factors (the
management structure) rather than to any technical problems. Thus the design of
electronic information systems, such as expert knowledge systems, needs to address
issues of context and structure, the human factor, before implementation.

6.3.5   Information and decision-making

Information is central to the decision-making process. The more relevant and
complete the information, the better an individual is able to make an informed

decision. It is rare, however, to have all the relevant information to hand and it is necessary to understand the information-seeking process that underlies decision-making. Typically, the person seeking information has an incomplete picture of the world and may have only partial knowledge of the information he or she wants. Christie (1981) has argued that at any given point in time an individual has five main behavioural options open:

1. To wait.
2. To act.
3. To generate information.
4. To seek information.
5. To opt out of the situation.

At all of these stages the individual will be exposed to a variety of messages. Many of these will be ignored: that is, the individual will exercise selective exposure.

6.3.6 Decision-making

The reflective thinking model discussed by John Dewey (1933) proposed six steps in effective decision-making. From (1) recognising an organisational difficulty to (2) defining the nature of the problem and (3) analysing the problem, the logical steps continue with (4) suggesting possible solutions and (5) selecting the best solution and then (6) implementing the solution chosen. Dewey's reflective thinking model is applicable to both individual and group decision-making. Another popular model used in group decision-making is 'brainstorming', during which as many ideas as possible are suggested before being evaluated, a hectic process that needs careful management if it is to be effective. A different view on group decision-making has been suggested by Cohen *et al.* (1972) called the 'garbage can model'. They have argued that problems, people, different choices and solutions sift about in a garbage can until enough of them make contact for a decision to be made. These random decisions may appear to be logical when seen retrospectively, but in reality they are due to chance.

6.3.7 Information and communication networks

Continuing the interpersonal communication theme, some work has been undertaken in an attempt to identify networks in urban renewal projects (Neary and Symes 1993). In all three case studies the entrepreneur, not the architect, was responsible for the direction of the projects. This was an important piece of work which identified the role of the various players during the development project, but it is important to note that the networks break down once a project is complete, thus disseminating any knowledge gained to new networks.

It is common practice to use network analysis techniques to determine the communication structure within a social system, from which communication networks may be represented graphically by a sociogram. Analysis of the frequency of communication between individuals within a social system can identify the most active lines of communication and gatekeepers. However, there is a methodological problem with sociograms, since they represent a network at a fixed point in time – they do not address the change in the network over time (Rogers and Kincaid 1981). Furthermore, there is a problem with the data collection in knowing exactly when the communication link reported by the respondent in response to a sociometric questionnaire actually occurred. Thus according to Rogers and Kincaid the dynamic process of communication relationships is 'so fleeting that networks cannot be accurately charted' (Rogers and Kincaid 1981:314). For example, an attempt to map information flow in a contractor's organisation by Norman Fisher and Shen Li Yin (1992) goes some way to highlighting some of the difficulties. There is a dilemma here. If communication networks cannot be charted accurately, how is it possible to manage the (temporary) communication networks that develop for individual building projects? It is an enormous challenge for the project manager. In building there are other difficulties. The communication networks are specific to individual projects and therefore temporary in nature; the networks are not stable since they change as the project develops and different individuals enter or leave the network, in part coincident with the stage of the project.

6.4   KNOWLEDGE

So far issues of communication and information have been addressed. It is important to be clear about the difference between information and knowledge. Earlier the knowledge-based firm was discussed in rather general terms, but what do we mean by knowledge? For the professional service firm, knowledge is its key resource; its core knowledge is the specialised knowledge that a professional would claim by virtue of his or her profession. Clients appoint professionals to apply that special knowledge on their behalf since they do not possess it themselves. An architect's core knowledge is building design – strangely given away for free in the hope of securing commissions. Such knowledge is closely bound up in professional values and beliefs which either tacitly or explicitly influence the professional's actions.

Traditionally professional service firms have stored their professional knowledge in the collective memory of the firm's staff, with supporting information contained in filing cabinets and plan chests. Digital information takes up much less space than plan chests and filing cabinets. Information must be manipulated into meaningful designs and drawings. We are all aware of Francis Bacon's observation that knowledge is power ('*Nam et ipsa scienta potestas est*'). However the challenge for the competitive firm is to manage information flow, knowledge and change to maximum advantage (e.g. Allee 1997).

6.4.1   Knowledge-based systems

The retention of knowledge is a challenge for the professional service firm, the majority of which walks into the office in the morning and out in the evening in the heads of individual members of the firm. The capture of this knowledge for future use is a challenge for electronic information systems and in particular electronic expert-knowledge-based systems. Knowledge-based systems should make it easier for employees to access relevant information. However, such systems need careful design and consideration before they can be useful. Systems also need policing for accuracy and currency of information. This is in itself a demanding job, which needs managing through the use of information audits, discussed above.

Good communication and information flow is essential if a client's requirements are to be translated into a competent design and well-built product. Architectural firms need easy and rapid access to a wide range of up-to-date information. Architects' information needs will vary through the different stages of the project lifecycle and must be carefully controlled to ensure that information is both up-to-date and relevant. Control is required to avoid information overload. Speed of access to relevant information is vital to both the efficient management of individual projects and the efficient use and maintenance of the building and its services. There are a number of distinct, but interrelated challenges facing the professional firm: the major ones are (1) information management in the office, (2) information management for individual projects, and (3) information management for the life of a building, discussed below.

6.5   INFORMATION MANAGEMENT IN THE OFFICE

To make informed decisions vast bodies of information must be transmitted, stored, processed and accessed by many people, a process facilitated by modern computer technology. Stamper (1973) argued that information technology was not being used effectively and put this down to the divide between the technologists (who do not understand the complexities of organisations) and the managers (who are unable to translate their wants into demands on technology) and suggested that 'between them a river of mistrust flows through the chasm of misunderstanding' (Stamper 1973:12). This situation has changed little since 1973 despite the phenomenal technological developments in the computer industry.

Professional firms have always had to manage information. With the adoption of computers and information management software, management of information may have become easier, but there has been an explosion in the amount of information that needs to be managed. The manner in which firms need to organise and access information will depend on the size of the office. At a CIB conference held in Trondheim, Norway (1997) three speakers demonstrated the difference in approach by firm size. A solo practitioner claimed that she needed information about specific parts of the job about twice a year. As such she needed a source of information that was updated by someone other than herself and one that she could rely on; this was sourced electronically from internet-based suppliers. In contrast, directors of two large practices talked about the challenge of designing their own information systems, based on intranet systems, and the difficulties of keeping the information current, given a finite amount of time and money. There is clearly a move away from paper-based to electronic systems, although there remain problems with compatibility, accessibility, cost and time, which must be addressed before everyone in building can communicate entirely via digital information.

6.6   INFORMATION MANAGEMENT FOR INDIVIDUAL PROJECTS

Effective communication and information management is not only vital to the efficient day-to-day running of the design firm, but also to the daily administration of individual projects, a role usually undertaken by the 'job architect' or project manager. Ineffective communication costs money and may add time to a project. From a project viewpoint there are two key areas where empathy is crucial: (1) the interaction of client and designer and (2) the interaction of designer and builder, both of which are addressed in further detail later. The gulf between designer and builder is also evident in the type of information they require. Information produced by the design team, the contract documents – drawings, schedules and specifications – describes the building as they want it to appear when it is complete. Such information describes the product, its size and its position in relation to other components. The contract documentation does not tell the builder *how* to assemble the various components. This information is held by the builder as specialist 'how to' knowledge.

6.6.1   The project team

Design is a participatory process. At its most simple the team will involve a client, an architect and a contractor. Usually the team involves a number of individuals who constitute an information network, made up of smaller groups or teams, for example the design team and the construction team. Each member of the team will have his or her own agenda, goals, individual values and experiences that may differ from the next individual in the project information chain. This will influence the interaction and participation of individuals, in particular the efficiency of communication between them. The building industry is notorious for its adversarial behaviour and distrust between different professional groups. At certain times in the life of a particular project these individuals will meet and communicate with one another, a condition I will refer to as a 'boundary condition', that may well have changing edges.

Construction industry professionals are primarily concerned with information exchange, dealing with drawings, specifications, cost data, programmes and other design and management information required for the successful completion of a building. Successful knowledge-based organisations have been shown to rely on the effective transfer of information (Winch and Schneider 1993; Boisot 1998). Similarly, good relations within the team depend on effective communication. However, problems have been identified in relation to the ease and effectiveness of communications even in small 'communication circles' where the process is relatively simple and the opportunity for interference is relatively low. The flow of information during the project will be through the project co-ordinator, an architect, project or construction manager, and the effectiveness of communication during the project will depend on the individual's ability to manage the process. Equally, members of 'periphery' groups associated with the project rely on the project manager's ability to listen to their requirements and concerns, incorporate them into the project knowledge base and transmit them to the relevant parties, thus providing a 'real' chance to participate in the project.

6.6.2 The cultural context

The problem with many communication studies is that communication is studied with little attention to culture. Culture influences communication on intrapersonal, interpersonal, intergroup, organisational and political levels. The problem with studying communication in building is that different individuals are drawn from a variety of educational and cultural backgrounds; thus barriers to effective communication are sure to exist and cannot be ignored. Furthermore, the culture of the social system(s) (networks) that form for building projects will influence how individuals within this system communicate.

The ability to share information is critical to expert knowledge systems and information management systems. While free access to information is possible within a firm (although the firm's culture may inhibit this) it becomes a problem when looked at in terms of the temporary project environment, partly because some members may withhold information as a means of gaining some form of advantage (i.e. acting as a gatekeeper) and partly because many of the project team members may well be competing for the same market segments. Thus security and the policing of the system become overriding, and restricting, factors. In practice the extent of 'managed information' may be (very) limited. In short, we have a complex technical and social problem.

To understand the opportunity for participation and empowerment in more depth it is necessary to look at the social structure of the temporary project team. Sociologists have argued that any social situation is a sort of reality agreed on by those taking part in it. Thus individuals will have preconceived constructs of what is expected of them and of others in the network. In building projects, the project team exists on three fundamentally different and potentially conflicting levels: the formally constituted network, the statutory network, and the informal local participants network.

1. *Formal network:* This is formally constituted through contracts. The members of the project team are clearly identified and their roles defined. Their aim is to produce a building project in accordance with the wishes of the client, usually within stringent time and cost constraints. The temporary project network is likely to contain individuals working to different agendas because of their training and position in the network. Interaction with the statutory network and the informal user groups may be sporadic and seen as a distraction rather than a help in terms of the project.

2. *Statutory network:* Various external contributors to the project are represented by statutory authorities, such as the town–planning officer, building control officer and fire officer. These may influence the planning of the project at different times and to varying degrees through, for example, the insistence on the submission of an environmental impact assessment (EIA) by the planning authorities. In the UK this network is usually perceived as protectionist and therefore restrictive in terms of the project.

3. *Informal network:* This will comprise local groups concerned with their own well-being and that of the local ecology. Local user groups may wish to participate in the project, through cooperation or through protest (often by way of the planning authorities). The opportunity for empowerment will depend on the timing of their intervention and the manner in which their concerns are communicated and accepted by members of the other networks.

Because of the different networks operating within any one project it is unlikely that any one individual will have a clear understanding or a complete picture because of the many processes occurring at the same time (see Figure 6.4). Not everyone in the team is linked together. Furthermore, communication loops within the project are not closed, thus there is scope for ambiguity, change, interference and misunderstanding. Individuals are likely to have different goals, values and priorities, whatever their position in the network. Each individual will also have a unique view of the project based on their own perceptions drawn from the information available. No single party is really in control of communication between the networks, but if effective participation is to be achieved, where everyone involved can get their individual messages and contribution considered, there is a need for a decision-making framework and leadership (Wulz 1986; Yoram 1996): an integrated team where all members, whatever their network, can provide their specialist input as part of a common goal, a true team that encourages and provides the opportunity for participation and empowerment.

An integrated, or deconstructed, design-led management team offers one way in which the opportunity to participate may be improved. This model is essentially a multidisciplinary team which designs, manages and builds. The advantage of containing the specialists under the umbrella of one company is that the potential for communication breakdown and/or conflict is reduced but not necessarily eliminated. Thus the prospect of good client briefing, effective communication between design team, construction team and between the informal participants may improve.

Projects are not hermetically sealed or static. They are made up of a multitude of individuals, some with greater input than others, some with greater influence than others. They are not closed, but open systems and as such particularly difficult to manage. It is easy to forget the social context in which technical activities take place. Project failure is often a result of a breakdown in communication, assisted by cultural differences. The greater the empathy between participants the closer they are in communication terms and the greater the potential for effective communication. Conversely the more distant they are in communication terms the greater the chance of ineffective communication.

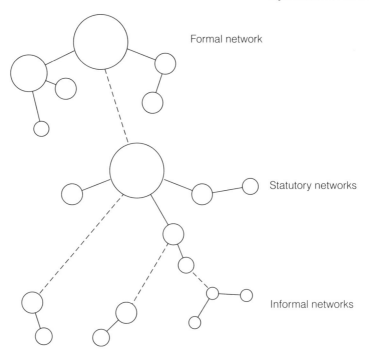

Fig. 6.4 Building networks

6.6.3 Boundary conditions

Each project will have an associated team development phase where individuals enter and leave the team at certain stages. Thus the team will constantly be changing in size and format. As such it will be particularly difficult to manage – but its effective management and direction is vital to the effective realisation of the building project, the finished building. Individuals in the project team are linked by interpersonal and written communication channels or information exchange routes. Information consists of drawings, specifications, schedules and programmes which are used to make decisions throughout the life of the project. Most of this information is task-specific and as such is unlikely to be shared by anyone other than those who need to use the information. Thus the information manager's task is a difficult one!

The generation, transmission and filtering of information as it passes around the network is a particularly complex area. Essentially, each project could be seen as a problem, broken down into a series of smaller problems to be dealt with by different individuals. In order to solve the problem and communicate the solution to the team leader, information has to be gathered, analysed, filtered, assembled and then transmitted on to the next link in the chain, who may or may not need all the information they receive; indeed, they may need additional information that the sender failed to send. The quality, rather than the quantity, of that information will ultimately determine the quality of the finished building and the service provided by the firm. The quality of the links between individuals, the nodes in the information network, is essential to effective communication.

6.7 PRODUCT INFORMATION

Of the vast quantity of information generated for individual projects, much is related to the process of building (project-orientated) with a small amount of information, such as drawings, specifications and maintenance logs being applicable to the actual finished building (product-orientated). Professionals involved in the building project will retain project information and product information primarily for legal reasons. Project information may have little or no value to the owners/ occupiers of the completed building. However, the product information such as floor plans, details of construction and legal consents are needed by the building owners (not necessarily the client or original owners). Such information is easily stored and accessed electronically. However, many designers are reluctant to release this information fearing loss of future business (copyright laws). Increased interest in both building and service maintenance, coincident with the growth of the facilities management discipline, has brought a greater awareness of the value of accurate, accessible information. At the heart of the facilities (asset) management discipline is effective decision-making, based on rapid access to current information. The discipline is information driven.

The post-project phase, or product phase, has traditionally been the domain of the building surveyor. Many architects have concentrated on the design and project phases, content to leave the building's demands in use to other professionals such as building surveyors, asset and facilities managers. With increased pressures to reuse existing buildings, through upgrading, extension and repair, architectural firms are starting to reconsider their role since there are opportunities to expand their service provision. As designers and possibly project managers the original design team (and in particular the information manager) is arguably in the best position to provide advice about the maintenance, repair and upgrading of the finished product because they should *understand* the building. This understanding is enhanced if the information manager is fully involved in the assembly of the building, for example through the use of construction management (discussed later).

As discussed in an earlier chapter, the interface between facilities management and design is important if a building's potential is to be realised. The maintenance of a current set of plans and a maintenance database is paramount if a building is to be cared for and utilised effectively during its various lives. The challenge for all parties concerned with building maintenance, asset and facilities management is one of collecting dispersed, often inaccessible, information; this may lead to a loss of design and technical expertise that first created the building. This is an area of growing interest to the asset and facilities management disciplines, often seen as an end in itself, but one that links back to initial design decisions. Perhaps the

Scandinavian 'total build approach' goes some way to addressing the fuller picture in calling for an integrated approach to a lifelong database (Haugen 1994). Efforts need to be made to convince promoters, owners, maintainers and building users that information for life should be their primary goal if sustainability is to move centre stage (Emmitt and Wyatt 1998).

6.7.1 Environmentally responsible design in an information age

It has been argued that the dilemma of networking for sustainable design is linked to the diffusion of information (Emmitt 1997a) and to the networks that form for any temporary building project: the social network, the project network, the product network and the information network (Wyatt and Emmitt 1997). The underlying theme of the Wyatt and Emmitt paper was communication, or rather the difficulty of communicating information effectively throughout all stages of the product's life. Information technology is a tool which can assist with the rapid transfer, storage and dissemination of information relating to a project, but this information (and the technologies employed) must be managed effectively if individuals in the project team are to avoid information overload and thus assist, not hinder, the communication process.

One reason why lifecycle design was largely neglected in the past lies in the inaccessibility of information – information that exists in the form of specialised knowledge – and which is held by a number of poorly linked players in the temporary project network. On the one hand, while progress may be achieved through new technologies making access to information easier and quicker, on the other the number of individuals involved in building continues to increase with the potential to hinder progress. Thus both information technologies, such as computer-based expert systems, and the number of people contributing and drawing on the information within the system need to be managed.

Whatever strategies are evolved to secure sustainable building they must embrace all the contributors to the building process, both in the project and the product phases (Emmitt and Wyatt 1998). Thus building product manufacturers and suppliers as well as the disassembly sector must be included within the whole life appraisal if an individual development's environmental impact is to be reduced. So while we must understand the temporary networks and the challenge posed by an information-driven environment, we must recognise that the role of the architect is changing. Whether the architect or another construction professional emerges as an information manager remains to be seen. What is important is to recognise that information management, not design, is the key to future development and the provision of competitive service provision.

6.8 THE INFORMATION MANAGER

Perhaps the biggest challenge to information management in the building industry is that information is generated for many different purposes, by different people for use by others, based on disparate definitions often resulting in the potential for conflict and inconsistencies. The problem is one of information transfer, codification and diffusion (e.g. Boisot 1987, 1998; E. Rogers 1995). Add to this the complexity of the networks that require complex information exchange and which are extremely difficult to model and the problems of inconsistent format – paper and electronic – and accessibility pale into insignificance. Arising from an investigation of communication networks and information transfer comes the concept of an information manager.

Like organisations, temporary project teams cannot be left to evolve: they must be designed so that they can use information effectively. Information holds firms and project teams together. Stamper (1973) called for an information specialist, with a balanced view and intellectual framework to harness the power of the organisation, something that is starting to happen almost 25 years later as firms have realised that knowledge has become their key economic resource. Naturally the question has to be asked: who is best qualified for such a role?

The case for an independent information manager has been put: for example, Li (1996) has argued that the IT manager is required but that the construction process needs to be re-engineered, with a re-engineered team, before IT can be applied successfully. The claims by Li and others are as much founded on optimism as hard fact; indeed, many of their models of the process are simplistic and potentially misleading. Rather than create yet another new profession within the building industry it may be more beneficial for an existing team member to take on this role. The independent project managers and to a lesser extent the construction managers may well see themselves as the most obvious candidates to become information managers. The important point is that the role requires an appreciation of the nature of the information transmitted and an overview of the process and the product. Because much of the information is concerned with design it has been suggested that architectural firms would be most suited to take on this role: a design-orientated information manager capable of harnessing the power of the temporary project networks and controlling the supply chain. Essentially this is an integrating role for the product champion (Wyatt and Emmitt 1996), a role likely to grow as client, designer and builder work towards an integrated team approach.

6.8.1   Competitive advantage through information management

Information management presents opportunities and poses threats for design professionals. The management challenge for senior managers and IT managers was discussed above: an information manager. Throughout this book the argument for integration between disparate team members has been made: IT as a tool has the potential to keep everyone informed, but with the potential of cohesion comes the threat of isolation. As part of a business strategy, information management can be offered as a professional service thus expanding fee provision and helping to retain and expand market share, while within the firm the management of information can help the firm to be more efficient in its use of time and more ready to adapt to changing circumstances. Information management also poses a threat because the architectural firm's competitors have equal access to IT tools and may also have the managerial expertise that allows them to offer the service. Furthermore and perhaps more importantly, ready access to building typologies and to 'free' design information makes it much easier for the designer's competitors to move into their market area.

Information and its management is a major driver and must be both understood and embraced if competitive advantage is to be secured. Firms that are able to get a grip of communication will have significant competitive advantage in an information-driven industry. It should be an essential part of the firm's business strategy.

CHAPTER 7

BUSINESS STRATEGIES

Although there is no single business strategy to suit all firms, this chapter examines a number of approaches to the development of an effective business strategy. The issue of fee-bidding and the development of new service provision is discussed against the need to balance risk and reward. These issues naturally lead on to a debate about how to achieve competitive advantage, either through specialisation or diversity. The chapter concludes with a look at possible approaches to the management of environmentally responsible ideals and practices.

7.1   SERVICE PROVISION

Every firm is subject to continual change since it is a living, growing social system that must adapt if it is to survive and prosper. Because the firm is both subject to, and dependent on, changes in its environment it needs to constantly monitor its size, market position and capabilities. It is useful, however, to look at architectural firms in terms of their size and approach to business before looking at business strategies for the design-orientated professional service firm. Earlier in the book the configuration and the culture of the architectural firm was discussed. These firms also vary in size, have differing workloads, and often differ in the type of services that they offer. Thus each firm will have its own identity, either by design or by accident.

Architect's firms were classified by the number of architects employed in the RIBA's first detailed study of the profession (RIBA 1962) which has since been used by others for comparative purposes. Broken down by firm size, the architectural profession comprises 70 per cent of offices in the 'very small' band (1–5 architects), 15 per cent in the 'small' category and the remaining 15 per cent in offices with 11 architectural staff or more. Since 85 per cent of architectural offices employ ten architects or fewer, many of the management books addressed to large firms are inappropriate. For example, the small firm cannot employ a personnel manager: this is a job done by one of the architects or directors within the office in addition to their other (more familiar) duties. Clearly size is important because the solo practitioner will be forced to act in a very different manner to the director of a medium-sized or large firm.

While architectural practices differ in size, they also differ in the type of service they offer their clients and the type of work in which they are engaged. This is more difficult to quantify. For example, architectural firms have been classified on a scale ranging from the practical to the artistic (Prak 1984). Others have attempted to define firms in terms of the type of service they provide, based on ideas, service or delivery (e.g. Gutman 1988; Allinson 1993). The problem with such classification is that firms tend to be put in one category. In reality many firms operate in at least two of these areas and may well alter to suit a particular client's aims and objectives. Furthermore, some specialist firms are set up to design one particular type of building only, for example medical facilities; other generalist firms will design any type of building regardless of size or location. Symes *et al.* (1995:61–2) reported that 80 per cent of the firms they surveyed specialised in at least one building type such as housing or industrial buildings. In business the key to success is to provide a service of superior value to a client at a competitive price in such a manner that the client will appreciate the value of the service and the end product. This is a simple statement, but is often hard to achieve. The service must fit the client's expectations and exceed them because clients will seek value by matching service and price.

7.2 CLIENTS

It may be an obvious statement, but without clients there can be no architectural business. According to Coxe (1980) the client must become part of the firm's organisational structure. Clients affect projects; ideas must be tested against a budget, regulations and a programme. Good communication between client and architect is crucial, not just to the success of a project but also to long-term client relationships. Satisfied clients are the most important source of new work, either through further commissions or through their recommendations to others (Kaderlan 1991). The importance of the link between architect and client was discussed earlier. If you want repeat business and good client relationships, do not allow an intermediary in the form of an independent project manager to come between because not only will communication be hindered by the presence of a gatekeeper, the independent project managers may also be after your business. Clients seek value in their choice of consultants by trying to match quality of service and quality of the finished product with price. Design is not the only differentiating factor. Service is just as important and the old adage 'you get what you pay for,' is worth remembering.

7.2.1 Client types

Clients vary in their experience of building, ranging from expert to inexperienced, and in the way they commission their consultants. Three types of client have been described by Kaderlan (1991:94):

- 'challenging clients', who constantly demand a high standard of service
- 'co-operative clients' who work with you towards a common goal, and
- 'difficult clients' who offer resistance and criticism and need careful management.

All three characteristics are often exerted by the same client at different times during a project's lifecycle. The secret is to manage the situation. Whatever the nature of the client, the architect–client relationship needs to be both nurtured and managed so that both parties benefit from the relationship. Client empathy is crucial to clear understanding and clear communications, which in turn is critical if everyone is to be happy with the finished product, the building. Management of the client–architect interface involves a number of specific skills, namely (1) listening to the client, (2) managing client expectations, and (3) building client trust (Kaderlan 1991; Maister 1993):

1. *Listening to clients:* The most critical skill and an important part of good communication skills is listening to clients. The better the understanding of clients' needs the better the competitive advantage of the firm (Maister 1993). It is a skill that requires a systematic approach.
2. *Managing client expectations:* The key to a good relationship is getting the expectations to match. Again, good clear communication skills will go a long way to highlight differences in expectations between client and designer, 'superpleasing' the client (Maister 1993). Clients often need educating about the building process. The more the client can be encouraged to become involved in the design process the easier it is to identify and meet their expectations. Quality management systems are a useful tool in this regard since they help the firm to keep the client informed of changes, especially changes requested by the client, and the implications.
3. *Building client trust and satisfaction:* The key word here is integrity. Clients place their trust and their money in a firm's hands. It pays to be open and honest. Satisfaction with a particular project will be related to the client's perceptions. The more involved the client is in their individual project the easier the management of the client–architect interface.

7.2.2   The client's view

Clients discriminate. It is useful to look at the firm from a client's perspective. What will the potential client see? A well-organised professional firm or a collection of professionals pulling in different directions? What image is the firm communicating to people outside the firm? They will be engaging a number of consultants to realise a building project and it is good practice to regularly review the firm from the client's perspective. Clients will be looking at the profile of the firm, their potential consultants. A useful check list is provided by Popovich (1995:39):

- Qualifications
- Experience

- Motivation
- Communication skills
- Maturity and emotional ability.

The client will be looking not just at the main contact with the firm, usually the principal, but also at the staff who will be engaged on its project – the profile of the whole firm. The messages that the firm gives out to its external environment, its promotional activity, needs to be managed, ranging from the drawings produced to the decor of the office and the manner in which telephone calls are dealt with by the office receptionist.

7.3   MARKET ANALYSIS

In addition to an assessment of the potential work from a variety of clients, both those known to the firm and those the firm would like to know, it is essential to assess the current market for professional design services and also to identify the firm's main competitors. These other firms pose a threat not only to a firm's market share but also to its survival. Time spent analysing the services offered by other building-orientated professional service firms and contractors is usually time well invested. The market analysis will involve an examination of the markets in which the firm operates and would like to operate – an external analysis – as well as an examination of the firm's own strengths and weaknesses – an internal analysis.

7.3.1   External analysis

Market analysis needs to be carried out to a schedule, for example every six months, because the market will be constantly changing and competitors will also be attempting to get an edge and increase their business. Firms close offices, open new offices, reinvent themselves and offer new services every day of the year: if the situation is not monitored the firm could very easily miss an opportunity or, worse, find itself in trouble because of new and unexpected competition. Anticipation is an important business skill. An external analysis of the market needs to consider the following:

1. *Economic and political climate:* Government policy, government spending and changes in legislation will effect building activity as will economic growth and interest rates.
2. *Social and technological climate:* Social changes may lead to a demand for certain building types while changes in technology may lead to new building products.
3. *Market for services:* The market for services is related to building types and service provision. 'Normal' services offered by architects are described in the *Architect's Appointment* (RIBA) which covers a wide range of activities. Other services, often offered by competitors, should also be considered. Growing markets and declining markets need to be monitored carefully with regard to client behaviour and client characteristics, referred to as market segmentation. A

large proportion of the information is available in the national press, specialist journals and from professional bodies such as the RIBA and RICS. However, information about client wants and needs is difficult to appraise without talking to them directly.

4. *Competition:* This comes from within the profession and from other trades' professions. Their strengths and weaknesses must be considered.

7.3.2   Internal analysis

Coinciding with an assessment of the market should be a careful audit of the firm's current skills, client contacts and opportunities. A regular analysis of employees' strengths and weaknesses will identify areas to be strengthened through further training and education, while an analysis of marketing activities and client satisfaction will help to identify areas to be consolidated. The firm will build on its collective experience, and a frequent evaluation of its successes and failures, its strengths and weaknesses, is just as important as an evaluation of the market for the firm's services. Potential clients will be looking at the firm in a similar manner, so it is important to recognise and manage the image the firm is giving out to people outside it.

7.3.3   Marketing objectives

Once information has been collected the firm can carry out an analysis of its strengths, weaknesses, opportunities and threats, known by the acronym SWOT analysis. The firm's strengths and weaknesses will come out of the internal analysis while opportunities and threats will emerge from the external market analysis. Information gathered needs to be analysed, discussed and acted upon; it should be used to set the firm's marketing objectives with regard to services and markets. Options may range from increasing market penetration, generally regarded as the safest option, through to diversification which carries the highest risk because new skills have to be developed. Management literature has identified four main strategies:

- Providing existing services to existing (familiar) markets
- Extending existing services to new (unfamiliar) markets
- Introducing new services to existing (familiar) markets
- Introducing new services to new (unfamiliar) markets

7.3.4   Benchmarking

Closely associated with internal and external market analysis is the concept of benchmarking, a management tool that can be used to help a firm gain competitive advantage. Benchmarking is a comparison-based system that allows a firm to carry out an assessment of three interrelated areas. First, the firm needs to examine its own working methods and make any necessary improvements, referred to as *internal benchmarking.* Second, the firm needs to look at the industry in which it operates, in this case the building industry, to learn from examples of best practice by other firms, referred to as *competitive benchmarking*. Third, the firm must look outside its own industry to learn the best practices from other industries, for example the advertising profession, known as *generic benchmarking*. It is the comparative nature of benchmarking (based on a comparison of the process rather than the product), especially the comparison with other industries, that separates benchmarking from other management techniques. Advocates of benchmarking claim that the true measure of a firm's performance can only be gauged by using competitive and generic benchmarking: it is not enough just to focus on internal benchmarking. As with the other principles outlined in this book, benchmarking must be planned, implemented, monitored and evaluated on a formal and regular basis if it is to be any use.

1. *Internal benchmarking:* For the architectural firm, internal benchmarking may be interpreted as a comparison between different projects where a quantitative comparison is possible based on an analysis of staff hours against profitability. This is the easiest to carry out since the information is, or can be, made available. However, it is often the most difficult one to come to terms with for directors and staff alike.
2. *Competitive benchmarking:* This area of benchmarking involves the comparison between the architectural firm and other firms operating in the building industry. The firm is able to compare its performance with other architectural firms and other service providers such as project managers or design-and-build companies, by comparison of competitive fee bids, for example. Care should be taken to compare the firm with one of a similar size.
3. *Generic benchmarking:* Although the benchmarking literature refers to generic benchmarking as a comparison between business processes regardless of the industry they come from, the architectural firm needs to exercise a certain amount of care here. Many manufacturing processes, based on mass production and repetitive processes, are not only inappropriate to professional service firms, but may also be dangerous if applied. Therefore, the architectural firm should concentrate on other professional service firm industries, such as accountancy and advertising, to see if lessons can be learned from their best practice. For example, the manner in which advertising agencies compartmentalise jobs to maximise individual talent offers lessons for architectural firms and is discussed in more detail later. By carrying out the benchmarking exercise on a regular basis a firm may well broaden its knowledge base and pick up different ways of doing things. It is the search for excellence which will help the firm to gain competitive advantage, a search that must attempt to balance the firm's exposure to risk with any potential reward.

7.4 RISK AND REWARD

Some of the strategies outlined in this book may be seen as carrying a certain amount of risk to the firm. If the firm is considering the provision of a new service, for example construction management, the risk will have to be assessed against potential fee income and the growth of the firm. New ideas and practices may be perceived as risky because they are not compatible with existing practices; the tendency for them to be resisted may be high, especially if they have legal implications and/or affect the firm's professional indemnity insurance premiums. There will be a learning curve and an associated time investment by members of the firm as it adapts to change. The greater the change the greater the amount of time and effort required to implement it effectively.

Generally speaking the success of a business venture is proportionate to the risk the directors are willing to take. As such it is essential to recognise the anticipated level of risk and set the goals of the firm within these parameters. New ideas represent a real enhancement in risk, but they often promise high rewards. The problem for many firms is to try to forecast the degree of return against the risk with uncertain information. A number of tried and tested techniques are available for forecasting from probability, to sensitivity analysis and scenario-planning. Scenario-planning is a useful way of considering likely outcomes to different variables, from the optimistic to the pessimistic. Questions about the firm's ability to respond to change, the applicability of the firm's skills and the client's reaction to any planned changes can be explored through such methods. The further ahead we try to forecast, the less accurate the prediction is likely to be.

7.4.1   Specialisation versus diversity

Whether a firm decides on or is forced into specialisation or diversity depends as much on the intentions of the directors and the firm's employees as it does on external market pressures. Whether a firm decides to be a design only firm, i.e. signature architects, or to offer a whole raft of diverse services is an issue for individual firms; clearly there is room for many configurations to survive and prosper. The well publicised 'secret' of business success is making sure the firm knows where it is positioned. Firms that attempt to sit on the fence are usually the ones that fail. That said there is a strong argument for diversity as a route to gaining competitive advantage (e.g. Herriot and Pemberton 1995) which is the underlying argument of this book. The clients interviewed for the purposes of this book were looking for single-point responsibility and a full range of services from one professional firm, tired of appointing many different firms for one project and dissatisfied with design-and-build contracts.

7.4.2   (Re)designing the firm

Only after the points discussed above have been considered can the firm be designed, if it is a new venture, or redesigned if it is an existing business. The design of the core business and the planning of the firm to achieve its aims and objectives should not be carried out until the directors have carefully investigated and evaluated the market for the firm's professional services, considered the balance between risk and reward, and investigated specialisation and diversity. The firm will then be in a position to plan its priorities and goals, instigate strategies for achieving them and write a mission statement.

Priorities should be established and considered against (limited) resources and then committed to paper as part of the business plan. However, Kaderlan (1991) has pointed out that directors of design firms are reluctant to plan for three reasons. First, because they fear failure and the ensuing loss of self-esteem; a very threatening situation for many people, especially those obsessed with image. Second, from a fear of success because they will feel an expectation to do better next time, and third because they feel to plan is unsuited to their creative temperament. The first two concerns are foremost in the minds of all business people; the third is a particular trait of the design professional. Designers must learn to separate the design side of the firm from the business side: a good business plan should allow a firm the freedom to respond to a situation spontaneously and creatively. A poorly considered plan is likely to inhibit, rather than assist, the firm's creative potential. There are a number of issues to address in the search for competitive advantage. First, the type of work – be it residential, retail, industrial, medical, educational – will influence the type of client and the specific marketplace for the firm's services. Second, the size of the firm needs careful consideration. Not everyone wants to manage or work in a large firm; staffing must be suitable and adequate for the jobs being taken on. Third, the location of the firm's office is important and needs to be considered in relation to its proximity to other consultants, clients, modes of transport and technology. There are many pros and cons of city centre, suburbs and rural locations. Add to this the potential of working from remote sites, the virtual office, and the location of the office takes on a new meaning.

At this point it is worth considering the legal constitution of the firm: should it trade as a partnership or a limited company? Usually the decision is made by the firm's principals, based on financial criteria. The culture of the firm, especially its collective ability to respond to change, needs careful consideration. A limited company provides more flexibility than a partnership because it is easier and quicker to change the directors as the firm evolves and adjusts over time. In any event it is an area in which expert legal advice should be sought.

7.4.3   Strategic plans

The managerial style of the firm's directors will influence the development of the strategic plan. For example, top–down management will determine the plan and impose it on the employees, while a bottom–up style of management involves all employees in the decision-making process. While there are advantages and disadvantages to both approaches, it is important that all members of the firm are consulted so that they can develop a sense of ownership by participating in the business plan and the ensuing strategies. Such an approach will help the firm move forward as a cohesive unit with well-defined, well-understood aims and objectives.

The strategic plan is a tool to guide the firm on a day-to-day basis, so it should be concise and accessible; a long document that employees ignore is of little use.

The strategic plan should form an essential part of the 'office manual' or the 'quality plan'. It should clearly show the aim of the business in the next 12 months and over the longer term, say the next three years. It is only by agreeing and committing these plans to paper that the necessary resources can be put in place, training programmes identified and marketing strategies established. Once agreed, strategic plans provide a useful framework on which human resources can be allocated and assessed against cash-flow projections.

7.4.4 Mission statements

The purpose of a mission statement is to put down in writing, clearly and concisely, the firm's direction, essentially its aims and objectives. Some mission statements are designed for use only by the firm's employees. Others are designed to be read by clients as well as the staff: they are designed to be part of a firm's marketing strategy. The mission of the firm can only be committed to paper once the directors and staff have a clear understanding of where the firm has come from and where it is heading, analysed the market for their particular services and discussed and agreed the strategy for the firm, the strategic plan. The statement must be realistic, for example does the firm have the resources to achieve its mission? It is only when the strategic plan and the mission statement have been committed to paper that the marketing strategy can be considered (see Chapter 13). The mission statement, like other aspects of the firm, must be constantly and systematically evaluated and if necessary updated to reflect changing market conditions.

7.5 FINANCIAL MANAGEMENT

One architect to another, 'What would you do if you won a million pounds on the lottery?' Reply, 'I'd continue to practise architecture until it was all gone.' Okay, it is a well-worn joke, but one uncomfortably close to the truth for many practitioners. Architects, in general, are not paid particularly well compared with other professionals (e.g. Burston 1995), no doubt because architectural firms are notorious for their inability to manage their finances.

A smooth running business must have a constant supply of money passing through its books to pay its staff, service its overheads and pay profits. Cash flow projections for both the short and the long term need careful consideration and constant monitoring. It is not uncommon for professionals to carry out a considerable amount of work before they are paid by the client. Workload forecasting is a very important part of any firm's business strategy, but given the nature of the services provided, often difficult to do with any degree of certainty. Profitability is important and some attempt to manage cash flow and staff workload is needed on a regular basis. Financial objectives must be set – otherwise financial data is of little use – to help the firm realise its goals.

7.5.1 Fee generation

Continuity of work and continuity of the firm's cash flow are linked. They are also important if the business is to remain healthy. The issue of fees, or more specifically how and what a firm should charge for its services, has caused a lot of angst over the years, as architects have been forced to drop their mandatory fee scales and experiment with different ways of fee generation. There are a number of ways in which a firm may charge its clients for the services provided and the benefits of one method over another will depend as much on the type of service provided as the wishes of the client.

Examples of service charges are:

1. *Percentage fees:* These are based on the final cost of the building work, and are common. The fee income will decrease or increase if the final cost of the project is less, or more, than that budgeted.
2. *Lump sum:* This is agreed in advance and is not negotiable.
3. *Time charge (hourly rate):* This is often disliked by clients because the time can (and often does) add up to a large fee that is often unexpected. It is good practice to agree a time limit that cannot be exceeded without the client's permission.
4. *Conditional fees, otherwise known as 'no hay, no pay':* There are instances where such arrangements may be entered into, for example some clients will commission professionals to obtain planning permission for them on a particular site. Because planning permission cannot be controlled by the architect some clients are happy to enter into a conditional arrangement; no fee if planning permission is refused, but 50 per cent extra fee on the production drawing stage if planning is granted. Conditional fees are popular with American lawyers and on the increase in the UK. Clearly an estimate of the risk involved needs careful consideration before such an agreement is entered into.

7.5.2 Fee-bidding

Whatever fee system is agreed with a client, it usually follows a period of discussion and negotiation to find the best approach for both parties. Over recent years and with the abolition of the RIBA's mandatory fee scale in 1986, it has become common for clients to invite architects and other consultants to tender for work, that is to submit a fee bid. Fee-bidding is not liked by many professional firms since it is often seen as being unprofessional, although these same professionals still expect contractors and sub-contractors to tender for work. On a more practical level it is also unpopular since it often requires the architectural firm to carry out a lot of work in preparing the fee bid without any guarantee of success, placing additional pressures on the firm's employees. It is not unusual for a client to invite tenders from at least three firms with specialisms in the same area. Thus firms find themselves competing against one another on the basis of cost and time. Although clients vary in the information they require as part of a fee bid, there are essentially two methods of submitting a bid:

1. *Fee only:* The title is a little deceptive because the firm will also be expected to submit details of their firm's track record, quality systems and often the qualifications and experience of its staff, in addition to the fee for carrying out the specified work and a programme. Depending upon the size of the project and the client's requirements it can take a great deal of staff time to prepare a well-presented tender document.
2. *Fee and design:* This usually requires the same information to be provided as a 'fee only' bid, but will also require the firm to submit some design work (sometimes referred to as 'no fee', since the sketch design is provided for free). The scope and nature of the design work will vary between clients and building types, but it is not uncommon for clients to request plans and elevations for commercial projects. Clearly this involves a lot of work for which the firm will not be paid and as a general rule of thumb will take at least three times as much time to prepare as the fee only bid.

Fee-tendering is a time-consuming activity and must be managed accordingly. For small firms such work has to be accommodated within the fee-generating work. For the larger firms it is often possible to employ at least one person to spend all his or her time on fee-bidding, falling within the firm's marketing activity and costed accordingly. There is a common misunderstanding that the cheapest fee bid wins. According to Derek Sharp (1991) a client's assessment is based on experience and creativity (50 per cent), project people (30 per cent) and management (20 per cent). The fee is not necessarily significant because it is usually discussed in detail after a decision to use a particular firm has been made. Clients will balance cost against likely performance because it generally holds true that you get what you pay for.

7.5.3   Costing systems

Financial information should be used as a management tool (Coxe 1980). Well-designed costing systems are important to monitor the progress of individual jobs and for assessing the efficiency of the firm as a whole. The most common tool to collect information is the staff time sheet. Time sheets provide information for analysis of individual jobs, a familiar strategy for assessing profitability and identifying areas for improvements in efficiency. The use of time sheets varies considerably among architectural firms. A minority do not use them. The majority use them but only refer to them if there is a problem, usually when a project has lost money, while a further minority refer to them regularly to monitor the financial pulse of the firm. The information is easy to collect, input to a computer-based spreadsheet and then analyse. But time sheets are disliked by designers. They are perceived as nothing more than a tool for management to control or restrain their creative urges, and filled in reluctantly. Staff costs can account for up to two-thirds of a firm's outgoings, therefore thorough analysis of time sheets is needed to monitor the amount of time spent on fee-generating work (chargeable to clients) and that spent on tasks associated with overheads. Analysis of time sheets tends to be job-specific, but client profitability is also important because some are more profitable than others (Maister 1993).

Data should also be analysed from a staff-specific view to identify which staff do particular tasks quicker, or slower, than others, with a view to reorientating their duties. To emphasise the point an example from a practice is used. Time sheets were filled in at the end of each week by staff (including the principal) and the data entered on a spreadsheet by the secretary. The data was analysed once a month by the principal and his associates on a job-by-job basis to compare the actual time spent by staff on particular stages against that projected and budgeted for. The firm was relatively well managed, with a dedicated team of professionals, and most jobs made either a small profit or broke even. The principal and his associates were keen to improve their profits, but were at a loss as to how to achieve it since analysis of time sheets per job indicated that staff were, for the most part, hitting their targets and were working hard. The problem was not with the data, but in how they were looking at it. A comparison was made of the hours spent per stage by individual architects on their past three jobs. When the time sheets were compared it was found that different architects varied in the amount of time they took on certain stages of each job. On the assumption that the competitive firm maximises its strengths and seeks to minimise its weaknesses it was proposed that individuals should concentrate on the job they do most efficiently. Theoretically, by redirecting staff to their most efficient tasks, there was a small, but significant increase in productivity.

7.6   MONITORING AND EVALUATION

Monitoring should be constant and systematic throughout all areas of the firm. Time must be scheduled for this important activity and designed into the firm's strategic plans. The performance of the firm then needs to be evaluated, at fixed intervals, against the strategies previously agreed, with adjustments made to suit changing circumstances. Evaluation involves the assessment of the current 'health' of the firm in terms of its specific aims and objectives. Before an evaluation can be undertaken the directors need to be clear about the aims of the firm. Only then is it possible to judge the performance of the firm as a whole in relation to the attainment of its aims. Evaluation should be undertaken for the following reasons:

1. *To assess the extent to which projects have achieved their stated objectives.* These should be related to previously determined standards of design, programme, resources, budget, profitability and client satisfaction.
2. *To consider the improvement of working methods.* Objectives may well have been met, but there may be scope for improving the way in which future projects are managed. For example, can the effectiveness of the firm and its profitability be improved? Has the client received value for money?
3. *To optimise the use of resources.* Has the firm been managed effectively given the resources available? Have the individual talents of the firms members been optimised? This area is linked back to the annual staff performance review.
4. *To assess the current standing of the firm in the marketplace.* Has the firm increased its market share?

The importance of systematic evaluation cannot be overstated. However, a word of caution is required. First, many people find this a stressful experience, but if the firm is to develop its staff must learn from collective experience. Sensitivity is required by the person(s) selected to carry out the evaluation. The firms with quality management and total quality management systems will have an advantage here because of the commitment to constant improvement. Second, the data is historical and should be used in a positive manner to shape the future direction of the firm. Third, it costs money because of the time it takes to carry out the evaluation effectively. The process should be kept as simple as possible: the production of a series of lengthy documents which few people have the time or inclination to read may well have a negative effect on staff morale. Fourth, there must be an effective and meaningful feedback system to all the firm's employees – remember it is a learning experience. Fifth, take action: do not put off difficult decisions until the next evaluation. Intervention may be the only solution.

Evaluation should be appropriate to both the size and development stage of the firm. The timing of the evaluation also needs careful consideration. Some firms may feel this should be carried out monthly, some quarterly and others annually. Again it will depend on the size and age of the practice. Evaluation can be carried out on a number of different levels:

- Evaluation of the entire firm, the complete system
- Evaluation of particular strategies
- Evaluation of particular projects.

7.7   MANAGING FOR ENVIRONMENTAL SUSTAINABILITY

Derek Sharp (1991) advises a dispassionate professional approach to business since overzealous personal, political and social characteristics can alienate clients. Such a view may be at odds with 'green' issues and an area that needs careful consideration as part of a competitive strategy. The word sustainability has a wide range of meanings. In management literature it is used to refer to the viability or maintenance of a business: thus if a business is sustainable it will continue to prosper. In building, the word sustainability has been used in connection with environmentally responsible or 'green' issues, ecological sustainability, and has been the focus of much debate in the building industry. The term 'sustainable development' came into common usage following the publication of the *Brundlandt Report* in 1987 (World Commission on Environment and Development) and further attention has been generated by the Rio Conference of 1992 and the widespread adoption of *Agenda 21*.

Despite the new use of the term the concept of ecological sustainability is not a new phenomenon and the public's awareness of environmental issues has been increasing since the 1960s with the influential publication by Rachel Carson, *Silent Spring* (1962), widely acknowledged as the catalyst to the worldwide environmental movement (Jackson 1995). More recently it has been acknowledged that the growing focus on environmental issues is associated with a cultural shift in society at large. However, building is notorious for its inability to change old habits and the relatively slow adoption of environmentally responsible ideals and practices in the UK has only served to reinforce this trait. For example, by the 1980s Lyall (1980) claimed that architects had not responded in any 'significant way' to the challenges posed by environmental issues.

Read any article about sustainable development and the message is clear: something must be done to change the way in which we develop, use and recycle buildings so that our natural environment is both protected and enhanced. Since the construction industry is, by and large, responsible for converting the 'natural environment' into an 'artificial environment' (Dicke 1995), contribution to sustainable development will come from the whole of the building team involved in both new build and refurbishment projects. Thus, the sponsors of building projects, the architects, the consultants, the contractors, the building product manufacturers and the building users all have a responsibility to implement a sustainable strategy. Within this team, the architect is, in my opinion, in the best position to make a positive contribution to environmentally responsible building. The architect's design philosophy and the architect's attitude to building product selection, together, will go some way to achieving environmentally responsible buildings, but only if the architectural firm is in a strong position to influence decisions at the individual project level.

Most literature concerned with 'green issues' has been criticised for having a strong environmental evangelism and lacking critical analysis (Newton and Harte 1997). In building, the literature has tended to concentrate on ways of reducing the emission of carbon dioxide to limit global warming. With the cement industry accused of causing more damage than emissions from aircraft (*New Scientist* 1997:14) such a focus is important. For example, the RIBA issued a policy statement about sustainable development which was largely concerned with global warming and ozone depletion, a policy that encouraged support from its members. These technical or 'hard issues' are relatively easy to measure, quantify and theoretically do something about through sensitive design and material selection. However, research suggests that although the techniques are available and familiar to some, the vast majority have not adopted a sustainable strategy (e.g. Vale 1994; Dicke 1995). A survey of 'green' practices and the largest 100 architectural practices by size (Eclipse Research Consultants 1996) found that most respondents had a 'narrow and parochial view' towards sustainable issues. The report clearly indicated that there is a long way to go, especially as approximately half this sample held themselves out to be promoters of sustainable design. Clearly, the adoption of environmentally responsible ideals and practices is a complex issue, driven as much by commercial concerns as ethical concerns for the environment (Emmitt 1997b). There is a need to investigate the more difficult sociological or 'soft issues', related to the way individuals communicate, interact and shape a building project during its life (e.g. Emmitt 1997b; Kruse 1997).

From a business perspective, architectural firms must decide how to respond to sustainable issues and state their intended actions. For the responsible professional service firm, environmental issues should form part of its business plan and be clearly stated in its mission statement and promotional material. But the manner and level at which this is pitched will depend to a certain extent on the firm's current and anticipated position in the marketplace. Some clients will be looking to appoint consultants who are committed to implementing environmentally responsible ideals and practices; others may perceive such an approach to be costly in terms of the finished product. The role of the client is very important, in particular their expectancy of the proposed building work; whether they desire a building that is as cheap as possible, or for a building that looks to the future. Work has been carried out which suggests that it is the responsibility of the architect to educate the client in this respect.

Sustainable development is a complex issue and one which should be considered from both an ethical and a business standpoint. Firms need to be realistic about what they can achieve since social and economic issues far outweigh technical issues. Whether we like it or not, we live in a consumer-orientated, throw-away culture. This is reflected in the attitude of building developers, demanding buildings with extremely short life spans (a 15-year design life is not uncommon). Given the amount of resources involved in the construction and demolition of such buildings this is an irresponsible approach, but we have to face facts. Not everyone will be interested in such issues; the pursuit of commercial gain is a powerful magnet, often at odds with environmental concerns. An environmentally friendly approach to building development will only come about if architects, developers and clients have the desire to pursue environmentally responsible ideas: it needs to be managed. Similarly, the pressures put on them by the general public and the building users, who are going to be affected by new developments, will influence the rate of adoption. Architectural firms have a significant role to play in both the promotion and implementation of environmentally responsible ideas and practices. Through greater interaction with building users and constant pressure on building sponsors, the implementation of environmentally responsible ideas and customs may become common practice sooner rather than later.

Part 3

ARCHITECTURAL
MANAGEMENT IN PRACTICE

MANAGING PROJECTS

Fundamental to the delivery of a well-designed and well-constructed product is the issue of procurement, client empathy and briefing. This chapter investigates the link between the client and the architect and the growing tendency for an intermediary, in the form of the project manager, to come between the two. Closely associated with the briefing process, it is an area in which the architectural firm must be proficient if it is to maintain contact with the client. The consequences of adopting or ignoring project management are addressed in the case study at the end of this chapter.

8.1   AN ADEQUATE FRAMEWORK?

The manner in which a building is designed and then built is rarely a neat, ordered process. There are many changes to both the design and the programme as the individual project moves from conception to a completed building. Architects are able to navigate this process because they have a conceptual framework in their mind which enables them to understand the process and also to accommodate changes which are often out of sequence (Hubbard 1995). The conceptual framework generally used to describe the design process is the RIBA's *Plan of Work* which implicitly divides the process into separate stages. Derived from the design methods work in the 1960s, the plan of work indicates a sequence of events, or stages, through which the design process should progress, from inception to completion and feedback: it forms the basis of most publications aimed at running a project, such as the *Architect's Job Book* (RIBA 1995) first published in 1969. Although the plan of work has been criticised because it does not allow for feedback loops, that would allow new information to be incorporated in the ongoing decision sequences (e.g. Broadbent 1988), it continues to be used by practitioners as a familiar guide to the organisation of projects in the office and as a guide for fee-invoicing. For example, research by Margaret Mackinder in 1980 found that some architects did not rigidly adhere to the detailed plan, but worked closely to the stages because the payment of fees was linked to them.

It is traditional to segment the design process into main phases, further divided into stages and then into detailed steps, as evidenced in the plan of work. Such models represent an idealised sequence of activities which, since reality is rarely ordered, are applied flexibly, but which form an excellent frame of reference from which to administer individual projects (see Chapter 9). Gradual moves towards a more environmentally aware society, focused on building activity, requires a fundamental reassessment of the plan of work to encompass the entire life of the project. The building and the plan of work needs extending (if not redesigning) to encompass the lifecycle concept of both the process and the product. This construct begins with the identification of a need, extends through the design, production, use, reuse and eventual disposal/recycling. It is important to note that at any time after the building is complete the stage of identifying a need to adjust, extend and modify may start again, thus necessitating a 'new' project team (see Figure 8.1).

Designers must be sensitive to the lifecycle construct since a lifecycle poorly co-ordinated, where no one individual or firm has overall responsibility for the lifecycle of either the process or the product, is flawed. The process, the product and the product service systems (logistic support activities) may be brought together by communication and co-ordination. It is not easy to achieve. Information is required at all stages: design is an information-processing activity and it must be managed.

The whole life building concept starts with procurement, an area once the domain of the architect but now under pressure from independent project managers. The increasing complexity of the building industry, combined with both increased demands and awareness of building sponsors, has led to the need for skilled management of the building process. This has resulted in the growth of a new management discipline, project management – a discipline which, it could be

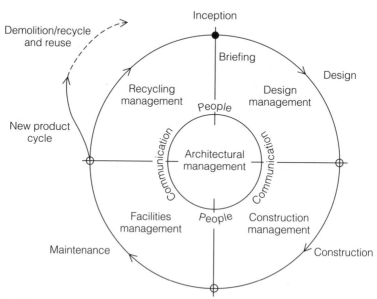

Fig. 8.1 The project framework

argued, is ideally suited to architects. However, it has been seen as a threat, rather than an opportunity, by the majority of architectural firms, to be eroding their responsibilities – and perhaps more to the point their fee-earning capacity. This is far from an isolated view. Most of the profession is aware that the architect's role is under increased threat, but seem unwilling, or unable, to respond to the competition. As the link with the client, the independent project manager role forms one of the greatest threats to architectural firms. Conversely, if offered as part of a firm's service portfolio, project management provides an excellent opportunity to deliver high quality buildings within an environmentally responsible framework and also generate additional fee income; it maintains the link between designer and client.

8.2   ARCHITECTS AND PROJECT MANAGEMENT

Traditionally architects have administered rather than managed building projects. At a CIB conference dedicated to the theme of 'project management by architects' the general concensus was that while architects may theoretically be in the best position to manage projects, given their design vision, generally they lacked the education and skills required to be effective project managers. Many architects move into project management roles as their career develops and there is scope for learning additional skills via professional updating (CPD) programmes. Taylor and Watling (1970) noted that project management is not easy, although they went on to say that it can be made easier by knowing the skills particular for the industry in addition to the methods of project management. Theoretically, the architect is well placed to become a project manager, but misconceptions exist within the architectural profession (Brandenburger 1995). On the one hand, the term is used to describe the role of the client's representative, the link between client and the rest of the project team; on the other hand the term is also used (incorrectly) to describe the management of the job by the architect. The *Architect's Job Book* (RIBA 1995:30) provides useful clarification:

> The role of project manager, for which some architects might well have the skills and aptitude, should be seen as separate and distinct from the architect's traditional role. It should not be confused with what many architects think of as simply managing the project.

The dilemma as to who should manage the project still remains an emotive topic and one difficult to discuss without the issue of leadership and fragmentation rising rapidly to the surface. There is nothing particularly new about project management: architects have always managed (administered) their projects. What is new is that the architect's competitors have been astute enough to realise that the discipline is a route to both increased business and increased control over the building process, and they have marketed their services accordingly. In the introduction to *Project Management*, Lock (1993:1) wrote that 'Project management has evolved in order to plan, co-ordinate and control the complex and diverse activities of modern industrial and commercial projects.' Project management has emerged as a distinct profession that has in turn led to further fragmentation of the building process (Smith and Morris 1992) and further loss of control of the building process by architectural firms (Pawley 1990).

8.3 PROJECT MANAGEMENT

Project management is concerned with the management of time, cost, quality and, most importantly, the management of people. There is nothing unfamiliar to an architect; what is important is the actual role and promotion of project management within an architectural environment. However, it is a separate discipline which requires particular skills and an understanding of management skills which have not been part of an architect's education. It is a discipline that should be marketed separately from, and in addition to, traditional architectural services. It can provide a source of additional fee generation and, more importantly, it maintains a vital link with the sponsor of a building project, the client.

Before looking at some of the issues in project management, it is necessary to state the obvious. First, all projects are unique, in that they differ from the one preceding it. Second, the project is a temporary task for the project participants. Thus not only does the site, product, objectives and application vary between projects, so, more importantly, do the project participants. Early work into project management tended to focus on project management techniques and tools to improve project delivery. Indeed, it is not uncommon to find this is still a primary concern for project managers in construction. While the effective application of project tools is still necessary, the focus of project management has moved to the people involved in projects (Ayas 1996). Regardless of the manner in which the project has been planned, whether it is judged a failure or a success will depend on the individuals involved. Hence getting the correct combination of people is crucial. The assembly of the project team is just as important as the briefing process, since the culture of the project will be set by the people involved and their interaction during the project.

8.3.1 Functions of project management

We can be sure of one fact in building: all projects, no matter how well designed and scheduled, encounter problems during their lifespan. Many problems are trivial, some have more serious implications. However, they all call for effective management and excellent communication skills. The ability to deal with problems effectively and clearly communicate decisions is a fundamental skill of the project manager. Such skill must also be underwritten by a clear understanding of the client's and designer's intentions. Failure to transmit this to the product may lead to compromise of the quality of the finished project which has long-term implications for the user. Case studies from England (Emmitt 1995) and Belgium (Douglas 1995) argue for the correct management of a project to deliver a better service; the background of the individuals, be they architects or project managers, is less important. A comprehensive list of 13 overlapping functions carried out by project managers has been provided by Walker (1996:147–51):

1. Establishment of the client's objectives and priorities.
2. Design of the project organisation structure.
3. Identification of the way in which the client is integrated into the project.
4. Advice on the selection and appointment of the contributors to the project and the establishment of their terms of reference.
5. Translation of the client's objectives into a brief for the project team and its transmission.
6. Preparation of the programme for the project.
7. Activation of the framework of relationships established for the contributors.
8. Establishment of an appropriate information and communication structure.
9. Convening and chairing meetings of appropriate contributors at all stages.
10. Monitoring and controlling feasibility studies, design and production to ensure that the brief is being satisfied, including adherence to the budget, investment and programme plans.
11. Contribution to primary and key decisions and to making operational decisions.
12. Recommendation and control of the implementation of a strategy for disposal or management of the completed project, including commissioning the building and advising on arrangements for running and maintaining it when completed.
13. Evaluation of the outcome of the project against its objectives and against interim reports including advice on future strategies.

What is clear from Walker's list of functions is that the design manager and project manager, often confused in literature and practice, are clearly different roles, demanding quite different skills and abilities. There are, however, overlaps between the project manager and design manager, best accommodated by integrating both disciplines within the same professional service firm.

8.3.2 Procurement

The procurement of design and construction services is paramount to the successful delivery of the client's goals. The client is not only faced with a variety of formal contractual routes from which to choose but also a wide variety of professionals from whom to seek advice. Architects (RIBA), construction managers (CIOB), consulting engineers (ACE), project managers (APM) and quantity surveyors (RICS) are all competing for the client's attention at the outset of a project. The choice of professional will influence the outcome of the project because of the social interactions set up. Clients need to consider a number of factors before a decision on procurement is made, ranging from timing and flexibility to make changes through to risk, responsibility and cost certainty.

All firms, regardless of background, will be able to offer a client advice on procurement routes and the firm may be asked to provide project management services in addition to its normal services. Project managers are better equipped to do this than their competitors, primarily because of the experience of programming and financial control. Financial control of individual projects is paramount in the minds of clients and a natural focus of project management. Although financial control and monitoring is important throughout the job, any decisions should be taken with due consideration for a building's design. A cost-orientated project manager may be concerned with the project cost and not the implications for the cost of the building in use. A balanced approach is required.

8.4   THE PROJECT NETWORK STRUCTURE

The design of the project organisational structure, the temporary project network, is an important function for the project manager. The composition of the team may influence the effectiveness of communications within the project team. The project team is formally constituted through contractual arrangements, usually appointed individually by the client or the client's representative. It is important to recognise that this formal team is influenced at various times by the contribution from individuals with no contractual link, for example the town-planning officer, the building control officer, local pressure groups and the building users, each with competing values, different goals and varying cultures. In Chapter 5 an attempt was made to look at the networks that develop for individual projects and a distinction was made between the different networks, namely the formal network, the statutory network and the informal networks. The distinction is useful to reflect on from a project manager's perspective since all three networks will exert different demands on the project manager's managerial skills (see Figure 8.2).

8.4.1   Team composition

The constitution of the first network, the formally constituted project team, is under the control of the project manager and depends on the individual's level of involvement, the client. It is the project manager's remit to assemble the best possible team for a particular project; that does not necessarily mean the consultants with the best credentials, but consultants who are best able to communicate with each other. The temporary project team is a social structure and the manner in which the participants interact will determine the effectiveness of their communication and the success (or otherwise) of the project. This is an important point to make: the project manager selects the designers, the structural engineers, the contractor (by way of the select tender list, for example) and some, if not all, of the sub-contractors (through nomination). There can be no hiding place if things go wrong. The initial choice of consultants will set the tone for the entire project.

The second network may be less easy to control since the network is determined

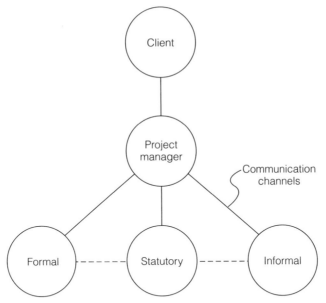

Fig. 8.2   The project networks
Formal network   Planned and designed by the project manager.
Statutory network   Largely known, can be anticipated and managed accordingly.
Informal network   Largely unknown, changes throughout the project's lifecycle
and is therefore difficult to anticipate and manage.

not by the project manager, but by the physical location of the site. Contributors to
the project, for example town planners and highway engineers, will be determined
by the local authority responsible for a particular site. However, the project
manager should be able to anticipate the contribution of, say, the planners based on
their experience of the particular local authority and any particular idiosyncrasies
they may harbour.

The third network, the informal network, is beyond the control of the project
manager. All they can do is 'manage' the relationships that develop to the best of
their ability. For example, neighbours and local pressure groups cannot be
influenced by the project manager, nor can the extent or timing of any contribution
be anticipated with any degree of accuracy.

8.4.2   Boundary conditions

This potentially very diverse group of people must be managed at different stages
in the project's life. In particular, it is where groups interact, the boundary
condition, that needs to be effectively managed so that there is no loss in the quality
of information transmitted from one group to another. Thus the project manager
must be aware of group dynamics and responsibilities throughout the project's
quite diverse stages. It is an area closely linked to participation.

8.5 PARTICIPATION

Participation in building projects and the adoption of ecologically sound ideas within the project are inextricably linked and influenced by the effectiveness of communication between the people in the network and the manner in which information is disseminated and managed within such a structure. More specifically, the complexity of the temporary project network will have implications for the level of participation and the way in which ecological ideas are taken up. The interaction of participants who are brought together in a temporary project team, or temporary network, to conceive, design and then implement a highly individualistic building is a particularly complex issue. Attempts to bring together various professionals as an integrated team have been developed. For example, large architectural practices offer multidisciplinary services and contractors offer design-and-build services. Clients are increasingly demanding improvements in quality, but package deals do not necessarily improve quality because production management and profit margins often conflict with the quality of the finished product. Some package deals have improved where architects hold senior positions in design-and-build firms (Franks 1995). Also within the small but growing field of architectural management, individuals concerned with issues of sustainability and the quality of the built environment have put the case for simpler procurement led by a design-orientated product champion, as illustrated by the case study firm reported in this chapter. The architect-led firm contained project managers and construction managers operating as an integrated team under an architectural management system. This architect-led team had actually started to construct its own designs in an attempt to achieve quality, reduce costs and improve communication, achieved at the expense of the main contractor. The only three players in this contractual arrangement were the client, the architectural firm and the trade contractors. Communication was improved and it was easier for 'real' participation to take place. Other models exist; for example, production industries have introduced systems such as total quality management (TQM) and concurrent engineering in an attempt to improve communications, quality, productivity and customer relationships through closer co-operation. The concept of 'partnering', a concept heavily reliant on quality assurance (QA) and TQM principles, has also been advocated and adopted in some instances. While this clearly has benefits over an adversarial system, the number of links in the product information chain have not been reduced: the potential for poor communication between intermediaries still exists.

An integrated design and construction management system offers the potential for implementing the ethos of concurrent engineering. Whether this integrated model is designer or contractor led will still depend on the type of project proposed and the aspirations of the client. What is important is that the number of links in the product information chain has been reduced and the opportunity for continuous feedback and continuous evaluation of design and production is provided. The prospect of improved feedback, so often lacking in the building process, will have implications for durability, will provide the opportunity to look at the total product lifecycle and may go some way to engendering a sense of ownership in all of the project's participants. The biggest advantage of a simplified procurement route is the ability of user groups to identify the project co-ordinator and get their views heard, simply because there are potentially fewer barriers to their messages. The project co-ordinator must have the responsibility and willingness to invite participation from the local community via his or her specialist interest groups at the start of the project, i.e. *before* design begins. It is then, and only then, that the specialist knowledge of the participants can be incorporated into the design process. With careful planning, such participation may not necessarily add additional time to the project's programme: indeed, the potential is also there to save time through the use of expert local knowledge. Early participation has another advantage in that differences of opinion can be discussed early in the project before potentially destructive conflicts of interest develop later in the design programme.

8.6   KNOWLEDGE RETENTION

The success of the firm will be determined to some extent by its ability to continually learn from its collective experience. The management of projects generates a wealth of experience which must be retained by the firm and disseminated to its members – a process much helped by computer-based expert knowledge systems. The acquisition, retention and dissemination of knowledge is a complex process requiring careful management and linked to quality management. The argument for offering project management as a service, rather than abrogating responsibility to an independent project manager, is discussed below from a business perspective. In terms of the development of the professional service firm and its ability to respond to external forces quickly and effectively, the knowledge acquired through the process of project management can contribute to competitive advantage. Thus the project management function is a particularly important one not to lose to competitors.

8.6.1   Project or product focus?

The primary aim of project management should be to deliver a quality service and a quality product on time and within budget. The project is a vehicle to deliver a quality building; it should not be a means in itself. There is the danger of placing too much emphasis on project management at the expense of the building. The building is considerably more important than the project since it costs more, lasts considerably longer and has an impact on the environment. The project is merely a means to an end.

8.7   PROJECT MANAGEMENT: THE IMPLICATIONS

It is recognised that the professional project management of clients' objectives is necessary. However, whether the project manager should be part of the architectural firm or an independent provider remains open to debate. Apart from the issue of responsibilities and associated risk, consideration should be given to the all-important link with the client and the likely effectiveness of communications within the formal project team. It is no secret that the trend for independent project management consultants has raised concern among architectural firms, partly because they form a barrier between themselves and their clients, with the associated potential loss of business contact, and partly because it adds another link to the communication chain. In researching this book it was difficult to find anyone other than independent project management consultants who felt that such a move was beneficial to the industry, although all those interviewed recognised the need for the professional management of a client's concerns.

8.7.1 An architect's perspective

All projects have an underlying element of risk, and it is not uncommon for design-orientated firms to limit their service provision to design as one way of reducing their exposure to risk. This book argues for strength through diversity and there are three fundamental reasons why architectural practices should resist the encroachment of an independent project manager and adopt it themselves, all concerned with the client and architect relationship. First, from a business point of view, the independent project manager poses a serious threat to architectural firms' workload and fee-earning capacity. Independent project managers, once appointed by a client, are in a very strong position since they can 'buy in' design services as and when they are needed. Thus the architect relies on project managers, rather than clients, for his or her commissions. This is an unpredictable dependency, since independent project management firms can, and are, taking on designers – architects, architectural technologists and building surveyors – as members of their firm, thus reducing their reliance on external consultants while at the same time increasing their own fee-generating potential. To a certain extent, the project management firms are becoming multidisciplinary professional service firms, but with a management background rather than design. We have to ask: are these the 'system architecture' firms of the future?

Second, from a communication perspective, the project manager acts as a node through which all communication should flow. As such it is without question the most important role in the project team. Empathy between client and designer is essential if the client's intentions are to be transformed into a quality product. Thus the project manager must be able to interpret the client's wishes and the only person capable of doing this is someone with design training. This is neatly summed up by Diana Rowntree (1994:76):

> The point where the communication gap must not exist is between client and architect. Just as the quality of architecture depends upon the joints between materials and the junctions between planes, so at a more profound level it depends upon a meeting of minds between client and architect.

The gatekeeping construct, discussed in Chapter 6, is important in illustrating the influence of an independent project manager, the gatekeeper, in the transfer of messages between client and designer. The independent project manager could be described as a happy gatekeeper, controlling information flow between the client and the architect, to the project manager's own advantage, and with a view to increasing their market share. More importantly, the link between client and architect is broken. Independent project managers are potentially in a very powerful position: they can direct individual projects to their own benefit by controlling the flow of information, i.e. by acting as a gatekeeper. It may be much easier for the management-orientated professional service firms to buy in design expertise than it would be for architectural firms to buy in management expertise. As such the firms offering project management services are in a very strong position from a business viewpoint. As design typologies become ever more freely available with the development of digital communication, there may be less incentive to include designers within the project team, especially since much of the specialist design is carried out by the manufacturers and suppliers of building components.

From an expert knowledge perspective, the point was made above about the project manager's role in the acquisition, retention and dissemination of knowledge. It is important to have this knowledge held within the firm if competitive advantage is to be maintained.

From a business standpoint it makes sense to adopt project management, helping to ensure the long-term viability and profitability of the firm while maintaining the all-important link between client and architect for producing good quality architecture. From a client's perspective, a situation where responsibility rests with only one firm is likely to be attractive (Walker 1996). The adoption of project management, however, has implications for the way in which architectural practices are staffed and managed. Despite the fact that an architect should possess the skills required to manage jobs, the complexity of building technology and methods of procurement require specialist training which is not taught at schools of architecture. Only 21 per cent of architects interviewed in a recent survey (Symes *et al.* 1995) thought they were adequately trained in project management and a survey of architectural students indicated they wanted more training in this field (L. Rogers 1995). So there appears to be a problem: architects are not trained in the skills necessary for delivering effective project management. Project management skills need to be bought into the firm through the employment of qualified and experienced project managers. One approach would be for the design firm to employ educated and experienced project managers, hence buying these essential skills and leaving the designers to do what they do best – design. From experience of recruiting staff it would appear that few architects have the skill or desire to dedicate themselves to project management. So recruitment of professionals other than architects may be necessary if a practice wishes to create and maintain its competitive edge (Emmitt 1995).

8.8   DELIVERING A QUALITY SERVICE THROUGH PROJECT MANAGEMENT

Project management is a natural vehicle through which to deliver a quality service. It should be seen as an extension of the marketing activity since it involves close involvement with clients. On an individual level, the design-orientated professionals who can make the transition to project manager are in a very strong position, since they have the all-important design skills to underlie their decision-making capabilities. It also follows that the professional design office with an integral project management section will have a certain degree of competitive advantage over its rivals. Project management is a tool that can be used to both retain and attract business by architectural practices. It is, however, a discipline which has threatened the traditional image of the architect and which may not be consistent with the image promoted by the RIBA. The case study below helps to illustrate the challenge and benefits of adopting project management. Adoption of project management led to a change in the staff skills, moving from design–orientated to management-orientated professionals. The benefits of maintaining contact with clients, control of project quality and contribution to the firm's knowledge base were clearly demonstrated.

Architectural practices will have to change, both in how they market their services and in the way their offices are staffed, if they wish to adopt project management, otherwise they will be demoted to a role of design consultants. The agenda for change put forward by Duffy (1993) called for architects to demonstrate the value of architectural knowledge and explain their services to clients. This is easier to achieve if the project manager is integral to architectural firm practices than if an independent project manager is acting as a gatekeeper. Duffy (1993) also called for the profession to improve management skills, a task that may be achieved via the adoption of professional project management. While there is no single business strategy for every architectural firm, project management offers a natural vehicle for architects to maintain the position of lead consultant, re-establish control of the building process and in turn regain respect from clients. It is only by adopting the project management role that they will be in a position to control design standards, material quality and cost control for the benefit of both client and building user. Project management is clearly a vital link between the client and the design team and a position that most professional consultants will continue to fight over as firms strive for the all-important client contact.

Case study   Project management

At the start of the 1990s the case study firm took a decision to invest in project management as part of a long-term business strategy, for two reasons. First, the firm recognised that the architectural profession as a whole was losing control of the building process and with it respect and credibility from the building sponsors. It had to respond to increased competition in order to retain control, and project management appeared to be the natural vehicle to bring this about. Second, the implementation of project management was seen as a tool, both to strengthen the service provided by the firm and to retain and attract business. At the time market share was being lost by architectural practices to other competitors in the marketplace (e.g. independent project management firms), a trend that has continued, and one that coincided with clients demanding a better service from their professional advisers. The desire to change both the way in which the firm was managed and the way in which it marketed its services came from inside the company. At the time there was no encouragement from the professional body to adopt project management or any promotion of the discipline to architects by the architectural press.

Experience of project management

The firm's experience of operating as architects, or rather design consultants, under the control of independent project managers had been a frustrating experience and in the firm's opinion it had not resulted in a better end product. There had been problems with communications, especially at the briefing stage, and the architects felt too far removed from both the decision-making process and the client. While the firm conceded that the independent project managers had done a better job keeping costs and programme in check, it had been at the expense of the finished product, with project managers often falling in line with contractors' requests to change materials to save time and cost (a policy normally rejected by the architectural firm because it was concerned with the long-term durability of the building). The problem, or so it appeared, was one of short-termism and an 'unhealthy' obsession with the project at the expense of the product.

Implementing project management

It would be misleading to suggest that the firm's implementation of project management was straightforward. At the outset there were a number of problems associated with a shortfall in experience; the design-orientated professionals that made up the firm did not have the relevant skills required. From the outset the firm was adamant that its project manager(s) should have a design background and project management qualifications/skills. The firm invested in project management training for one of its staff who took over the project management side of the firm and took steps to employ design-orientated professionals with project management skills/experience in future (which in the event proved difficult). Thus at an early stage new staff were brought into the firm with project management experience at the expense of technical/design orientated staff (who had moved jobs voluntarily). As a result the firm's staff profile started to change, with an increase in staff with managerial skills and a decrease in the proportion of those with design skills.

   One of the biggest concerns of the firm at the time was its ability to convince clients that an architectural firm could project manage just as well, if not better, than an independent firm of project managers. In many respects this was overcome through a process of gradual implementation combined with active marketing to both existing and potential clients. The first project management services were provided to oversee the firm's own designs and it was not long before the firm found itself providing project management services for schemes that it had not designed. This trend has continued and has strengthened the firm's fee generation and business prospects.

Improved control

For the case study firm their combined experience as project managers and designers has led to improved control of the building process, which has had benefits for the business and clients alike. Projects have seen better cost control, better management of individual contracts and greater adherence to programme without compromising the design resulting in buildings of improved quality. This has come about because the firm has been able to dictate the culture of the temporary project team (under a variety of contract types), essential for developing synergy between (theoretically) disparate parties to the contract. The project culture has helped to maintain efficient information exchange through amiable relationships and to a subsequent improvement in feedback from building site to design team. As such the firm claims to have benefited from increased knowledge retention which, combined with its ability to assemble a competitive, cohesive, project team in line with the philosophy of partnering, has increased the firm's competitive advantage.

Another benefit has been an increase in the firm's ability to adopt environmentally responsible ideas and practices, mainly because the project management side of the firm has empathy with the design side; it can control any changes made to the design, thus the design vision can be maintained from sketch design through to implementation on-site in the majority of cases. More importantly, the personal link with the client, essential to effective briefing, a quality building and for future commissions, is maintained via the project management role.

The adoption and promotion of project management has been closely linked with the desire of the practice to work to a certified quality assurance scheme as part of an overall business plan. Because the firm had developed a project management section, closely integrated with the architectural side of the business, it was in an ideal position to offer new services such as construction management and the planning supervisor role. Both services are closely related to the project management skills, thus adoption was relatively easy. Thus experience gained through project management has led to the provision of other services and a rapid increase in the firm's knowledge base, some of which has been captured in the firm's management systems. That said, the firm openly admits that it is in need of a well-designed expert knowledge system to take it into the future in a competitive mode. Perhaps, more importantly, in the context of this book, the provision of project management services has helped the firm to remain competitive and has helped to increase the firm's fee income during a period of economic stagnation, thus strengthening its position in the marketplace.

CHAPTER 9

MANAGING DESIGN

Two contrasting approaches to design management are described and compared in this chapter. The familiar method of one individual administering a job from inception to completion is contrasted with a sequential model where individuals are responsible for clearly defined segments of individual jobs. A case study is used to illustrate how an architectural practice changed from the traditional model to the sequential model and how this impacted on time, cost and quality control.

9.1   DESIGN MANAGEMENT AND THE CREATIVE PROCESS

As competitive pressures increase, so does the pressure to plan design work efficiently and administer projects competently. Design, like anything else, can be managed. However, because of its unique characteristics it needs to be managed in a particular way if creativity is to be encouraged rather than stifled. Design, or rather the manner in which it is managed, has significant implications for the competitiveness of an architectural firm; the context in which designers work must be understood before it can be managed effectively. Designers should operate within normal managerial constraints. However, research and experience indicates that few are capable of constraining their creative pursuits. The problem stems from the design studio where architectural students rarely experience any time controls or budgetary limits on their creative endeavours. But for managers, design is just another resource and needs to be managed to ensure the profitability of the firm. There is clearly a difference in culture between designers and managers. As with business, the difference between good and excellent design is in the detail: in the small but important differences.

9.1.1   Design: the core skill

Architects pride themselves on their creative abilities. And why not? It is the one trumpet they can blow with confidence. Design, the core skill, has to be managed with just as much skill as the rest of the business. Successful firms are committed to 'superpleasing' their clients through the provision of good design, technical expertise, delivery to programme and to budget. Successful firms have clear business objectives through a balance of design, technology and management. Those who are over enthusiastic about design at the expense of the other elements make design an end in itself: design for design's sake. The act of designing can be both intoxicating and addictive, but design is not the only differentiating factor when clients make their choice of consultants.

Most published literature that has investigated the way in which architects make decisions has concentrated on the *design process* with emphasis on the resultant *design* (Rowe 1987). This body of literature goes back to the 1960s and is commonly referred to as 'design methods' literature (e.g. Thornley 1963; Heath 1984). Concerned with creative problem–solving it sought to provide theoretical constructs which in the event were poorly supported by observation of the actual process. The literature has been criticised for paying too much attention to the process and not enough to the product (e.g. Lyall 1980) and has been criticised by practising architects as irrelevant to their working methods (e.g. Mackinder 1980). There is clearly a distinction in the design methods literature between the initial *design idea* and the detail design process in which the vision is translated into documents from which to build. This break is reflected in the literature, whose authors would appear to lose interest when the design process enters the detail design stage, despite the fact that this is the stage when important decisions are made about material selection and specification.

Writing from experience of various architectural practices, architectural management as a tool tends to be applied as and when it suits the architect, or when forced to do so by external agents such as the client. Perhaps, then, it is not too surprising to find that the concept of a management system that documents every action, such as quality assurance, and forces the architect's creative genius into a management structure has met with resistance. But the design process must be managed. While it is true that learning can take place through making mistakes, in business mistakes are extremely costly and need to be avoided or at least minimised. This contrasts with design education and the act of designing where learning through mistakes (wrong turns) is fundamental to the development of good design. This contrasts with the logic of good management where efficiency is important.

The question of whether design can be managed is often raised, usually by people who do not want to be managed. The answer is of course yes it can. We must not get carried away by the mythology of design; much building work and hence much design work is mundane, repetitive and boring. That said, it still takes a great deal of skill to carry out. Design is a group effort, based on degrees of compromise. As such it must be managed through the use of management systems that support, rather than hinder, the efficient production of drawings and specifications during the design process. So whatever model of the design process is used – whether simple linear models or more intuitive models allowing for feedback – design is a process, constrained by time and cost. Its purpose is to produce a product.

9.1.2   Problems with the management of design

Traditionally architects have moved away from the act of doing design to the act of managing design as their careers and status in the firm have advanced, learned through doing rather than through education. It could be argued that it is the architectural firm's inability to manage the design process, and hence the project, which has led to the development and proliferation of independent project managers. There is a need to question an architect's competence in design management and to consider whether a manager would be a better option. Architects are not taught design management. There is nothing unusual in this, it is not taught to designers either. It is a skill picked up through experience in the workplace. Architects are also trained to take all job decisions themselves – to control their own decision-making process, rather than manage or be managed by others (Coxe 1980). An alternative is to add expertise to the firm by hiring additional staff with specific competences in design management. Such a strategy is not without its problems because managers are not taught design and therefore are not privileged to the special language of design. A good design manager should be concentrating on releasing the potential of those being managed and at the same time removing the fear and stress that often arises through poor management and working to unachievable deadlines. Design management is not so much about the management of people as the management of processes; the better the framework for managing the processes the better the result. Within these processes the flow of work must be continuous and not obstructed by inefficient communication or unnecessary bureaucratic barriers. The design manager must be familiar with and able to design. The management skills need to be built on top of these skills.

9.1.3   Design control

The *plan of work* provides a framework by which an individual project is administered, rather than managed; and it is important to make the distinction. A better management tool is provided through the use of well-designed quality management systems (see Chapter 10). There are three distinct phases to be considered in the management of an individual project. First the briefing process, second the conceptual design stage, and third the detail design stage. Each requires different and conflicting skills. As time progresses the creative zone, that is the amount of design freedom, narrows. It is at its most diverse at the conceptual stage and at its most restrictive when the project is on site (see Figure 9.1). Care is taken in this diagram to show that the design may not be fixed when work starts on site, since problems arise and materials, products and details are often revised as work proceeds. This is not necessarily a problem (if the contingencies have covered it) as long as the design manager recognises the need for continued monitoring and management at this stage.

9.2   CLIENT BRIEFING

Without doubt, the most important phase in a building's life is the client-briefing stage. The argument as to who should be involved in the briefing process was explored earlier, where it was argued that a design-orientated professional should

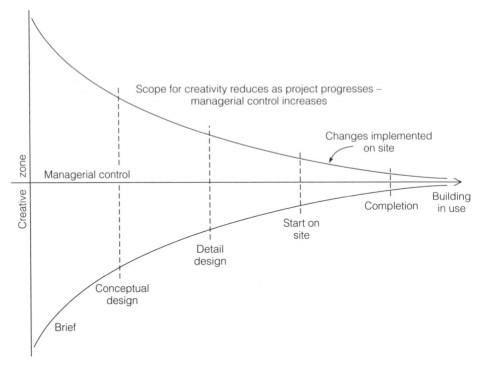

Fig. 9.1   Design control

be involved in the briefing process because of the importance of effective communication between client and designer. Instructions agreed during the briefing process will influence the scheme. It is important to consider ecological design here, since any cost implications can be assessed against the running costs of the building.

9.2.1   Two arguments

Client-briefing is a complex area. However, it is generally accepted that the better the briefing process, the better the resulting design: excellent briefing relates to an excellent product. The greater the involvement of the client during the briefing stage the greater the success of the outcome (Salisbury 1990). Time spent on data-gathering at this stage is seldom wasted since information is required before the design processs can begin.

There are two schools of thought about briefing. The first believes that the brief should be established and agreed before the design begins. Thus briefing is separate from the other stages in the design process, and all relevant information should be collected and the brief fixed before design begins. This is a sensible policy from a management and client relations perspective since it is one way of reducing the gap between client expectations and those of the design team and it is central to a well-designed quality management system. However, in practice, and despite everyone's best intentions, it is rarely possible to fix the whole of the client's brief before design begins given the time pressures that are often brought to bear by the client and the enormity of the task. It is good practice to clearly state what has been agreed and what is still to be agreed by a certain date to the client. The second school of thought maintains that briefing occurs throughout the design process. As such it is an ongoing activity and extends throughout the design stages (e.g. Salisbury 1990). In many respects this view represents the classic creative and chaotic stereotype of design as a creative process and is used by many architectural firms. It is, however, very difficult to manage, both at the briefing stage and through the design stages. Although informal (chaotic) methods can work in some situations, good design comes from a well-managed brief. Vague briefs waste time because additional effort is required to define the problem further down the line, leading to the possibility of an unsuitable design which in itself will need time to resolve. The importance of the design review cannot be overstated. The design review should be implemented as an important element in the briefing process. This is a chance for client and consultants to check and agree that the brief is as complete and accurate as possible before proceeding to the next stage.

Both views are valid and some practices use both, or a combination, to suit a particular project or client. There is no doubt that the briefing process is a creative activity during which the client and the designer need to understand each other. If empathy is missing the briefing process can go wrong. Whatever the school of thought followed, it is important for the designer to get as close as possible to the client in terms of understanding their requirements. Regardless of the client's experience of building, the designer's past experience of brief-writing and awareness of architectural possibilities is vital at this stage. If it is to be successful, briefing must be carried out by someone with a design background.

9.3   SETTING THE DESIGN AGENDA

Briefing techniques are outside the scope of this book. However, a good brief should contain the client's objectives, the project timescale, the cost limit and an indication of the client's expectations of the finished quality of the building. Where more than one professional is involved it is essential to establish who is to act as the 'design team leader' at the start of the commission to avoid confusion with responsibilities and communication at a later stage.

9.3.1   Project timescale and costs

A well-managed project starts with careful consideration and agreement of both programme and cost at the briefing stage. The aim is to reduce the number of uncertain aspects relating to the job so that they do not crop up later unexpectedly. Quality assurance is a very useful tool in this regard where such issues are established via the project quality plan. At the briefing stage the programme for the job should be discussed and agreed. The programme should clearly indicate critical dates and establish a schedule for design team meetings. This is when the architectural firm must carefully consider its available resources for the job. The risk associated with cost, time and delivery of design must be evaluated by all participating parties before design begins. For the architectural firm this means giving consideration to the human and non-human resources, themselves determined by both the fee income and the project timescale. Both funds and time will be limited. Thus the firm must utilise its design skills to best effect through effective design management if a profit is to be made from each project.

9.3.2   Responsibilities

Architects have a responsibility to educate their clients about or at least draw their attention to 'sustainable design', particularly important at the briefing stage and before design begins. Closely associated with sustainable design is the Environmental Impact Assessment (EIA). This is another essential element of the briefing process since the architect will need to assemble information about potential environmental impacts in anticipation of a submission to the local planning authority. What, for example, is the approach to biodiversity going to be for a particular project? In line with the lifecycle construct, the maintenance systems must be considered and defined at the briefing stage so that support for the finished project's planned life can be budgeted and considered throughout the design stages.

9.3.3   Approval for the brief

Care should be taken to ensure that the brief has the client's approval before proceeding to the next phase. This should be a relatively straightforward procedure if the client has been involved during this phase. Again, if an intermediary is involved (independent project manager), it is important to ensure that the architectural firm's input is clearly defined and approved by the client. Such procedures are central to quality management. Once the brief has been agreed (the problem formulated) the design specification from which to work can be produced. The interface between the project manager and the design manager should be established and roles defined before proceeding with the conceptual design stage.

   An example drawn from practice helps to highlight the issues. As part of one firm's quality management system it developed an extensive briefing document which formed an essential part of the job quality plan. Aimed at reducing uncertainty as the job progressed, it helped to manage the time and cost constraints of the project. The briefing process was carried out via a meeting (or a number of meetings on large jobs) between the client, the firm's designer and project manager and the planning supervisor, a minimum of four people. The philosophy was about including the client as much as possible and starting with a brief that had attempted to address important issues of safety, time, cost, and design quality *before* the design process began. At the end of the briefing process was perhaps the most important question of the whole process: 'Now what do you want?' An important question since the perception of both client and architectural firm may change during the briefing process, as possibilities are narrowed down. The firm found this to be an excellent management tool that helped to reduce unnecessary work further along the design process, thus making individual projects much easier to manage. However, it was heavy on resources early in the project and an area many clients were a little uneasy about paying for – especially those clients who were used to working with other architects who would provide a sketch design before starting to charge them. The briefing process was at the heart of this firm's philosophy on design and the firm is able to produce high quality products efficiently and profitably because it sets the design agenda before design begins.

9.4 CONCEPTUAL DESIGN

Once the design agenda has been set by way of the briefing process, the firm is then in a position to proceed with the design process. Feasibility studies and sketch designs are vehicles in which the most creative design may flourish and an area in which managerial control is often unwelcome. But for a design firm to be successful this stage, just like the others, must be carefully managed to ensure timescales and cost parameters are not exceeded. However, the management controls should be as loose as possible so that design may be encouraged, not stifled, early in the process, tightening as time progresses (see Figure 9.1). Despite being one of the most heavily researched and written about areas of building design, there is much less literature about the management of the conceptual design stage. Perhaps it is because architects are most emotive about this stage, claiming to be creative individuals and beyond the bounds of conventional management control. Such claims have little credibility. If architectural firms are to be competitive the amount of time spent at this stage needs very careful monitoring and control. Designers must be capable of designing within time constraints and not exceed these limits. It is not uncommon for firms to lose money at this stage, necessitating often costly short cuts further along the process. These are not well-managed firms. Good design does not necessarily take a long time if the management structure is there to support the designers.

9.4.1 Planning approvals

Towards the end of this stage comes the planning submission: an art in itself and one that many architects do not manage effectively for their clients. Planning consent is decided on by a planning committee. It is outside the control of the applicant, but that is not to imply that the application should be submitted then forgotten about until the planning committee makes a decision. Without approval there is no building project and successful architectural firms pay a lot of attention to the application, monitoring its progress and being ready to take action if delay is imminent. Firms that know how to get development approvals in difficult circumstances will have the competitive advantage. Double-tracking and even triple-tracking with slightly different proposals, with a view to appealing, is disliked and perceived as aggressive behaviour by town planners; clients on the other hand have quite a different view. It is no secret that the official planning system is conservative and 'anti-architectural' (Lyall 1980:146): spats between architects and planners are often reported in the architectural press.

9.5   DETAIL DESIGN

For many designers and researchers the conceptual design stage (RIBA stages A to D) is the most interesting and more fully researched than the more mundane detail design stage. Heath (1984) was unable to describe how far the design process extended, but separated schematic design from detail design. Separation of these two stages can also be seen in some larger architectural offices in which the design architect often delegates responsibility for the detail design to an architectural technologist whose primary skill is detailing. Detail design involves the production of many drawings and schedules which will enable the production of the bills of quantities and from which the building design will be built. As such quality control should be foremost in the design manager's mind. This stage is often seen as being concerned with implementing the design quickly, accurately and as cheaply as possible (Maver 1970). Although poorly researched compared with the conceptual design stage, it is arguably the most important stage from the viewpoint of the future durability of the completed building: any building is only as good as its detailing.

'Standard' details

The use of 'standard' details by architectural firms is common practice. Sometimes criticised for stifling innovative design, they are used to save time and reduce the risk of failure. Not only do they save time in generating the same drawing over and over again, they also encourage good practice since they are usually based on experience of detailing/materials that are known to perform well – or more specifically known not to fail. As such the standard details form an essential part of a quality control system. They form part of the firm's collective knowledge. As such they can be implemented by less experienced staff as long as the process is monitored and checked.

9.5.2   Product selection

Closely linked to detailing is the issue of product selection, an area poorly researched given its importance in terms of the durability of the building. There are approximately 20,000 building product manufacturers, many of whom offer more than one product for sale (Edmonds 1996). Every year manufacturers introduce new products and make improvements to existing products in response to competition, changing architectural fashion and revised codes and regulations. Thus the specifier is faced with an enormous range of products from which to choose. Specifiers of building products have traditionally been architects, although more recently with the move to different procurement methods such as design-and-build there has been a move towards greater product selection from other members of the building team. Although *The Barbour Report* (1993) indicated that architects' responsibility for building product specification was declining, they remained the most influential and important specifier because of their influence at the design stage. This point is noted by Pawley (1990:5) who claimed that while architects had lost status, they retained 'one important power, and that is the power of specification'. Manufacturers are aware of this and constantly bombard architects' offices with their trade literature in the hope that the specifier will select their product rather than that of a competitor. Research into product selection by architects (Mackinder 1980; Emmitt 1997a) found that the process was extremely complex. From a management viewpoint the biggest challenge was found to be the management of information as it came into the office, with senior management acting as gatekeepers, filtering the information before it got to the specifier, in an attempt to reduce the firm's exposure to unnecessary risk and reduce information overload on behalf of the specifier. Thus the tendency was to specify familiar materials in conjunction with standard details to reduce exposure to risk and save time (Emmitt 1997a).

9.5.3 Quality control

During this phase the design manager has a number of responsibilities. Not only does he or she have to ensure that target dates are met for the production of relevant information, but the quality of the information must be constantly monitored and checked for compliance with both the firm's standards and those of the client. More specifically:

1. Design changes should always be referred back to the client for approval, a fundamental aspect of any quality assurance system.
2. Drawings should constantly be monitored for accuracy. It would be reckless to issue drawings to parties outside the office without checking them for accuracy. It is surprising, then, how many drawings do get issued without going through any formal checking procedure. The control of drawings in architectural offices often leaves something to be desired, especially where jobs are being run to tight time constraints. Good control can reduce potential claims and avoid the need for additional work at a later stage.
3. All project information should be co-ordinated through the use of drawing registers. This is equally important for electronically generated/stored images as for information on paper. While great ideas may be created by individuals, buildings are complex products requiring input from many different individuals with different skills.

Co-ordination is a fundamental element of design management: not just co-ordination within the firm but the co-ordination of consultants – other designers – from other firms. Within the temporary structure of the project team people need to have a certain degree of empathy and respect for one another if communication is to flow. Co-ordinating communication within the office and with outside consultants is problematic and calls for particular skills.

The detail design stage is primarily concerned with transmitting the design intent to the people who are going to assemble the building on site, via the contract documentation. However, the first use of the documentation is to prepare the bills of quantities for the tender stage. The contract documentation has two functions: it will be analysed for the purposes of assembling a contract sum *and* used to build the building.

9.6   CONSTRUCTION

The management of building construction is discussed in Chapter 11. However, a number of issues deserve attention from a design management perspective. First, changes to the building design are often necessary when the project is on site, because of unforeseen circumstances. These changes need to be referred back to the design manager and checked against critical documents such as planning approvals and the client's brief before implementing them. Requests to change building products and details have implications for the durability of the building and must be given careful consideration. The process needs to be monitored. Second, it is vital that empathy exists between the design manager and the construction project manager: this is important for the project's success and also for feedback.

9.7   MODELS OF DESIGN MANAGEMENT

Design management is inextricably linked, but often independent of, the management of the firm. It is an area in which, more than any other discussed in this book, the conflict between designers and managers is potentially greatest since design management is concerned with finding a balance between creative freedom and managerial control. Adequate preparation is the key to successful design management. Direction and control of the design come through good briefing and good management throughout the design stages. Good design needs a supportive environment in which to flourish. Design deserves specific responsibility – a design manager – delegated at director level. Design, although all-pervasive, needs special treatment.

There is an implication, certainly in education, that an individual architect starts at stage A and proceeds through to stage M, a 'job architect' supported by technical staff. This model is often employed in practice, but there are other ways in which design can be managed. Derek Sharp (1991:166) has outlined three different methods of managing projects as they pass through the office, described as (1) the traditional whole man team, (2) the process method, and (3) the functional specialisation method. He then discusses their relative pros and cons from the perspective of small to large offices. For the purposes of this book and since Sharp's process method and functional specialisation models are similar, two models, the 'traditional model' and the 'sequential model', are described here in terms of their potential contribution to achieving competitive advantage.

9.7.1 The traditional model

The traditional model is used by the majority of small- and medium-sized firms in the UK (Sharp 1991). When a commission is received a 'job architect' is appointed to take the project from inception through all of its, quite different, stages to practical completion, often acting by default in a project management role. Depending on the size of the project and the size of the office, the job architect may receive some assistance from other less experienced members of the firm. However, an individual is required to exercise skill throughout all stages of the project, thus becoming a generalist rather than a specialist.

While this is the only option for solo practitioners and very small architectural firms, it could be seen as wasteful of skills and time in a larger office. The reason behind this argument is that it is rare for an excellent designer to also excel at other quite different functions, such as detailing, contract document preparation or project administration: tasks that could be carried out by someone who has better skills in this area. Thus there may well be a weakness in the service reflected through an inappropriate use of resources: it certainly is not cost-effective and not a strategy to employ if competitive advantage is required. Another problem arises if a member of staff leaves the firm, taking knowledge of the job with them that may not necessarily be recorded, or for some reason has to be replaced with another job architect. Thus continuity is lost and time is required for another architect to pick up the project.

The benefit of this system is that it is familiar to architects. It is consistent with the manner in which they are taught, with little interaction with other disciplines through their training. Each individual job is carried through by an architect, sometimes with support from technologists within the office, from inception to practical completion and final certification. Thus each individual project is managed by the job architect (or indeed could be seen as self-managing within the RIBA *plan of work* framework). The individual architects within the office are overseen by the design manager, sometimes and perhaps more correctly referred to as the office manager, who is responsible for overseeing programmes and checking on progress/ target dates. Thus the design manager tends to be concerned mainly with problem-solving and reporting progress to the firm's directors: a reactive role, more of an administrative one than a management one in the strictest sense of the word.

9.7.2 The sequential model

The alternative approach is to assemble a team of individuals with a variety of specialist skills who are capable of working as a team under the control of a design manager. With this system each individual is responsible for clearly defined segments of the project, and since their administration duties are reduced there is more time to specialise in their chosen area. The sequential model is based on the earlier observation that every project has four distinct phases: briefing, design, production information and site supervision and each phase requires individuals with specialised skills (Sharp 1991). Such a system demands individuals not just with different abilities and interests but also with different training. It is unrealistic to expect qualified architects to be the best people for all the jobs. For example, a simple sequential model would require individuals with the following skills:

1. *Briefing phase:* This requires project management and design skills: architects with additional project management experience or project managers/ construction managers with design experience (see Chapter 9).
2. *Design phase:* This requires design skills: architects.
3. *Production information phase (detail design):* This requires detailed knowledge of construction, materials and building methods: architects and architectural technologists.
4. *Construction phase:* This requires contractual, legal and time management skills: construction managers and project managers (see Chapter 11).

Although Sharp contests that such a model is only applicable to a medium-sized to large practice, from the breakdown above it is clear that four individuals could operate as a very effective firm. Add an additional member to deal with the financial/administration side of the business and the total is five: a small practice, and one with considerable competitive advantage over a similar sized office employing the traditional model. In larger offices it is possible to delegate specific tasks within a certain phase. For example, design departments have specialists in feasibility studies only (Sharp calls this 'functional specialisation'), production information may have individuals who specialise in specification writing only, etc. Such a model has parallels with the building industry, where specialist sub-contractors are employed to supply specific items, cladding or brickwork, for example. Strange then that architects expect building product manufacturers and sub-contractors to be specialists when they themselves try to be generalists.

Good managerial skills are required to ensure such a system operates smoothly and the links between the specialist disciplines is as seamless as possible. This requires a dedicated design manager, capable of getting the best out of the team, which itself must be fully integrated. Good, clear communication is essential, as is the ability to keep everyone informed of decisions. This is where the design review operated as part of a quality management system becomes an essential tool, because it provides regular meetings where all those concerned with the project are brought together. Thus regardless of the stage at which the project is at, the project manager, designer, detailer and construction manager will all be present to contribute to the design and maintain its integrity as it proceeds from conceptual scheme to finished product on site. The case for involving the client or the client's representative in the design reviews is also made.

The advantages of the sequential model are that individual skills are maximised and utilised: there are no frustrated designers working on contract administration. Designers can concentrate on the latest trends and developments in design, technologists can keep up-to-date with the latest developments in materials and products, and construction managers can know their contracts as well as, if not better than, the contractors, thus reducing claims against the firm. It also allows a more structured approach to the planning of work within the office, since individuals will know how long a particular task will take because they have done similar tasks before. With the traditional team, the project is limited to the speed of the individual, who may be a fast designer but a slow detailer, and as a result the programme may be difficult to manage. Clearly such a system can help to produce a more consistent and higher level of both service and product; usually more profitably for the firm and more cost-effectively for the client. Quiet periods can be usefully spent researching and updating individual skills, knowing that such effort will be of use on the next job. This is not something that can be guaranteed with the traditional model, where the next project tends to be given to the individual with the lightest workload rather than the person who is best suited to the job.

Such a model is not without its critics. The production-line approach analogy is often wrongly drawn, usually by architects who have not experienced such a system. Architects are still trained on the assumption that they will be 'running the job' and actively involved in all stages of the project from inception to completion. Many interviewed have confirmed they do not like the idea of losing control, although this assumes that they had control in the first place. This is, perhaps, unusual to architects. Other creative professions such as advertising appear to have no difficulty in working with such a model. Consider the following example of a typical small architectural firm and a similar sized advertising firm, both of which comprised five professional staff plus secretarial support.

The architectural firm comprises four architects (three of whom are directors) and a technician. Individual jobs are administered by individual architects with technical support to all four architects provided by the technician. In this example each architect carries out all aspects of the job function, from design to technical to contractual to site, along with issues relating to the day-to-day running of the firm. Each architect could be described as a generalist, skilled in design but engaged on a number of other issues at which it should be noted the architects were competent but not specialists. This firm is being run as a series of individuals with individual projects, albeit in the same firm. There is little team work.

Now consider the advertising firm: its five employees are each specialists. All are called 'directors', namely, creative, accounts, production, technical and marketing directors, although only three were legally directors of the firm. Each job was worked on as a team, with clearly defined but flexible boundaries. There is a marked difference here between how the offices are being run. The advertising firm has an effective structure that maximises the individual's talents; the architectural firm does not. So, as argued earlier, for the architectural firm to become competitive it must rethink how it is constituted (see Chapter 12).

9.8 MANAGING DESIGN TIME AND DESIGN COSTS

Individual jobs may vary significantly in size, complexity and timescale. Time and cost control through careful programming is necessary if the firm is to operate at maximum efficiency. To do so requires a full understanding of all the employees' strengths and weaknesses and their effective deployment to maximise the strengths and minimise the weaknesses. Only when such an exercise is complete and constantly monitored can time and cost management be effective.

9.8.1 Time management

Time management is critical to the smooth flow of work through the office. Achieving a balance between the amount of time allowed by the client and that required to carry out the work is a difficult but essential managerial task. All stages of the job need to be planned, critical dates identified and design review dates fixed. It then has to be monitored and adhered to as part of a quality service provision. Time management is an important activity for all members of the office, therefore the planning and co-ordination of all employees' daily activities is essential to the smooth running and competitiveness of the firm. Scheduling the work needs to be carefully considered: it is just as dangerous to give an employee too little work as it is to give them too much. All programmes should have clear aims and objectives. It is essential to anticipate problems and allow 'time windows' in the programme in which to handle them. A programme of work that does not allow for the resolution of potential problems is a programme that will fail and may lead to overrun problems. If, on the other hand, things go well, and the time window is not needed, it can be used positively, perhaps for some additional CPD activity for the staff or more time to reflect and analyse the current situation.

The way in which a client is charged for the services provided will depend on a number of factors. Whatever method is agreed – percentage, lump sum or time charge – the fee distribution should be planned so that each stage makes a profit. If a profit is to be returned at each stage of a project, care must be taken to manage time efficiently. Meetings, though essential, should be kept to a minimum. Their purpose should be clear and only those who really need to attend should be invited. A good rule of thumb is to try to avoid unnecessary meetings; a well-designed project quality plan with carefully scheduled design review meetings is one way of achieving this. However, no matter how well planned the project, problems will arise. The manner in which they are resolved needs careful consideration so that they can be dealt with in the most cost-effective way.

Also linked to profitability is the issue of delegation. Delegation of work can only be done effectively if the people employed are capable of doing their job: this goes back to effective recruitment and continuing training through CPD activities. All the firm's employees, from managing director to trainee, should take time out to reflect. This must be programmed into the daily routine because it is too easy to be swamped by other equally important demands and not do it. Regular, positive feedback sessions are essential if the firm is to grow stronger from its collective experiences. There is a need to control the quality of the process and communication between individuals. This is best achieved by implementing a quality management system where the *design review* is used as a control gate and as a vehicle to improve communication and feedback within the team. This is described more fully in Chapter 10.

9.8.2   Attributes of the design manager

So what special qualities are required for an individual co-ordinating and managing the team based on a sequential model? The following skills are seen as critical to success:

1. *Motivation and leadership:* Able to stimulate and motivate team members through commitment and personal enthusiasm. Ability to establish and build effective working teams and clearly define responsibilities within the overall project framework.
2. *Planning:* Managing meetings. Assessing and managing individual workloads with due concern for other team members. 'Helicopter perspective', to stand back from the immediate concerns and take an overview of priorities.
3. *Communication:* Communication skills to explain concepts and ideas as well as to transmit changes in individual tasks, responsibilities and project goals often through drawing and sketching. Interpersonal skills include the ability to listen to the team members and include feedback. Communication is essential, especially where design is separated from the production team. The importance of integration, teamwork and effective communication cannot be overemphasised.
4. *Flexibility:* Flexibility in responding to changes, both from external and internal sources within the framework of a quality management system. Tolerance of working in uncertain areas.
5. *Problem solving:* This is where an individual with design training has the advantage over one with managerial training.
6. *Ability to soak up stress:* Demands on time have increased over recent years as clients expect buildings to be designed and built faster than the last project. This may result in an increase in stress. The sequential model does offer one substantial benefit here since each individual within the team has assigned boundaries, controlled by the pre-programmed design reviews: there is more stability in the system and therefore less uncertainty. The stress must, however, be absorbed by the design manager. It is important to manage stress through effective and considerate delegation to avoid a negative stress situation.

9.9   IMPLICATIONS

The manner in which design is managed within the firm will be influenced by its managerial style and culture. The sequential model outlined above offers one route to achieving quality and a competitive edge. The case study, overleaf, helps to illustrate the potential of the sequential model in terms of providing improved consistency of service. By assigning responsibilities and maximising individuals' different skills to the full, the framework is then in place to look beyond traditional services to construction management from a sound financial footing. But this approach has implications for the staff structure of the firm since they cannot all be architects. Such an approach has implications for the composition and management of the design-orientated professional service firm.

Case study   A sequential model

To take an established architectural firm and move the design team from the familiar traditional model to the unfamiliar sequential model is a challenge, both for the directors of the firm and its staff. It cannot be done overnight, but must be carefully planned and discussed both with staff and existing clients before the change is implemented. Since many architectural businesses start as small firms, it is likely that the traditional model will have been used. Thus to move to the more competitive sequential model requires commitment on behalf of the directors, the design manager and the staff. In this case study the directors of the firm were aware that they needed to improve their productivity and, perhaps more importantly, their rate of response in all areas of their business, a strategy seen as providing a competitive edge over their immediate rivals. Their aim was simple, if not challenging: to improve the performance of the firm by improving the management of both the conceptual and the detail design phases. The following case study describes the change and identifies the problems and benefits of such a transformation.

Assessment

The balance between cost, time and quality had to be correct. The firm already had a good reputation for delivering a quality building, within budget and time constraints, but its clients were constantly looking for savings in the time it took to design projects, without compromising quality. By analysing the then current structure of the firm it was found that improvements were not possible with projects administered under the traditional system because all the staff were fully committed and working extremely hard, usually on two or three projects concurrently, but largely in isolation from one another. There was very little sharing of experiences, despite the use of a weekly team meeting, from individual projects. Changes were necessary if the firm was to stay competitive. The quality of both the service provided to the client and that of the finished building had to be maintained, if not increased.

Implementing change

A decision was taken to use the sequential model, but the directors were concerned because the change-over had to be done on all projects concurrently. It could not be experimented with on a trial basis, so there was a great deal riding on the transition. Clients and staff were informed of the impending changes and the reasons for adopting them in advance of the changes being made; in the event the switch was relatively painless, though stressful.

This development led to the separation of the design team and the contracts team, each with its own manager, with all handovers carried out under a quality management system. Natural staff movement over time provided an opportunity to reorientate existing employees into areas that best suited their individual talents;

recruitment for replacement staff was implemented for very specific roles. As such, the implementation of change was a relatively smooth transition. The reorientation of the staff into a sequential model led to the following structure. Between each stage handover there was a formal design review, in accordance with the firm's quality management, with formal intermediate reviews before drawings were sent out of the office for statutory approval. The model implemented was divided into the following stages:

Team 1
Stage 1. Briefing/feasibility studies
Stage 2. Conceptual design
Stage 3. Detail design

Team 2
Stage 4. Contract documentation and tendering
Stage 5. Site operations and feedback to Team 1
Stage 6. Ongoing monitoring and maintenance

Staff resistance

The sequential model was initially disliked by staff, even though it had been discussed by staff and management on a number of occasions before implementation. The resistance partly stemmed from the unfamiliar nature of the model, but more importantly it was seen as eroding the individual (bespoke) character of the job, seen by some as depersonalised design and compared unfavourably to a factory production line. Although staff admitted to disliking certain aspects of jobs – for some it was writing specifications, for others it was dealing with contracts – they still expressed a strong desire to do these 'chores' since they were part of 'the job'. They expressed a desire to see jobs through from start to finish; there was clearly a strong sense of ownership for individual projects. One mistake was made. At the time it was felt that the refurbishment and maintenance projects should be left outside the sequential model, since they accounted for less than 10 per cent of the firm's work and their particular characteristics seemed better suited to an individual approach. This caused a great deal of resentment in the office since only one member of staff dealt with work to existing buildings and he was excluded from the sequential model team. Once the model was running the argument for keeping the refurbishment projects separate appeared less persuasive and so these too were included.

Conclusion

The outcome of changing from the traditional model to the sequential model was beneficial for this firm. Projects were easier to control in terms of time and cost, while the quality of the finished drawings and the finished products improved. There was a small increase in productivity which meant that more jobs could be handled competently with the same resources. The profitability of individual jobs was improved, with a couple of exceptions. In spite of their initial resistance, the existing staff were quick to appreciate the benefits of the sequential model once it was running correctly, and it has become an important tool in the firm's business strategy. The system does, however, place a great deal of responsibility on the design manager, since it changes the individual's responsibilities, and the firm was quick to point out that the smooth running of the system depended on their skills. Thus recruitment and retention of this key member of the firm is important to the firm's culture and ongoing competitiveness.

CHAPTER 10

MANAGING QUALITY

This chapter deals with issues of quality, from quality control to quality assurance (QA) and total quality management (TQM). Some of the reasons behind the slow rate of adoption of QA by architectural practices and the implications of this resistance for future improvements within the construction industry are considered. The problems of implementing managerial control over the creative process and more specifically over creative individuals is addressed and then illustrated by the case study. This describes the implementation of QA and the adoption of the TQM ethos.

10.1   QUALITY MANAGEMENT

Architectural firms must give their clients confidence both in the quality of the service they provide and in the quality of the buildings they produce. They must also be able to do this cost effectively in order to stay competitive (Taylor and Hosker 1992). Although professional firms have a duty of care to their clients, the service they offer can be enhanced and improved through the adoption of quality management. For example, efficient design can be encouraged through quality management systems such as QA while total commitment to quality is seen as the best way of consistently delighting the customer through quality service and quality products (Macdonald and Piggott 1990). The level of service must be defined before it can be managed and delivered to consistent standards. Although it may be convenient to equate inconsistent service delivery with creativity, inconsistent service is a clear indicator of poor management control. Quality assurance has been neglected by design firms. According to Coxe (1980) this is partly because of a misunderstanding about what it takes to sustain the creative process.

Quality management evolved from early work on quality control in the American manufacturing industry but it was the Japanese who took quality management to new heights, inspired by the work of Deming and Juran. From the 1950s they contributed to the Japanese revolution in continuous quality improvement which has culminated in a number of Japanse gurus of total quality management (TQM) such as Kaori Ishikawa and Genichi Taguchi (Macdonald and Piggott 1990).

127

Quality management has an interesting background, it appears to travel well and is a constantly evolving philosophy that demands change.

Despite the considerable volume of literature dealing with quality management, there is often a degree of confusion over the use of the word 'quality', especially within the construction industry. For example, when people talk or write about quality the term is often used subjectively. Quality work does not mean quality service; similarly, quality service does not necessarily mean quality work (Maister 1993). However, the two should be inseparable. Before proceeding further it is necessary to look at some of the definitions from the perspective of the professional design firm.

10.1.1 Quality control

Quality control is a managerial tool that ensures work conforms to predetermined performance specifications, a management tool developed and associated with manufacturing rather than with service industries. In manufacturing industries quality control procedures work well because it is easy to check products against predetermined standards both during and at the end of the production process. The intangible nature of a professional design firm's output makes quality control particularly difficult to achieve and it is not uncommon to find quality control applied as a checking procedure only to the drawings produced before issue. Such control is often influenced by the personality of the directors and senior staff within the firm rather than by any predetermined set of controls; as such it can be somewhat varied in its implementation and effectiveness. A more appropriate quality management tool for design firms is provided in the form of formal QA systems.

10.1.2 Quality assurance

This is a formally implemented management system that is constantly monitored by an external agency, either the BSI or one of the other UK certification bodies, to check that the firm is conforming to ISO 9000/9001 (formerly BS 5750). Care is needed here to explain exactly what constitutes a QA system since it has been, and continues to be, subject to a number of misconceptions and myths. According to Stebbing (1990) it is not quality control (although this forms part of a QA system), it is not a massive paper-generating exercise, it is not a major cost area, nor will such a system be a panacea for all ills; instead it is a cost-effective aid to getting it right first and every time. Hence it forms an aid to productivity and makes good management sense. More specifically, QA means assurance that the process is managed. It does not assure a quality service (Taylor and Hosker 1992) nor does it assure either a quality design or a quality building. It is a hard management tool that can offer a reliable, consistent quality of service to the client while helping to reduce risk and minimise negligence. Like quality control, it has its roots in manufacturing but it can be effectively transferred to the professional service firm. Essentially, QA comprises a series of procedures, a uniform system of working which is reviewed on a regular basis, has senior management support and is utilised on every contract (Stebbing 1990).

To become certified, the firm must set up and maintain a formal QA system which comprises a series of controls designed to ensure the delivery of a quality service to the client. These controls include the appointment of a senior member of the firm as a quality manager and the writing of a quality manual. Most firms already have the basis of such a system contained in their office manual, although considerable investment in time and money is required if the firm is to achieve and maintain certification. An informal quality system could be based on the RIBA's *Architect's Job Book* (1995) which sets out a series of stages and checklists. Indeed, most firms still use this. But a QA system needs to identify key actions to be taken and identify responsibilities which go way beyond guidance. Hence the need to write a quality manual that is specific to the firm. Derek Sharp (1991:113) makes it sound easy when he suggests that 'all that is needed is to introduce new controls and training systems to conform'. Those architectural firms that have decided to try to achieve certification will testify that it is not such a simple transition and many have not pursued QA to full certification.

10.1.3   Total quality management

In contrast to QA which may only be applicable to certain parts of a firm's activities, total quality management (TQM) encompasses everything the firm does and where the quality of the working environment is seen to be an important influence on the quality of what is produced. It is a people-focused management concept that aims at continual improvement and greater integration with a focus on increased client satisfaction. As with QA, TQM has its roots in manufacturing; it is a simple, holistic approach to quality that transfers well to professional service firms because it is a philosophy rather than a technique – essentially a soft management system. However, the philosophy of TQM needs to be introduced to everyone in the firm and extended to include suppliers, contractors and even the client which in many cases may require a cultural change. Within the architectural firm a change to TQM can be achieved through a combination of leadership through management, the implementation of systems (QA), continuing professional development and, most importantly, employee involvement through teamwork. The Japanese refer to this as *Kaizen*, a step-by-step approach to continuous improvement; it has similarities to the often forgotten concept of having pride in one's work.

10.1.4   Quality of life

While the adoption of quality management is important from a business viewpoint, it is also important to look at it in terms of the quality of life for those employed in the firm, the sponsor of the building project, those involved in the assembly of the building and indeed the building users. A well designed quality management system has the potential to make life at work easier and more enjoyable and to allow more time to be spent on delivering exciting buildings.

10.2 RESISTANCE TO QA

QA is a management innovation that offers one method of controlling, or managing, the consistency of architectural service provision. It is, however, an innovation that has been met with resistance by architectural firms in, for example, England and The Netherlands, despite the growing demand from potential clients and in spite of the architect's reputation for poor management. Resistance to planned organisational change is a recurring theme in management literature and certainly an issue likely to upset the creative individuals who constitute an architectural practice. The perceived threat of change is unsettling to the majority, but spare a thought for the architect: five years spent in a school of architecture learning to be individualistic, creative and unmanageable, the threat of a QA management system, with its procedures, manuals and controls perceived as akin to a straitjacket. Surely it is impossible to behave like a creative architect under the burden of such a restrictive system. Such a view has led to the misguided belief that QA is acceptable for the building component manufacturers and even the builders, but not for designers.

It is not surprising then that the majority of professional design firms have been relatively slow to adopt QA systems. The number of architectural practices that have certified QA systems is a very small percentage of the total number of firms. Resistance to this management innovation is not restricted to UK practices, for example The Netherlands did not record its first certified architectural firm until 1995. QA has been given little coverage in the architectural press, and on the rare occasion when it is been addressed the tendency is to dismiss it as little more than a marketing badge (e.g. Lucas 1995). While it could be and is used as a marketing tool, the adoption of quality management has far-reaching benefits for architectural firms and the quality of the finished building. Work carried out by the RIBA (1992, 1993) highlighted a number of areas in which architectural firms were weak, many of which could be improved by a good quality management system and the adoption of a TQM ethos.

The slow uptake of QA by architectural firms may have surprised and no doubt dismayed the promoters of such management innovations. Anyone familiar with literature about the diffusion of innovations (E. Rogers 1995) would recognise that within any social system, there will be a small proportion, the 'innovators' and 'early adopters' who will adopt an innovation ahead of the rest of the social system. The innovation, however, may not always be fully diffused within a social system, despite what appear to be obvious advantages to their promoters. Diffusion literature has identified a number of factors that are influential in the diffusion of an innovation. The main factors identified are the communication of information about the innovation to a social system, the perceived characteristics of the innovation and its compatibility with existing social system norms which will affect its rate of adoption. Put simply, if the architect perceives QA, from the information available, as incompatible with existing values and practices there will be a tendency to resist adoption. Diffusion studies have shown that this resistance is likely to continue until a critical mass have adopted, at which time the rest of the system tend to adopt it and the innovation is diffused within the social system. If this critical mass is not reached, the innovation will not become fully adopted and its diffusion will have failed. Architectural firms are currently a long way from this critical mass.

10.2.1 Change agents

Despite what would appear to be obvious benefits, there has been relatively little exposure or debate in the architectural press about the pros and cons of utilising a QA system in an architect's office. Indeed, in conversations with practising architects there is often a degree of confusion about the differences between QA and quality of the finished building – quality control. Although the subject is debated at international conferences, research has indicated (Bardin *et al.* 1993) and has been confirmed by experience of practice, that the proceedings of such meetings are rarely transferred to the people who would benefit most, the practising architects. Thus architects may remain unaware of relevant literature relating to this management innovation, information which could help them in their quest for competitive advantage.

Pressure to adopt or resist quality management will come from both inside and from outside the architectural profession. The RIBA clearly has a role to play. They addressed the issue of QA in their 1991 publication the *Architect's Handbook of Practice Management* and issued guidance on quality management to practitioners. There have not been any incentives in terms of lower professional indemnity (PI) insurance premiums for those firms that operate a certified system. While there has been no quantitative assessment of the promotion of QA to architects, it has been suggested that the professional institution has taken a very conservative view in the promotion of management innovations such as QA to the profession, leaving it to practitioners to make their own decision about such issues (Emmitt and Neary 1995). Literature addressed specifically at architects also tends to be in short supply and is primarily concerned with how to set up a system (e.g. Taylor and Hosker 1992), rather than specifically tackling the usual concerns of architects which tend to relate, not surprisingly, to design-related issues.

External pressures to adopt have come, and will continue to come, largely through client pressure for better service and better value for money. Large institutions and local authorities have started to request that professionals have a certified QA system before they will be allowed to bid for work from them, but smaller clients have, to date, not made such demands. The programme of CPD, although initiated from within the social system by the RIBA, has been left very much to players from outside the system to organise. Thus seminars are presented by building product manufacturers and by management consultants, where issues relating to QA (and other themes addressed in this book) are rarely promoted. Since there is no clearly identifiable change agent and there is currently no great pressure to adopt, the rate of adoption is likely to remain slow.

10.3   THE PERCEIVED EFFECT OF QA ON THE CREATIVE PROCESS

While setting up the QA system in an architectural practice and experiencing the change from an 'it will do' attitude to a total quality philosophy/environment, I was conscious of both bemusement and hostility from other practising architects to the concept of quality management or QA. The few architectural firms that had adopted a quality management system were very positive about its benefits to their business and were moving towards a TQM philosophy within their firms. It was the architectural firms who had not adopted that appeared to hold intransigent views on this issue. There is nothing unusual in this. The promoters of TQM are aware that certain groups, including designers, always have difficulty in associating themselves with its philosophy because they see themselves as having unique, highly specialised and individual skills. As such, management is viewed as an unnecessary intrusion into their creative endeavours (e.g. Macdonald and Piggott 1990).

Most of the case studies reported in the quality management literature are concerned with its successful implementation by manufacturing and service industries and focus on the positive benefits it has brought to a particular firm. Few studies have attempted to look at why quality management has been resisted within the building industry and by architectural firms in particular. Evidence of the architectural professions' strongly held beliefs and conservative attitudes to change was identified in research based on interviews with directors of medium-sized architectural practices that had not adopted QA (Emmitt 1995), summarised below.

10.3.1   Awareness of QA

It was important to allow the practitioners freedom of expression during the interviews, so semi-structured interviews were undertaken with the director of each architectural firm in their working environment, their offices. This allowed an informal exchange of views which, from experience, tends to allow greater openness on behalf of the interviewee. Of the firms visited, half of the directors claimed to be working towards the implementation of a quality management system but had no intention of attempting to achieve certification, while the other half declared that they had no intention of adopting any sort of quality management system whatsoever unless it was absolutely necessary, i.e. specifically requested by a client.

None of the architects could remember where they had picked up information about QA, although they all claimed to have read about it in management literature, rather than in the architectural journals. Indeed, four of the architects interviewed noted that in their opinion the RIBA should have done more to debate the topic within the journals. With regard to interpersonal communication, there was little interaction with fellow professionals because of the fear of competition, so the chance to discuss QA with peers was largely denied.

All the architects spoken to were concerned about the additional paperwork and administrative cost that a QA system would impose on their already overburdened office routines. They all had office systems which had been developed in accordance with the RIBA *Office Manual/Job Book* which was described as more than adequate for their purposes. There was no discernible difference between the attitude of the part-adopters and the non-adopters. The part-adopters felt they had to 'make an effort' to keep their clients happy, a view which perhaps resulted in the observation that QA is only a marketing badge, while the non-adopters had more integrity (in my opinion), in that they had refused to adopt, unless forced to do so by client pressure; there was no pretence of adoption.

None of the architects spoken to were happy about someone from outside their practices advising them on a suitable system, or auditing them. Unprompted, they all claimed that 'only they' knew how to manage their practices, a somewhat arrogant view, and thus QA would not benefit them, especially if it was set up by someone other than an architect. Indeed, one architect had sacked his QA consultant 'because he did not understand design'. These views (prejudices) were deeply held, but the concern which raised the most comment was the perceived clash of management and creativity.

10.3.2   Creativity

First, all of the architects saw themselves as creative and therefore outside the bounds of a 'restrictive' management system, a fear imparted during architectural education where management issues are given very little time or respect in a design-centred learning environment. This view had been maintained in practice, where management was seen as something which had to be done, rather than a tool to help the practice. Half of the sample confessed 'off the record' to being highly disorganised, but saw this as a sign of their creativity rather than anything to be concerned about. A management consultant may take a different view!

Second, there would appear to be great resistance from practising architects to a management system that specifically manages the design process, from design generation through to detail design, in particular resistance to a system that imposes additional deadlines in the form of design reviews. Perhaps surprisingly, given the recent Strategic Study reports, all the architects expressed discomfort with working to deadlines. It was noted that it was difficult enough getting the drawings completed to go to tender – which usually went out incomplete. Recording such comments, it is not surprising to see that professionals other than architects have seized the project management domain.

Interestingly, these views were expressed based largely in ignorance of QA. All the architects interviewed were articulate, competent and radiated an air of professionalism. However, only a third of the sample had actually fully investigated QA literature and none of them had read or were aware of any conference proceedings relating to QA. Perhaps more worrying is that one of the practices which claimed to be working to QA, a point stated on their practice brochure sent out to clients, had no intention of adopting and had not investigated it. In these examples, quality management was only mentioned for marketing purposes. The old adage never trust what you read in promotional literature unfortunately may also apply to professional service firms.

10.3.3   QA and the design process

Given the comments noted in the interviews reported above and my own experience of QA in an architectural environment a look at the apparent conflict between QA and the design process is required. QA and management depend on time, which continues relentlessly in a linear process to and beyond previously determined deadlines. Design, in comparison, is not linear, involving feedback loops and creative leaps. It is, however, a 'process' and as such subject to programme and time constraints. It is easy to believe that the two are incompatible, and the architects interviewed clearly had convinced themselves that this was indeed the case. But whether the architects like it or not, deadlines are imposed by clients and from a need to manage the project, usually by RIBA work stages. The question is, therefore: Can QA be accommodated within the design process without hindering the process?

10.4   ADVOCATING QUALITY MANAGEMENT

As illustrated above, many firms have questioned whether QA is worth the investment and critics have claimed that it is little more than a form-filling exercise, a fashion that will pass or is just a marketing badge to attract clients. But they have overlooked both the demand from their clients and the benefits such a system can bring to an architectural firm. Implemented correctly a QA system can reduce the time taken to ensure quality and also reduce the firm's exposure to risk, thus freeing up time for more creative pursuits. Sharp (1991) believes that the adoption of QA is worth the investment because of the improvement in efficiency, reduction in waste and generation of new work. Advocates of quality management within the architectural literature (e.g. Coxe 1980; Cornick 1991; Taylor and Hosker 1992) certainly put up convincing arguments for its adoption, an argument supported by those firms that have taken the time and effort to adopt a quality management system. Indeed Gray *et al.* (1994:32) state that 'if the design process is to be managed successfully it must be subject to control within the framework of Quality Management.' According to Coxe (1980) quality service can be achieved by giving attention to the following:

- consistent standards for individual projects
- consistent approach to client relations
- consistent quality review process
- clear responsibility.

All these areas should be covered in a well designed and implemented quality management system.

10.4.1   Keep it simple

In discussion about quality management systems the term 'well designed' has deliberately been used in this book. This is because a badly designed and poorly implemented quality management system may well cause more harm than good to the firm and its relationship with its clients. One of the most important attributes of a simple, well-designed and easy to use QA system is that it can be used as an underlying framework for all the firm's activities. Such a system provides the firm with:

- A clear management structure that is understood by all the firm's members.
- Policy and procedures to enable the delivery of the service promised to the client.
- Control and review of the design process and production information.
- Control of job documentation via the 'job quality plan'.
- A training policy for all staff and directors.
- A comprehensive risk management system.

The problem of knowledge retention was raised earlier and QA can help to retain some of this experience within its system. This both saves time and reduces the firm's exposure to risk. Perhaps the best advice, yet the hardest to achieve in practice, is to keep the procedures as simple and as flexible as possible so that they are used.

10.4.2   Programme and budget

The implementation of a QA system will need to be carefully programmed and budgeted. The development costs relate to the appointment of an external consultant, the purchase of reference documents, the production of the quality manual, training, formal certification, auditing and maintenance costs. This is a daunting list but, seen in the context of the overall development of the firm, its improved service delivery and reduced exposure to risk, it should be an important investment. The programme is also important, since it would be unwise to implement quality management in one big step. Instead it needs to be introduced gradually so that the firm's members, external consultants and clients are comfortable with resulting changes and improvements in service delivery.

10.4.3   Quality education and training

At the heart of quality management is the total commitment of all the firm's members to quality. Commitment comes from initially raising staff awareness about quality management, through specialist training for both the quality manager and the auditors to general training and updating as jobs progress through the office. The secret of success is to get all members of the firm to appreciate, understand and agree with the philosophy and drive for quality. They must also understand that this is a team effort. If they fail to meet quality standards they are not only letting themselves down but also their colleagues and the firm. However, TQM cannot be enforced through management checks and instructions, it has to be desired and worked for with examples set by senior management. The firm must invest in adequate education and training if this is to be achieved.

Education and training needs must be planned and tailored to the firm's own needs so that step-by-step everyone in the organisation is educated, trained and comfortable with the systems and tools to make TQM happen. Summed up by Macdonald and Piggott (1990:188), 'A TQM education system is a principal agent of change in management behaviour, introducing both new attitudes and the practice of new skills.'

10.4.4   Feedback

Each individual must make the aim of continuous improvement central to all his or her activities and feel free to contribute to the process through feedback to senior management. The use of feedback through 'quality circles' or 'suggestion systems' is central to the Japanese philosophy of TQM. Employee involvement in all levels of the architectural firm have been advocated earlier in this book, to promote a sense of ownership and the desire to continually improve the performance of the firm; the literature on TQM advocates the use of 'quality circles'.

Quality circles are used to bring together employees, managers and directors to discuss and analyse aspects of the firm's service provision through the use of group problem-solving. The American consultant Joseph Juran introduced quality circles to Japanese organisations after the Second World War, since when they have become a popular management strategy for increasing worker participation. Quality circles function at their best as small groups (between five and 12) where the firm's members meet on a voluntary basis for approximately one hour a week. In addition to helping to solve job-related problems, quality circles also seem to increase an individual's satisfaction with his or her firm by increasing participation in important decision-making activities (Kreps 1990). They are best scheduled to a regular timetable, rather than assembled to deal with a particular problem, and need careful management if they are to work for the firm. Caution is required since quality circles can have a negative effect if ideas and decisions are seen to be ignored by management. It is through continuous education that the firm's members are able to provide better suggestions because they better understand the environment in which they operate and are better able to analyse problems. A well-managed firm will recognise the individual's contribution.

The motivational factor was discussed earlier and with quality management the quality manager and the directors of the firm must be able to set examples and motivate all the firm's staff because TQM is a team effort. The use of in-house training sessions and CPD are essential factors in the education and motivation of all the firm's members.

10.5   THE DESIGN REVIEW: GATEWAY TO A QUALITY SERVICE

One of the great strengths of a QA system is the value of internal quality reviews, the 'design review'. The design review is a formal assessment of the design against the client's brief to check that the design meets the client's requirements, is in line with the firm's own standards and conforms to relevant regulatory requirements. The concept of the design review is not new to architects since design critiques are a familiar part of an architect's training and are used in practice to control design standards. Design critiques tend to be relatively informal events conducted within the sanctum of the office so that drawings can be checked and approved by the firm before they are released, e.g. shown to the client. Care is needed not to confuse the two since there are two important differences between the informal critique and the formal design review. First, design reviews are planned events, forming an important part of the programme and the project quality plan. Second, design reviews should include the presence of the client and consultants working on the project so that the design is reviewed by the project team and any alterations can be agreed by the team and recorded in the office plan.

Design reviews are carried out at predetermined stages in the project. To work at their best they should include the project team, consultants, the quality manager, the planning supervisor, and the client or the client's representative. The term 'design review' is a little misleading since the review should be carried out at key stages throughout the life of the project. The review system is essentially a series of gates in the design process through which the project cannot pass without a thorough check from the quality manager and the approval of the client.

The design review provides an opportunity to discuss and agree the design before proceeding further. More specifically it should address the following:

- Design verification
- Design changes
- Statutory consents
- Health and safety
- Environmental impact
- Budget
- Programme.

The design review is important on a number of fronts. It is a very good system of detecting errors and omissions. It provides a checkpoint for ensuring that the design meets the client's requirements and the architectural practice's standards. It also gives the planning supervisor an opportunity to check the scheme for compliance under the recently introduced CDM regulations. Even more importantly, it also provides a window for debate, while feedback from and for other projects can be introduced. In the examples studied in one architect's practice a great deal of benefit was derived from the design reviews, ranging from the practical, such as picking up errors and saving time further along the process, to the creative, such as allowing time to debate design quality and feedback from previous jobs. Thus the design review was far more than a paper-generating exercise in terms of the benefits it could provide an architect's office. It is important to keep these meetings organised but as informal as possible so that ideas can be discussed freely and all members of the project can participate in the process.

In particular the importance of the first design review, to confirm the client's brief, cannot be overstated. This review in many ways establishes the quality of the finished job. It is a stage which confirms and refines the brief from which the product quality chain will follow. In this situation, the quality manager becomes the keeper of the gate through which the project must pass in order to be realised as a building. The project can only pass through the gate if it meets set requirements, and may well be denied passage or only allowed through with a number of conditions which must be met within a certain timescale.

10.5.1   Health and safety

Health and safety legislation, especially the CDM regulations in the UK, place stringent responsibilities on designers. Planned design reviews where client, external consultants, designer, design manager, project manager and the planning supervisor can review, discuss potential problem areas, and take appropriate decisions, should form an essential part of a health and safety strategy.

10.5.2   Environmental assessment

The design review has another purpose which is often ignored in the quality management literature: the check for compliance with environmental/sustainable policies and practices. These may be a combination of the client's requirements and the firm's own pursuit of environmentally responsible policies and will have been discussed and agreed at the briefing stage. As the project proceeds many situations arise and change, so it is important to constantly review the project's environmental impact against the predetermined criteria. The design review is a particularly good opportunity to include such a review.

10.6   A QUALITY FRAMEWORK

The formal QA framework provides an excellent frame of reference in which to design and detail buildings. It provides a certain discipline which has an affinity to the recently introduced CDM regulations in the UK. It also has a number of other advantages.

10.6.1   Risk management

Perhaps the biggest risk to the professional service firm is that someone will claim against it because they are dissatisfied with the service provided by the firm. While there is no guaranteed way of preventing this, the risk can be reduced by assessing it and taking appropriate precautions. The implementation of formal systems that require the adoption of sound working methods will limit the risk of unsatisfactory service and hence reduce the risk of a claim being brought against the firm; QA could then be viewed as an effective risk management tool. The firm should not be complacent, for however good the system and however talented the workforce there will be occasions when things may go wrong and formal procedures not implemented. Legal advice should be sought.

10.7 COMPETITIVE ADVANTAGE THROUGH QUALITY MANAGEMENT

This chapter has attempted to highlight both the potential and the threat that QA poses to the practising architect. There is clearly a responsibility on the schools of architecture to encompass both a management and a QA philosophy, promoted while the architect is learning the craft of design rather than leave it entirely to the practitioners to tackle. This will require a sea change within the UK architectural schools where design is taught in isolation, or abstraction, of its true intent: the design and production of buildings. Effective utilisation of a QA system can help the designer in his or her task and has serious implications for assessment of the design by the planning supervisor under the recently introduced CDM regulations. The case study overleaf helps to highlight the point that QA as a philosophy is essential to the competitiveness of the architectural firm. It provides the backbone of a well-managed practice and may allow a firm to adopt other management innovations.

If a firm is to achieve competitive advantage through TQM both its customers (clients) and its suppliers (consultants) must be involved in the process. The goal is to superplease the client through anticipation of their needs and the addition of 'that little extra' to delight them. Once such an approach has been adopted it is important to maintain the momentum through review of the quality business plan and the commitment of all staff to continuous improvement. Quality concerns all those involved in building. Continuous improvement is a managerial style that can improve the quality of life of all concerned. It is not a quick-fix solution but a long-term business strategy. The management of change is also a complex, difficult area.

The implications for architectural firms are considerable, given a competitive market. Design is essential to the quality of the finished product, the building – but what use is design ability if it is poorly managed? Those architects who have bucked the trend and adopted QA, and all the benefits it brings, should be congratulated and perhaps rewarded with lower professional indemnity (PI) insurance premiums. Those who are playing the system should get off the fence and go through the pain barrier to adoption or, alternatively, stop fooling their clients and themselves and drop the pretence. The decision to adopt or resist, client permitting, is the architect's.

Case study   Implementing quality management

The case study firm was quick to realise the potential benefits of implementing quality assurance, seen both as an underlying framework and philosophy in the delivery of the firm's professional services. This case study briefly charts the implementation of quality assurance within the firm, highlighting some of the challenges and opportunities that arose in the process.

Before adoption

A risk assessment was carried out by the designated quality manager before the implementation of the QA scheme. There were three main questions to be addressed. First, was it worthwhile financially? This was difficult to assess since the firm knew it could not charge more for its services. However, it was accepted that a reduction in unnecessary work (correction of errors) should make individual jobs more financially viable. On balance it was accepted that the implementation of quality management would cost the firm money in the short term, money that might be difficult to recoup in the longer term. Second, would there be an adverse reaction from the staff? Resistance from the staff was anticipated, despite the fact that they already worked to a set of tried and tested procedures laid down in the 'office manual'. The implementation of an office-wide education and training programme was required to minimise the risk of disruption and/or resentment. Third, would it be required by clients? According to the literature available at the time there was a need for a more consistent approach to the professional delivery of design services. The firm felt that it may gain a certain degree of competitive advantage if it adopted QA and its competitors did not.

Implementation

Before the implementation of the QA scheme the firm went to great lengths to inform the staff about what it was doing, why it was doing it and when the changes were to take place, via staff meetings and internal memos. This is regarded as good practice. However, some staff remained uneasy with the concept, perceiving QA as a management tool to constrain their creative work, an attitude that softened as more information became available and staff grew more familiar with the terminology and what was expected of them. One of the biggest mistakes made by the firm was the relatively small amount of input from staff at the early stages in the development of the quality manual. The quality manager did consult staff, but mainly towards the later stages in the development of the manual, by which time many of the procedures and paperwork were relatively fixed. The result was a relatively large, albeit comprehensive, quality manual that the staff found too onerous to work with, thus causing a degree of resentment. The quality manual has since been reduced in size and complexity.

The scheme took two years to implement, from the decision to adopt, through implementation, to certification. The main differences to the way jobs were administered before implementation lay with the project quality plan for each job, the formal use of design reviews and a greater openness with clients. In particular the quality system was designed to increase client participation in their projects.

Benefits

As part of the process of monitoring the impact of the QA scheme a number of similar projects, administered under the old office management system, and administered under the QA scheme, were compared. Analysis of the data confirmed that the biggest advantage to the designer was a reduction in the amount of time spent on correcting errors. Offset against the additional time spent checking work, there was a net saving in time. Thus jobs were more profitable and the firm's exposure to risk reduced since errors had, for the most part, been identified and dealt with before information left the office. Most errors and omissions were identified during the formal design reviews: an invaluable tool in the quest for quality.

The design review

Although reviews were used on projects before the implementation of QA, the formal implementation of QA placed additional emphasis on the design review. Design reviews were scheduled as part of the job programme: they were fixed. Although the number was adjusted to suit the size of projects, as a minimum on all projects design reviews were carried out at the following interfaces:

- Brief: sketch design
- Sketch design: detailed design
- Detailed design: tender documentation
- Tender documentation: contract
- Completion/feedback.

The more structured design review was welcomed by staff, since they had a fixed target date to work to, while also acting as a useful management tool to control individual design projects. The design review was also welcomed by some of the firm's clients who were happy to become fully involved with their projects and contribute through the review. Other clients felt less willing or were less able to participate.

Much more than a marketing badge

Once the QA system was operating and the staff had contributed to in-house seminar sessions relating to the TQM ethos, staff motivation improved. In the first few months after implementation (and before certification from the external body) there was a tendency for staff to read the quality manual only when necessary, i.e. when there was a problem. The quality manager spent a lot of time talking to the firm's members and eventually got the message home: the quality manual should be used as a tool. These conversations, sometimes on an individual basis, sometimes as small groups, were important in identifying areas of concern. The feedback from the staff identified a number of problems with the quality manual, largely associated with procedures that were difficult to implement, and these were redesigned to make the manual easier to use. In line with the ethos of continuing improvement the quality management system has been refined and adjusted over the years following certification. The scheme is now an embedded part of the firm's service provision and staff are comfortable with its use.

The management of the firm felt that adopting quality management had been the right thing to do. Clients were receiving a far more consistent level of service and staff had a greater awareness of the service they were expected to deliver. The managing director was not aware of any situations where having QA had helped them gain new commissions and was unsure of its benefit as a marketing badge. However, he was convinced of its benefits in terms of improved design quality and service quality within the firm. The firm's management were also quick to realise that the management structure provided by the QA system provided the rigour and the flexibility to adopt other management innovations. The general view was that adoption had been worthwhile and had helped the firm to maintain its competitive edge.

CHAPTER 11

MANAGING CONSTRUCTION

The management of the construction process is an area from which many architectural firms have withdrawn or been pushed out by other disciplines. While architectural firms have been slow to realise the potential of project management, by the same token they have been slow to realise the importance of construction management. This chapter discusses the importance of the link between the design office and the building site, an important link for achieving environmentally responsible design principles. The case study illustrates how an architectural firm can manage the construction process and reduce the cost of the finished building through effective management. The adoption of such an approach has implications for the quality of the finished product and feedback to the design process. In particular the link back to procurement strategy and client empathy is discussed as part of the firm's business strategy.

11.1   MAKING BUILDINGS

Architects often talk of 'making buildings' but very few architects build in a physical manner. The buildings they design are built by others in a process where architectural designs represented by drawings, specifications, schedules and models are used to translate intent to physical artefact. This was not always the case. Before the drive for professional status, 'architects' as directors of the work, were in direct touch with the workmen; there was no intermediary (in the form of the general contractor) between architect and tradesmen; drawings were rarely needed because of the empathy that existed between designer, tradesmen and materials. A combination of more complex technologies, an ever-increasing choice of building products and a growth in the number of intermediaries involved in building has resulted in architects becoming disengaged from the physical act of building. Again, this is not a recent phenomenon but coincident with the architect's drive for professional status and exclusivity. Writing in 1955 Eggleston noted the architect's retreat from the building site during the preceding 50 years, concluding that 'The architect is no longer both designer and builder, but is now to some extent separated from the practical side of the work' (Eggleston 1955:6).

Most architectural firms have little real control over production, regardless of the contract used, although they are often judged on the quality of the finished building as well as on the quality of their service provision. From a business perspective, architectural firms seem insufficiently attached to the buildings they design. Such detachment is unsettling since it emphasises architects' vulnerability in the order of things. For the firms that have concentrated entirely on providing a design service, such detachment is inevitable (and not necessarily a problem for them); for others the detachment from the physicality of building is a problem. Attempts to get back in touch with the assembly process have been made by a few firms, keen to regain control of site management and costs through the use of construction management techniques (Emmitt 1995, 1997b). It is an unfamiliar area which must be understood if advances are to be made in the drive for environmentally responsible approaches to building.

11.1.1   Buildability

Not wanting to be left out of the creeping tide of jargon the building industry has come up with the words 'buildability' and 'constructability'. During the early 1980s the Construction Industry Research and Information Association (CIRIA) published *Buildability: An Assessment* (CIRIA 1983) which defined buildability as 'the extent to which the design of the building facilitates ease of construction, subject to the overall requirements for the completed building'. This work highlighted the separation between design and production in the British building industry, identified in earlier reports (e.g. *Emmerson Report* 1962); it advocated greater simplicity, more standardisation and better communication between designer and builder. A similar argument was made by the architectural profession with the proposal for the Alternative Method of Management (discussed below) that eliminated the main contractor from the process altogether.

To many architects the term buildability is synonymous with good design and good detailing, and something that architectural firms have always taken seriously. However, the CIRIA's well-intended publication, based on a survey of building contractors, has been used as an effective weapon by architects' competitors to claim a greater share of the market. Paradoxically the CIRIA report and the following publications have resulted in designers (architects) becoming ever more detached from building as the management professionals have relentlessly pushed architects further into a design-only role, with the intermediaries acting as gatekeepers. Arguably, for buildability to improve designers need to be more, not less, involved in site operations. If quality is to be achieved in construction, a simpler model with fewer links in the chain is required: a model that relies on close co-operation between client, architect and tradesmen.

11.2   CONSTRUCTION MANAGEMENT BY ARCHITECTS

One way of overcoming the potential problem of conflict and ineffective communication is to build using a limited number of intermediaries. Some have claimed that design-and-build is one method for achieving this, although this contractor-led system of building has often been criticised for the poor quality of the finished product and tends to be disliked by architects because they are not in a contractual position to control quality. An architect-led method of reducing the number of intermediaries is to use construction management: a procurement route that allows the architect to communicate directly with trade contractors and eliminates the main contractor. In the books dedicated to describing procurement routes the term *design and manage* is sometimes used to describe an architectural practice that also manages the building phase of the project, although in architectural literature the term construction management tends to be used and is the term favoured here. Through the employment of an individual with contracting and management skills – a contracts manager – the architectural firm is in a position to manage, administer and co-ordinate the sub-contractors, taking advantage of the minimal capital outlay required. Using construction management, the architectural firm can control the whole construction process, thus ensuring continuity in the product quality chain, while also charging a management fee for their efforts. The contract, agreed between client and architectural firm, provides the client with single point responsibility while the independent selection and control of sub-contractors provides the opportunity theoretically for improved completion times, improved quality, reduced costs and improved communication within the temporary project team. Communication routes are more direct, with sub-contractors being in contact with both client and architect. Another advantage is that the designer is in direct contact with the sub-contractors so problems can be solved more quickly, reducing claims and variation orders. Communication may also be improved through the elimination of an unnecessary layer of management: the main contractor. Such a system of procurement has many similarities with design-and-build but the biggest difference is the architectural firm's design vision which separates it from the more familiar contractor-led design-and-build option, in that the team is led by a design-conscious professional rather than just a cost-conscious one.

The arguments for a design-led form of contractual arrangement is not new. In the 1980s there was a proposal for an Alternative Method of Management (AMM) from the architectural profession, a model in which the main contractor was eliminated and the architect took on the central role of design and management. AMM was important because it recognised the growing importance of sub-contracting with architects, not contractors, benefiting from their management. Such a system is, theoretically, well suited to architectural firms since the ability to communicate their ideas directly to the sub-contractors and the ability to learn directly from them on-site can go a long way to improve the quality of the finished product. The problem comes from the environment in which construction takes place, an adversarial, fiercely competitive environment, in which main contractors will not readily relinquish control to architectural firms. Certainly in the 1980s AMM was not adopted widely, partly because of the architect's weak position and partly because the system relies on co-operation which contractors were not prepared to accept (Ball 1988).

On first impressions, the thought of architects dirtying their hands with building may be, perhaps, a little unusual. Architectural education does not teach architects to build, it teaches them to design. The adoption of construction management by architects is a new direction in architectural management. Indeed, writing on the subject of management contracting, Bennett (1981) concluded that such methods are quite unsuitable for architectural firms because they introduce overheads (management staff) that are difficult to justify. His caution is echoed in the *Architect's Job Book* (RIBA 1995:32) which states that 'acting in the role of construction manager is unlikely to interest the majority of architects directly, who will only rarely have the necessary experience, skills and aptitude'. As with much of the literature produced by the RIBA, such statements tend to assume that it will be qualified architects who may take on this role, rather than qualified contracts managers in the employ of an architectural firm as advocated above.

A small but growing number of architectural practices find that such methods are possible to implement and have adopted management contracting and/or construction management techniques in pursuit of better building quality. For example, Michael Hopkins and Partners have used construction management to ensure that quality is transferred from the architect's office to the building site and hence to the finished product (Slavid 1996). Such methods may be ideally suited to architectural firms. The challenge lies more in how the firm is able to utilise different skills and abilities. However, for most architectural firms this is not such a natural management innovation to adopt as, say, project management, because it involves a greater readjustment in the knowledge and skills base of the firm to implement it.

11.3   IMPLICATIONS FOR ADOPTION

From a client's perspective the concept of single point responsibility is, on the surface, appealing since the client only has to deal with one firm, regardless of when queries or problems occur, be it at the design, assembly or occupation stage. From the architectural firm's perspective such an approach represents a large increase in both responsibility and the exposure to risk that accompanies it.

11.3.1   Risk and reward

Risk and reward go hand-in-hand. Such a venture does expose the firm to additional responsibilities and thus additional risks, but it also provides another avenue for fee generation. The adoption and provision of these additional services represents an increase in the architectural firm's exposure to risk, and is an area in which the directors/partners of the business should take legal advice before proceeding. But the provision of extensive services with a suitably qualified and experienced team, especially where the full service is being provided, could also be seen as one way of reducing exposure to risk. Certainly the prospect of claims by a main contractor during the contract has been removed and improved communications within the integrated team is likely to reduce (but not necessarily eradicate) mistakes. It may also be easier to deal with any problems directly with a trade contractor rather than through an intermediary in the form of the general contractor.

11.3.2   Professional accountability

The thorny issue of accountability needs to be addressed here. Architects have often found themselves in a difficult position: appointed and paid by a client, but charged with managing the project and the contractor fairly, a difficult but correct path to follow from a professional standpoint. Once an architectural firm starts to build its own designs it is potentially open to claims of misconduct and must be careful to make sure everything is open to scrutiny. The 'open book' policy is recognised as a sensible approach, combined with charging a management fee for services provided.

11.3.3   Site operations

The thought of organising construction sites, hiring site huts and safety equipment and being liable for the employee's tax is an unfamiliar area to the majority of architectural firms. But the architectural firm must be prepared to venture into unfamiliar territory (usually the contractor's domain), from planning the site to accommodate equipment, materials, temporary buildings and insurance. The secret is employing a diverse range of professionals, some of whom are experienced in such matters. For example, the scheduling of resources should not be beyond the skills of a construction project manager. The setting up of the site, the employment of the clerk of works (often under the architect's remit anyway), the appointment of a contracts manager and a site agent/manager is an area in which many architects become involved, whether they want to or not. It is certainly an issue that may affect the project and the quality of the completed building.

11.3.4   Quality

The challenge of maintaining a quality design through the building stage to the finished product is considerable. With traditional contractual arrangements compromises are often made before a start on-site or during construction, with pressure from the contractor to change products to save time or money. To a certain extent such control is in the hands of the designer. However, in design-and-build contracts and where an independent project manager is pulling the strings, control of design quality by the designer becomes difficult. For a book concerned with the delivery of quality work and quality service the detachment from the actual process of building is not a particularly good policy.

11.3.5   Cost control and payment

One problem associated with the building industry is the length of time taken by the main contractor to pay the sub-contractors (Cheetham *et al.* 1995). Delayed payment is recognised as leading to company failures, conflict and poor morale in the industry. Construction management techniques can overcome this problem by direct payment from the client to the trade contractor once the work has been approved and certified by the architect. It was noted as a positive benefit in the case study.

11.3.6   Communication and control

Improving communication through the reduction in the number of competing intermediaries is difficult to achieve since the designer must be in a position to influence the procurement route. The argument for effective communication within an information-driven environment was made in earlier chapters, but once again it comes back to control. Separation of design from production has been highlighted as a problem in achieving quality because of the communication barriers that exist (Higgin and Jessop 1965; Harper 1978). Construction management by architectural firms, based on the integration of client, architect and tradesmen, may go some way to improving the transfer of information within the temporary project team. Designers must stay close to both the client and the product.

11.4   BUILDING LIFE

For the design-orientated professional service firm there is a natural link between operations on-site and the longer term issue of maintenance, repair and reuse. Architects have long been criticised for walking away after the building is complete with scant attention paid to feedback or indeed to the use of the building in the years after completion. This is not a particularly good policy. Experience of the building process stands the 'builder' in good stead to carry out repairs, alterations and maintenance, often without reference to the team responsible for its original design. Since the design firm has empathy with the building's assembly there is greater potential for offering maintenance/asset management/FM services: better control of original design intentions.

11.4.1   Maintenance

Both maintenance and the management of property is a field traditionally associated with the building surveying profession and more recently the facilities management discipline. From an economic viewpoint buildings represent substantial assets to their owners and users, frequently requiring maintenance, repair and upgrading. Responsible owners have long recognised the long-term financial benefits of regular maintenance of their often substantial assets. Maintenance management has long been overlooked by owners and it is still an area in which many property owners have no provision: surprising, given the costs in use. More surprising still is that a building owner who has gone to great lengths to employ professionals to design and oversee the construction of the building, taking great care in the selection of the contractor, should then employ a wide assortment of firms – often with no professional input – to carry out alterations and maintenance, often without reference to the original design philosophy (Paterson 1977). From an asset management viewpoint such an approach is not particularly sensible. From an environmental viewpoint the aim of the design team should be to extend the building's life for as long as possible, through careful design and material selection, in order to conserve the scarce resources that are locked into the fabric. Once constructed there is a need to consult the original documentation (if not the original team) before alterations or maintenance is carried out. This should be an area offered by the architectural firm, especially if it has direct experience of the building and the relevant information to hand.

11.4.2 Additional services

Once the architectural office has been assembled and has gained some experience it may then be in a position to further expand the range of services it provides. The natural extension to construction management would be to offer management services for the whole construction process, ranging from site identification and land assembly through feasibility studies to completion and feedback. The architectural firm will act as an enabler, where a client appoints a professional to manage the entire construction process on their behalf: a role also claimed by independent project managers. We have come full circle, from the initial argument that the project manager role was an essential link between client and architectural firm.

In order to offer such a service, the office would need additional expertise to deal with the land identification and assembly, ideally a chartered building surveyor. Thus the firm is now completely multidisciplinary in terms of the different qualifications and expertise held by its individual members. The argument that the various individuals should work together to improve communication and ultimately the quality of the finished product, the building, is addressed by this model, because the initial planning, design and construction phases are integrated rather than segregated. Thus design quality is possible within a project delivered to programme and offering value for money: advantageous to the client and to the society in which the building sits. However, the architectural firm will be competing with many other providers within the marketplace, so competition for service provision will still be present. The model proposed above, in addition to offering the full service, will also be in a position to unbundle particular services to suit certain client requirements: the best of both worlds.

Case study   Design and manage

Once the case study firm had implemented its quality assurance scheme and had established its project management service provision it was then in a position to adopt other management innovations. Of particular concern to the firm, and its clients, was not only the quality of service delivery but also the quality of the finished building. Over the course of some months the architectural firm and one of its repeat clients discussed various options of reducing both costs and construction times, while at the same time improving the quality of the finished product. The architectural firm felt that there was a limit to the amount of money and time that could be saved through careful detailing, constant revision of the specification and careful programming; a limit which had been reached using a traditional procurement route. The most radical proposal at the time was for the architectural firm to adopt construction management as a procurement route and thereby eliminate the need for a main contractor. Feasibility studies carried out by the firm indicated that there would be a cost saving to the client and the architectural practice would be able to charge a fee for carrying out such a service. Such a venture was not without risk for either party.

Apart from the obvious dangers of exposing the practice to additional risk, which had to be balanced against additional income, there were two more fundamental problems to address. First was the difficulty of convincing the client that such a procurement route could be managed by an architectural firm: a difficult task since at that time the firm was unaware of any other architects using similar techniques. The client's principal concern centred around the firm's lack of experience. Second, the firm knew that it was an innovator and the service had to be implemented from scratch. Adoption of construction management techniques required considerable investment, with no guarantee that the venture would be successful. In an attempt to reduce the amount of risk to both parties, early forages into the world of construction management were restricted to small projects where the risk of failure was reduced.

Ownership and accountability

The construction management system used by the architects placed a great deal of emphasis on co-operation and understanding by the client. For example, while the payment of trade contractors was certified by the architect, payment was made directly from the client to the trade contractor within a set time period. This meant that the client had to be conversant with the way in which the building industry functioned (the client's previous experience of the industry helped in this case) and also prepared to act, essentially, in the role of the main contractor. The construction management service provided by the architectural practice was agreed on a lump sum basis with the client. As for the contract itself, this was administered on an 'open book' policy, where the client could see exactly what was being purchased and at what cost: there was no price mark-up by the architectural practice. The open book approach was important in maintaining trust between client and architect, encouraging the concept of 'ownership' to develop. It also ensured that the architectural practice did not have any conflict of interest (it would be easy to abuse this system and design for profit) and thus retained its professional integrity.

The client was encouraged to take part in the decision-making process throughout both the design and the construction processes. There was a considerable learning curve for the client, but the feeling of greater involvement and greater responsibility for the project contributed to the client's satisfaction with the finished product. Thus the sense of 'ownership' of the project by all parties was particularly important in quality terms.

Cost control, delivery and the quality of workmanship

Direct payment from client to trade contractor had two positive contributions to overall quality. First, the tradesmen provided a cheaper price to the architect than that previously submitted to the main contractor for carrying out the same work, primarily because they were told that they would be paid within 14 days of submitting an invoice for work carried out – and they were. This meant that the quality of the building, assessed against cost, improved because the client was paying less money for the same product. Second, because the tradesmen were paid quickly, as promised, the quality of the work on site improved. When the tradesmen were questioned about this they associated prompt payment with job satisfaction: since they were keen to tender for further work they felt that it was worth putting in the extra effort.

There was a considerable cost-saving to the client, compared with the traditional route, despite the payment of a construction management fee (lump sum) on top of the contract sum. Comparison between a traditionally administered contract and the construction management route showed a saving to the client of 23 per cent. This is a figure approaching the magical 30 per cent proposed by Latham (1994), achieved through closer liaison with the tradesmen and closer negotiation with the building product manufacturers. However, the largest contribution to cost reduction was the exclusion of the main contractor from the team.

In terms of delivery, comparison showed that there was no overall saving on the contract period, although a few subtle pointers are illuminating. The snagging list, prepared one week before practical completion, and the snagging list prepared at practical completion were more indicative of the delivery and quality aspects of the project. Both lists contained just over 50 per cent less defects/outstanding work on the construction management contracts than the traditional contracts. On closer inspection the list compiled under the construction management contract contained items of a more minor nature: for example, chips to paintwork. Therefore the reduction in defects was closer to 70 per cent. Although this was a relatively rough method of comparison, it did indicate that there was a cleaner handover of the building to the client.

Information flow and control

Construction management is an inherently simple system because there are fewer intermediaries involved in the process. One obvious benefit was the reduction in adversarial behaviour, by removal of the main contractor, which allowed the architect time for more creative or productive pursuits, normally spent dealing with claims from the main contractor. There was also the potential for greater communication exchange between the client and architect and between the trade contractor and the architect; the quality triangle illustrated in Figure 11.1. The architectural firm felt that through improved communication it was able to make better informed decisions during the design and construction phases of the contracts, a decision-making process that included the client. A direct benefit of face-to-face communication with the trade contractors was an improvement in feedback between the building site and the design office, so often lacking in the product quality chain. Feedback, often transmitted by the architect's own site agent, had been encouraged and suggestions to reduce cost or save time made by trade contractors had been adopted where applicable.

A positive benefit to the architectural firm came from being the team leader, in control of finances, in control of programme and ultimately in control of quality. Control of the process was seen to be important, not because of prestige or social status, but to ensure that the building was built as designed and specified. For example, it eliminated the main contractor's penchant for switching specified materials for cheaper, and often inferior, products, thus reducing quality.

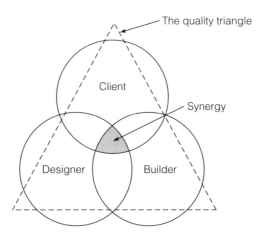

Fig. 11.1   The quality triangle
Designer has empathy with client site – synergy in the quality triangle.

Conclusion

The philosophy of the architectural firm was to reduce the number of players involved in the building process in an attempt to improve communication, to improve cost control and ultimately to improve the quality of the finished product. In addition to the significant cost reduction achieved, a major benefit to both the architect and the client was the removal of the main contractor from the building chain which had eliminated conflict from the building project. The firm also found that it was in a position to exert more control over site procedures, thus assisting in its environmentally responsible policy. Another benefit was reported by the people involved in the various projects who claimed that their quality of life had improved, in part because their work was more enjoyable, because of a regained pride in workmanship and in having a sense of ownership in the finished building. Other factors, such as a reduction in conflict were noted, and a desire for the whole team to strive for quality in the finished product. It is a system close in philosophy to TQM and one which has achieved similar objectives to those claimed by the promoters of 'partnering' techniques (e.g. Baden Hellard 1994, 1995).

In terms of promoting the service to clients the case study firm claimed there was resistance from clients to this procurement method. First, it is still an innovative procurement route for architectural practices, therefore the client's perception of risk is high because of lack of knowledge. Thus the architects now have a role as educators, providing the client with enough information to enable him or her to make an informed decision. Second, the system requires a great deal of involvement on behalf of the client. Not all clients are prepared or have the time to be involved in the design and construction decision-making process, and as such these clients still favour a more traditional, supposedly less risky procurement route. Promotion of construction management techniques to clients, both new and existing, is less of a problem now that the practice has some experience and has proved it can deliver. The firm now has a number of both new and existing clients who have commissioned buildings using this method since it has proved to be beneficial to both client and architect in a fiercely competitive environment.

The adoption of construction management (combined with other areas of diversity in service provision) resulted in an adjustment of core staff skills with more emphasis on qualified construction managers, site agents and administrative staff. In the process of adopting construction management, the office had become truly multidisciplinary.

Part 4

COMPETITIVE ADVANTAGE

THE DESIGN-ORIENTATED PROFESSIONAL SERVICE FIRM

Following on from the issues raised through the theoretical debates and the case studies, this chapter puts forward a model of the architect-led professional service firm, the product champions, focusing on staff structure and the multidisciplinary skills base. Such an approach leads on to questions about the traditional office base and the possibilities of networking staff from remote sites. Transformation from a traditional architectural practice to a firm employing architectural management systems, a firm with competitive advantage, is illustrated by the final case study.

12.1 COMPETITIVE ADVANTAGE IN PRACTICE

Up to this point in the book a number of issues have been explored and illustrated with examples drawn from practice. Many of the ideas presented, either individually or together, may help the design-orientated professional service firm to achieve a degree of competitive advantage over its rivals. The assets and strategies employed by a firm and the way in which different architectural management systems may be implemented were discussed in Parts 2 and 3 respectively. The challenge for the firm's directors comes from knowing *how* to put it all together into a cohesive firm, a challenge for those about to set up a new firm and also to those who wish to bring about change within an existing firm. As discussed earlier, just as there is no one business strategy to guarantee competitive advantage, neither is there an ideal method of structuring the firm. The concept of competitive advantage is well established (Porter 1985) and has been widely applied, but what gives the design-orientated professional service firm competitive advantage? A number of examples drawn from practice help to illustrate the complexity of what appears on the surface to be a straightforward question. A firm in three size brackets is used to illustrate the point. They are not meant to be representative of the architectural profession as a whole, but are selected because they were known to the author, they have all been trading for approximately ten years, and they are financially successful and well respected by their clients for providing both a quality service and a quality product.

12.1.1   Firm A

The solo practitioner had been trading as a limited company for more than eight years. The architect claimed competitive advantage by concentrating on one very specific area of development, limiting his service provision to feasibility studies and scheme design up to and including planning submissions. He had established a good reputation for dealing with planning applications for difficult sites and claimed that he could operate in this area because few architects had the competence to deal with planners (they did not know the planning regulations well enough), and planning consultants could not provide the design input. Thus he had very little real competition. Once planning was achieved the project was passed on to a number of other small firms that work together as a small, informal network: first to an architectural technologist who deals with the detail design and contractual issues and then on to a contract manager who oversees the sub-contractors using construction management techniques. Work also flows the other way, from the contracts manager and the architectural technician. The solo practitioner claimed to be doing well financially and had no ambition to expand or change the manner in which he worked. He did not use any promotional material, relying solely on interpersonal contact with clients and word of mouth. He claimed to use no management tools whatsoever other than working in a very pragmatic and organised manner which he associated with being a good professional.

12.1.2   Firm B

The five-person firm described itself as a typical architectural practice and traded as such: one director was an architect, the other a quantity surveyor and the three other members of the firm were architectural technicians. Its specialist area was residential work, comprising a variety of projects, both new build and refurbishment. The office was fully computerised; a drawing board was positioned in the office window for promotional purposes only. The firm claimed its reputation was based on delivering projects on time, to cost and with a high level of design: it had won local recognition for its buildings. In an attempt to maintain the quality of its buildings the firm always tried to work with the same contractors, and three were mentioned. It had contemplated the adoption of construction management but was concerned about the additional responsibilities and risk it posed; it would only adopt this method of procurement if it could persuade its clients to take on board some of the risk. All projects were project managed, for which a separate fee was charged. The management system was based on individual project quality plans, although there was no quality management system in place and the firm's philosophy was to do everything to the best of its ability and make a profit. The firm had been designed from the outset and had deliberately stayed the same size. Additional work in busy periods was outsourced to a number of professionals who worked from home. Promotional material was modest, but the firm's logo and corporate identity was all-pervasive, from letterhead and drawings through to the colour scheme of the office.

12.1.3   Firm C

The 20-person firm comprised a variety of staff experience and qualifications, trading as chartered architects. Only five of the staff were qualified architects; the remainder were technologists, project and contracts managers, a building surveyor, a planning consultant and a clerk of works. The two directors – both architects – described their firm as a diverse team and saw their job as keeping the multidisciplinary firm focused. They had developed very competent and comprehensive marketing literature, designed by marketing consultants, and claimed to offer all the standard services plus project management, planning supervisor and energy management. The firm only dealt with commercial projects: housing was not perceived as being profitable. The firm had an excellent reputation for delivery and design quality among its clients. The sequential model had always been used, combined with a flexible workforce – contract staff when needed. The firm operated an internally designed and administered quality management system, specifically designed to allow the sequential model to operate and to accommodate a transient workforce.

What was evident from these successful firms was their dedication to their carefully selected clients, i.e. their market niche. They were very clear about what they were offering by way of services and also very clear about what they did not offer, either because they felt they could not make money from these services or because the services were beyond the firm's current level of expertise. This contrasted with their less successful competitors: firms in similar size brackets who, by their own admission, were 'scraping a living'. These firms were operating in similar areas and offering similar services to the firms highlighted above but were far less successful in attracting clients and running their businesses as profitable undertakings. For these firms life was tough and getting tougher. The successful firms appeared to be well designed and well balanced. The less successful ones appeared to me to be somewhat disjointed and unbalanced. Presumably clients were picking up the same messages and voting with their feet. It is a small sample, but it does help to illustrate the point that architectural management is not just about management systems and slick marketing. It is about getting the culture of the firm, the type of job, the right clients and the message the firm gives out correct; it is a matter of balance.

12.2   GETTING THE BALANCE RIGHT

David Maister (1993) has argued that the most successful service firms are distinguished by the skills and behaviour of the firm's leader, transforming his or her vision into reality through effective leadership and management skills. Earlier, when discussing the best way to manage both projects and the professional design firm, it was argued that a well-balanced team would comprise a number of individuals with different education and a wide variety of skills, drawing on the combined knowledge of the firm, a point illustrated by the case study firm at the end of this chapter. There are a wide variety of ways in which a design firm may be comprised. Some firms will employ only architects, some more design-orientated, some more technology-orientated; others have a combination of architects and technologists; a few (other than the large firms) employ professionals from a variety of backgrounds. In architectural literature it is common to focus on the skills of the individual architect, listing a raft of quite diverse skills required for practice (e.g. Eggleston 1955): the architect as 'general practitioner'. This professional combines architecture, technology and management in roughly equal measures. Let's call this individual our balanced professional (Figure 12.1): a mythical figure?

At this point it is worth looking at the attributes of a variety of players in the building industry based on the skills learned during education and training. By the very nature of their specialised training, individuals are not balanced; they will have a particular bias towards design, technology or management.

Figure 12.2 illustrates the point graphically, based on the education of architects, architectural technologists (building surveyors), construction managers and project managers. Once aware of this bias, it is then possible to look at the composition of the firm. Again a diagram is used to illustrate a firm's bias based on the individuals employed (see Figure 12.3). Three firms are used, the all-architect firm (firm A), the architect and technologist firm (firm B) and the multidisciplinary firm (firm C), all based on five individuals. It is clear from Figure 12.3 that there is a difference in bias.

The argument throughout this book has been in favour of the firm which harnesses the skills of a variety of individuals – the balanced firm. But that is not to say that the firm with a design bias does not have a degree of competitive advantage. Of course it does. But it is not necessarily a good policy to pursue, given the change being brought about by information technology.

A modern, competitive architectural practice requires professionals with different skills, all working towards a common goal within an architect-managed office. They do not need to be, nor can they all be qualified architects. In this model, the term 'architect' is no longer used to represent an individual person who is a generalist,

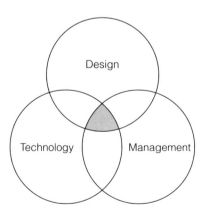

Fig. 12.1   The balanced professional
A mythical figure?

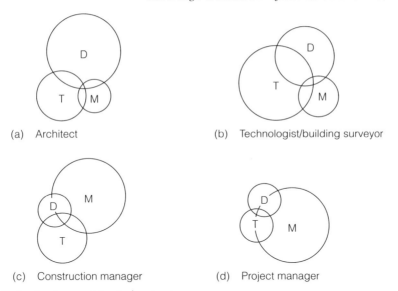

(a)   Architect   (b)   Technologist/building surveyor

(c)   Construction manager   (d)   Project manager

Fig. 12.2   Attributes of the four main players
Clearly illustrating a natural bias as a result of education.

but to describe a group of specialists working together to ensure both a quality service and a quality product, managed by the product champion, the architect. Indeed, it has been suggested that the environment awaits a simple, integrated product quality chain, led by a professional with a design pedigree (Wyatt and Emmitt 1996) and competent in architectural management. In most literature the emphasis is on the architect: that is, the individual. In this book the focus has been on the firm, more importantly a firm made up of individuals with different but complimentary skills (see Figure 12.4).

12.2.1   Talent is not enough

The design firm with competitive advantage needs to harness a number of skills in addition to talent in design. The firm needs clear direction and effective leadership, but above all it needs the ability to anticipate future markets and the ability to adapt to changing circumstances. Any management systems employed need to be simple and flexible to allow the creative side of the business to flourish within a well-organised and competitive framework. A combination of hard and soft management systems is required: a more organic approach. The hard management system is the formal structure and systems employed by the firm and is task-orientated. The soft management system sits within this and is concerned with the informal, intuitive nature of the firm, concerned with individuals' values and feelings. Both systems should ideally work together if the firm is to be effective. For many existing firms the adoption of architectural management necessitates a change both in the way things are done and in a change of attitude.

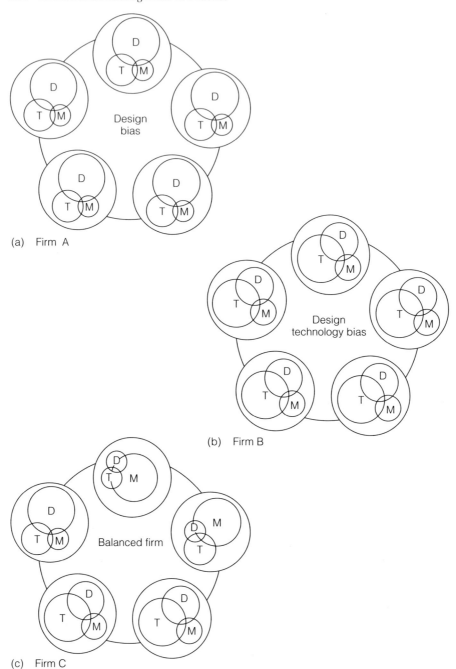

(a) Firm A

(b) Firm B

(c) Firm C

Fig. 12.3 A question of balance
Firm A All architects.
Firm B All technologists.
Firm C Multidisciplinary firm.

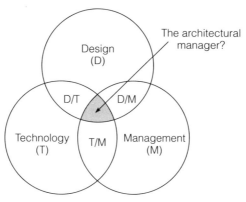

Fig. 12.4   The balanced firm

12.3   AGENTS OF CHANGE

Within the professional design firm's turbulent environment there are a number of drivers pushing things in the direction of change. To a great extent market forces will determine the fate of architectural firms, but architects are also motivated through a desire to stay in business. The best firms realise the worth of investing in their most valuable resource – their staff – and encourage them to take every opportunity to increase their skills and enhance their knowledge. But change is a complex issue, influenced by attitudes, beliefs and existing behaviour.

12.3.1   Attitudes, beliefs and behaviour

Attitudes affect the way in which individuals, groups and social systems respond to ideas that are new to them, are linked to beliefs and behaviours, and are associated with status. The establishment of attitudes takes place (to a lesser or greater extent) during education; in the case of the architect they are developed mainly in the design studio, therefore the role of the design tutor may be particularly important. Attitudes themselves are difficult to measure, but are evident in related traits such as beliefs and behaviour. They are not fixed, rather they are 'relatively stable', therefore they change and can be changed, through for example the acquisition of knowledge. Attitudes are characteristic of individuals, but they are influenced and determined by societal and situational as well as personal factors. A positive approach to the adoption of architectural management can only come about through knowledge, change in attitudes and a corresponding change in behaviour.

12.3.2   Change agents?

There is an assumption that people can organise themselves to identify realised goals. They do, however, require advice from an enabler or facilitator, which Spence (1994) has described as the role of the 'change agent'. This is a person or organisation who attempts to stimulate change within a social system once the felt need for change has been recognised. Thus the change agent will attempt to influence the attitudes and behaviour of the profession by helping people who need assistance to help themselves. The change agent's role has been well documented in the large body of diffusion literature (E. Rogers 1995), where the change agent is regarded as essential to the diffusion of innovative ideas and practices. Essentially, the change agent acts as an educator, attempting to change attitudes by the dissemination of information, while providing the encouragement to develop new skills. From the initial step of raising awareness of a problem, the change agent will assist with analysis, provide the initiative to acquire knowledge and provide the stimulus to adjust working methods. Although the change agent has been described from a design viewpoint (Ottaway 1982), where the change agent is responsible for affecting changes to design, the term has only recently been applied to the architectural profession. Emmitt and Neary (1995) argued that the change agent was missing from the architectural equation, leaving architects to make their own way in a rapidly changing marketplace. Clearly change should be promoted by the professional institution, but it is hindered by its historical baggage.

12.3.3   Overcoming resistance to change

Kaderlan (1991) noted that people in practice have only a partial understanding and interest in what the firm is doing, with designers primarily concerned with design, production staff with production drawings, etc. This fragmentation of viewpoint is often reinforced by the firm's organisational structure and hierarchy, leading to ineffective information flow between directors and employees. In such a situation the implementation of change may be difficult. Managing change is an important skill and a rich area for authors of change management literature. One of the secrets of change management is good preparation. This includes the careful selection of staff (discussed earlier) and the creation of a flexible structure that encourages change, through frequent opportunities to discuss issues openly at all levels within the firm. It is important for all members of the office to share the same goals, ideally through good communication and leadership, perhaps reinforced by reward systems based on an individual's and the firm's performance.

12.4   (RE)DESIGNING THE FIRM

From the arguments and the case studies illustrated above, it is clear that a modern architectural practice needs the skills of a wide range of individuals. The final case study helps to illustrate the change in structure required, a slow transformation or metamorphosis, from a traditional firm to a firm with multiple skills and a diverse approach to business. Change has to be implemented with care and the homily 'evolution not revolution' should be borne in mind, if not adhered to. To progress, the firm must learn from its past experience, learning not to repeat the same mistakes and learning to repeat and improve things it does well. An evaluation of the firm's performance is not easy, especially when the pressure is to complete jobs on time, but this must not be neglected if the firm is to improve and not stagnate. The case for adopting a policy of continual development based on reflective practice was made earlier. In line with the ideas expressed, this self-assessment should involve all the firm's employees. This helps to keep everyone informed and, more importantly, is an excellent opportunity for generating new ideas and re-evaluating ones which may not have worked three months earlier but may now be relevant to the firm and the market. If new ideas are to be accommodated, the firm must be so structured as to be flexible enough to allow minor adjustments with minimal disruption.

Following this argument the management and organisational structures used by the firm must be flexible enough to allow for adjustment and adaption and not be constrained by convention. More specifically the firm must be:

- willing to take risks
- goal-orientated
- client-centred
- flexible and adaptive
- capable of learning
- quality driven.

12.4.1   Beyond the brass plate

The concept of the office is changing and will continue to change as information technology improves. Not so long ago setting up and running an architectural business was easy: one found suitable accommodation and put a brass plate up outside the door to announce one's presence. We are now faced with rapid advances in information technology that has presented the opportunity of working from remote sites, i.e. from the building site and from home. The question has to be asked: Does the service firm need a physical place to work from, i.e. office space that has to be paid for? The technology already exists to allow individuals to work as part of a networked team from remote sites (e.g. internet and intranet), perhaps only coming together for design reviews and other meetings: the 'virtual office'.

Remote working has a number of advantages and disadvantages. The principle of remote working should be familiar to most professional design offices which use external consultants to help in busy times and/or to add specific talents for certain jobs. These flexible workers often carry out work outside the firm's office, either from their own offices or from home. From an environmental standpoint, the less staff have to commute the less the congestion and pollution in our towns and cities. Working from home can improve one's quality of life. There are, however, a large number of people who enjoy the social interaction afforded by working together in an office. Communicating by telephone or by email fails to satisfy their desire to be with other human beings. For the directors of a firm the main issues, in addition to the cost of accommodation, centre around trust, quality and delivery, i.e. control. Telecommuting can be employed effectively. If appropriate management systems are in place and the available technology utilised, there is the opportunity to reduce the amount of floor space rented or purchased along with the reduced overheads. Another bonus is the flexibility afforded to the firm's members. Happier employees equates to a better quality of work.

12.4.2   A utopian view

One of the clients interviewed for this book expressed his frustration with the whole business of building, claiming that there was a desperate need and opportunity for a professional firm to offer a 'one-stop' shop. He wanted a design-orientated professional service firm to do everything for him, from site identification, through design to construction, maintenance and disposal. Such firms do exist, although they are in the minority at present, and have evolved largely in response to competition and a desire to offer both a better service and product. A Utopian view would be to see the development of a series of integrated professional service firms within the building industry; firms that have the experience and expertise to carry out a variety of management functions throughout the whole life of a project; firms committed to the improvement of the quality of the built environment and with it the quality of life for all those concerned. The thrust of this book has been for an architect led professional service firm, the product champion. There are a small number of architectural firms pursuing this route at present and more may follow, but there are some stiff challenges ahead.

First, the balance in the building industry is moving towards management-orientated, not design-orientated, disciplines which have gained the competitive edge. Their instigators will be keen to both retain and expand their market share. Second, the professionalisation of the building industry has led to an increased compartmentation or fragmentation of the industry. This does not help clients, nor does it help in the drive for environmentally responsible design because there is no real team effort. Third, for the architectural profession as a whole to change, there needs to be a fundamental reassessment and reorganisation of the professional body and with it a redefinition of the term 'architect'. In pursuit of competitive advantage professional boundaries need to be redefined and the concept of the professional design firm reconsidered. The computer industry – an industry obsessed with information – were quick to realise the importance of the words 'architecture' and 'system architecture', and the architectural profession, instead of continually moaning about them hijacking the word architecture could learn a lot from the computer industry. Fourth, many of the issues discussed here require a precious commodity: time. Time to assess, plan, implement, monitor and evaluate.

12.5   TOWARDS AN ENVIRONMENTALLY RESPONSIBLE APPROACH

Designers must provide leadership and seize the position of product champion if 'quality', in terms of aesthetics, function and sustainability, is to exist within the product quality chain. The problem facing the architectural profession is that so many architects have abrogated responsibility for management and building quality to their non-design trained competitors, and it will be difficult to regain lost ground. The case study firm illustrates one way forward in a competitive environment, an approach that requires considerable effort, vision and commitment on behalf of both client and architectural firm. The case study also helps to show that quality in building is achievable if both client and architect are prepared to work closely together and share in the ownership of both the process and the product. While the model may not be to everyone's liking, the opportunity for architects to claim the role of the product champion and deliver quality is there to be seized.

The argument developed in earlier chapters has been for both an integrated project team and a professionally managed design firm: a synergy between project and product. The thrust of the book has led to the notion that one, if not *the*, firm of the future will be an architect-led professional service firm: a firm comprised of individuals with differing but complimentary skills who are capable of adapting to changing circumstances, at ease with building in an environmentally aware, information-driven society; the product champions. Through the integrated model, proposed above, the establishment and maintenance of environmentally responsible ideals and practices is possible because the whole project is controlled by a design conscious (not just cost or time conscious) professional. This has implications for lifecycle costing, material selection and reduction of waste on site. It is clear that if environmentally responsible ideals are to be adopted it requires individual responsibility and control of the whole building process to ensure such approaches are not compromised. Control is needed from inception, through the design stages, through assembly on site to use, maintenance, reuse and eventual disposal. Synergy is needed between people and their environment: an environmentally responsible agenda in an information-rich world.

Case study   Transforming the professional practice

The case study firm has evolved considerably over the period of observation. Starting as a relatively traditional architectural firm, with a desire to both resist competition and expand its service provision, the firm has become multidisciplinary, offering its clients a quality service within a quality management framework. The firm is remarkable because despite its large service provision portfolio it retains the same number of staff, but staff with different skills to those at the outset of its transformation. The adoption of architectural management tools and techniques has allowed efficiencies and opportunities to grow, while the challenge for the future will be to harness the potential of information technology. The case study firm helps to illustrate some of the theoretical issues discussed in the book. In particular it goes some way to showing what is possible. But the case study firm does not fall neatly into any of the models promoted by the professional institution or architectural education: so what has the firm become?

The jolt

It is one thing to report on a successful transformation of a business, but it is not always as easy to identify the factor(s) that resulted in change coming about. At the outset the firm was an (average?) architectural practice. It was not losing money, nor was it generating very good profits given its fee income. It had a good reputation with its clients and was regarded as treating and paying its staff well. The business had been running for some years and despite a few managerial changes was unlikely to change the way it went about its business to any great extent. Although the directors of the firm have different recollections of what caused them to change the way the firm was managed, they were unanimous in their view that three key factors influenced their thinking at the time. First was a couple of repeat clients, who, while relatively satisfied with the service they were getting from the firm, were constantly complaining and requesting improvements, so much so that they were described as 'demanding clients'. The firm found it very difficult to make a profit from their commissions because of the extra work expected and provided. In particular, clients were looking for accountability and single point responsibility *with* quality and value for money. Second was an interest in quality assurance and its application to a design office, which at the time was seen as a major driver for change and one way of helping to deliver a better service. Third was the economic recession at the start of the 1990s and an increase in competition from other, management-orientated, players in the market.

   Combined, these three drivers provided the jolt that resulted in the desire to change and the evolution of the business into one with competitive advantage. The firm's initial strategic plan was simple, if not ambitious:

1. *Start providing project management services*: To retain the client link, to dictate the project culture and to deliver a quality design.
2. *Implement a quality assurance system*: To provide the framework for quality work and to deliver a quality service.
3. *Build the firm's own designs*: To deliver a quality product.

These have been discussed earlier in the case studies reported at the end of Chapters 8 to 11. However, it is worth mentioning that the firm initially set itself a timescale of two years to effect change, which in the event was far too optimistic. Transformation takes time and commitment, 1 per cent inspiration, 99 per cent perspiration, and the case study helps to illustrate the point. Change took more than five years to implement and is still occurring as the firm adjusts to external pressures. Although the three aims were straightforward, they immediately led to discussion about *how* to implement the plan and *how* to redesign the firm's culture.

Structure of the firm

Over the study period there was a considerable change in the staffing and structure of the firm, but not in its overall size, which has remained relatively constant. In addition to the provision of training to enable staff to change the way they worked,

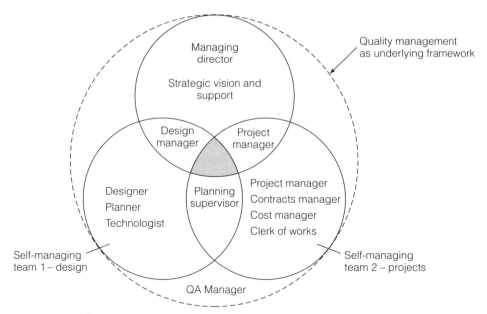

Fig. 12.5 The case study firm

the firm also ran in-house seminars to carefully and clearly explain to the staff how the firm intended to change in both the short and long term. Staff input, both suggestions and criticism, was sought through the use of regular quality circles. In many respects this was the most difficult period for the firm, because some of the staff had been with the firm for some time and were resistant to change. Within 12 months of the decision to change the firm, two members of staff left to take up positions with other more traditional firms. Although this was seen as a problem at the time – they took knowledge and business contacts with them – it provided the opportunity to bring a design manager and a contracts manager into the firm. Combined with the staff training programme the firm had started to 'improve' its assets, redesign its culture and shift its emphasis.

During the firm's metamorphosis a decision was taken to split the firm into two closely related teams, the 'design' team and the 'project' team, each with a manager, a design manager and a project manager respectively. In effect the two teams have grown into self-managing teams, both currently ten members strong (see Figure 12.5), and although the self-managing teams came about more from circumstance than from strategic planning, the two teams do work particularly well for this firm. Communication between teams is maintained through the use of design reviews, internal communication, and monitoring from the planning supervisor, all within the quality management framework. So, although there are occasional breakdowns in communication, the managerial framework allows such events to be recognised early and corrective action taken before any problems become too serious. The sharing of information and the firm's expert knowledge base has also increased significantly through the sensitive management of the teams.

The importance of professional project management as a link to the client was always realised by the firm. However, project management has grown in importance with the implementation of the planning supervisor role (unforeseen at the outset) and construction management. Now the firm has a structure that allows for a reflective learning ethos and the potential to develop further through greater use of information technologies. The directors felt it was important to get the firm's staff structure and managerial ethos in place *before* developing and investing in information technology. In many respects this strategy has paid off, since the past five years has seen considerable advances in the technology with reduced costs and, more importantly, a big increase in the number of firms and clients employing these technologies. Thus electronic interchange via the internet and intranet offers real potential. However, it is still a matter of balancing investment against potential economies. What is clear is that any investment in information technology (whether purchased or leased) must be to support and enhance the firm's growth, i.e. the technology must fit the firm.

Service provision

The firm has developed into a lean, efficient, strong service provider without compromising design excellence. Its service provision has grown from traditional architectural services to project management, design management, contract management and facilities management, available as a complete package or as discrete elements, depending on the client's requirements. Sold separately, or as part of bespoke packages, these services have all contributed to an increase in the firm's fee income. The list of service provision is not marketing hyperbole; the firm can and does provide all these services very successfully because it is able to offer an individual service from site identification, design, construction and maintenance through to reuse. As such it is ideally placed to deliver not just a quality service but also a quality product, with the scope to make a real impact in terms of delivering environmentally responsible buildings. With the change in focus has come an increased awareness of commercial issues and an increased reliance on the firm's marketing activity. In addition to a careful targeting of potentially profitable clients, the firm spends a lot of time preparing and submitting fee bids (the majority with design). This strategy has paid off in the long term and is seen as an essential part of the firm's business promotion strategy.

Keeping it going

Despite its successful transformation the firm's directors and staff recognise the need for continuous development if they are going to be able to respond to change in the future. Three specific challenges were identified. First is to keep apace of information technology as a means of improving both the efficiency and the quality of service provision. Second is the continual problem of knowledge retention, developing the firm's collective experience. Third is the challenge of promoting the firm's services to clients who may be confused by the number of different procurement routes open to them and the number of competing professionals knocking on their door. These challenges are set alongside a continuing willingness to respond to changes and adjust both its position and culture accordingly.

There was an assumption or hope that once the management systems, culture and service provision were in place, the directors and staff could sit back a little and enjoy a period of relative stability. This has not happened. The firm now acknowledges that its competitive position will only continue if it continually strives to improve every aspect of its service position, responding to anticipated change as quickly as possible with the resources available. As the firm heads into the twenty-first century it is looking at introducing a series of project/product guarantees: in effect becoming a guardian of the structure.

What has the firm become?

The transformation has caused a few problems. There has been resistance from some clients who refused to contribute to the process. Some contractors have removed the firm from their tender list for design-and-build work because they are now competing directly with them for some projects, and some architects have accused the firm of being too commercial and no longer a 'proper' architectural practice. So what has the firm become? To answer the question is not easy. On the one hand, the firm is a chartered architectural practice and still refers to itself as such. On the other hand it is clearly much more than a traditional architectural practice; when marketing its services to clients the firm uses a whole host of terms to describe more fully what it does; for example project managers, planning supervisors and facilities managers are terms used, in addition to that of chartered architects. To a certain extent, this reflects the fragmented nature of the industry and the competitive marketplace, but it also reflects a response to client demands. In many respects, the firm reported here, and others that operate in a similar manner, have been doing for some time what reports by Latham (1994) and Egan (1998) have proposed as the way forward, working closely with client and manufacturers and controlling the supply chain through effective management.

The firm has adopted a commercial, management-orientated approach to the business of architecture that has been successful: an approach still not liked by a large number of professionals. However, throughout the firm's metamorphosis the directors have been careful to retain their professional integrity, balancing commercial pressures with professional ethics. The firm now competes just as frequently with surveyors, project managers and contractors as it does with architects for their commissions. In my opinion, the firm is carrying out services that were associated with the architect/surveyor role before the rise of the professional institution: they are architects as true controllers of 'the works', the old 'master builder', the sole point of responsibility.

Conclusion

The case study firm has shown that transformation takes time and commitment from both staff and directors. For this firm it also required its clients' involvement. Such a model reported here will not suit all firms – especially those which still like to distance themselves from their clients – nor will it suit all clients. 'New' clients need to be educated so that they understand *their* contribution to the whole building process; it is about ownership and partnering in the truest sense of both words. The firm has considered, but rejected, the temptation to outsource because it was concerned with the quality of service provision. In many respects this decision is consistent with the firm's philosophy of reducing sub-contracted and sub-sub-contracted services, so we should not be surprised by this.

Whether or not the case study firm prospers or fails in the future will depend not only on its internal management, but also on the quality of the contribution from the other members of the temporary project team, whether they have adopted partnering or not: a temporary project team whose 'design' is firmly in the hands of the architectural firm, the controllers of both the information and the supply chain.

CHAPTER 13

BUSINESS PROMOTION

It is of little use developing a competitive professional service firm if potential clients are unaware of the services on offer. This chapter contests that the challenge for the architect-led firm will be to sell services to clients who may well have a fixed view of what an architectural practice can deliver, a view reinforced by other players in the marketplace. Effective promotion is an essential element of the competitive firm and various strategies are discussed.

13.1 PROMOTION

Promotion has been reserved for the last chapter of this book for one simple, but critical, reason: the firm must 'know its business' before any marketing strategy is put in place. Or, more specifically, the firm's culture must have been designed and its aims, both short term and long term, agreed, *before* a promotion strategy can be implemented. The three core areas of individual job management, staff management and client relations, the firm's culture, will influence the type of message given out by the firm. Promotion is concerned with sending and receiving information, communication with people external to the firm. With the exception of the highly regarded work of Weld Coxe (1980; Coxe *et al.* 1987) there are few books that specifically address the issue of marketing, advertising and public relations to architectural firms. One of the most comprehensive guides for the architectural profession was published under the title *The Marchitect* (RIAS 1990) in which architects were urged to develop a structured approach to attracting and retaining clients. *Marketing and Communication Techniques for Architects* by Lynne Choona Ryness (1992) provides a wide selection of examples drawn from practice. More recently Richardson's (1996) *Marketing for Architects and Engineers* offers an alternative approach based on scenario-planning and synthesis. Many authors use the generic term marketing to cover all three elements of service promotion. According to Kreps (1990) advertising, marketing and public relations efforts are complementary and interdependent forms of external communication. They are discussed below.

13.1.1   Public relations

Public relations is concerned with the management of external communication channels, of which marketing and advertising are key elements. Essentially, public relations could be seen as the management of communication between a firm and its clients: a complex and demanding activity. To be effective, public relations information must be carefully considered, well designed, planned and well implemented, i.e. it must be managed. Public relations is most commonly associated with press relations in the form of press releases and feature articles. Press releases are essentially news items, such as a new commission or the completion of a project while feature articles are longer than press releases and can cover a topic in greater detail, usually in the specialist press. Another form of public relations covers the sponsorship of events or causes associated with any specialist areas of the firm's activities that may help to raise the profile of the firm and may lead to new commissions.

13.1.2   Marketing

The main purpose of marketing is to bring the firm's services to the attention of clients. In architectural circles this activity is often described as 'attracting' or 'getting work'. Marketing comprises strategies for identifying and developing services to match or create market demand; it is a business philosophy based on the orientation of the firm to the wants and needs of its clients. The aim is to achieve client satisfaction and to make a profit (RIAS 1990). This includes the use of market research to help target new markets, identify new services and adapt to changing market conditions. Marketing is influenced by the market awareness of the firm's managers (Coxe 1980). As such the marketing performance should be measured and must be managed (Maister 1993).

13.1.3   Advertising

The implementation of creative communication strategies, often in media communication campaigns, to bring services to the attention of potential clients is known as advertising. Advertising campaigns should be designed to both reflect the general marketing strategies and be consistent with the image established for the firm. Advertising can be used to establish and maintain the firm's image by raising its profile and separating it from its competitors. The architectural profession was restricted by its own Code of Conduct from advertising until 1986, and even now many within the profession feel that advertising is not something professionals do. Such caution is understandable, but carried out with the same professionalism that is reserved for other activities, advertising is an essential part of a professional service firm's competitive strategy and survival in the commercial world of building.

13.2   COMMUNICATING WITH CLIENTS

Whatever term is used, be it public relations, marketing or advertising, the process is concerned with communication: the communication of the firm's culture to its clients. Everything a firm does has a secondary function as promotion. The way in which designs are presented, meetings administered, problems attended to, are all part of the promotional initiative. Every letter, every telephone call, every drawing says something about the firm. They provide people outside the firm with information about the firm's approach to every aspect of its business. Richardson (1996) uses the term 'synthesis marketing' to cover four interrelated areas, namely (1) the marketing activity before client contact, (2) after client contact but before commission, (3) during the commission and (4) establishing and maintaining repeat business. A tried and tested way of looking at the firm is from the client's perspective. Does the client see a well-designed, consistent, professional corporate image?

There are two distinct client groups to consider here: the firm's existing clients and the clients the firm would like, its potential clients. The issue of client profitability, discussed earlier, needs considering *before* marketing is directed at them. If the client is unlikely to be profitable it is a waste of resources trying to communicate with them. Marketing to existing clients is often taken for granted by professional firms, yet existing clients represent the most probable source of new business (Maister 1993). Existing clients need to be nurtured and much of the effort of developing the business around existing clients will be of an interpersonal nature, supported with targeted promotional material. This is especially true where the firm seeks to make the client a cohesive element of the firm's culture, requiring input from the client as well as the firm. In contrast the business of attracting new clients takes a different form of effort and is more demanding of resources. Many potentially profitable clients may well already have an established network of contacts, so the firm must recognise that it will be trying to dislodge a competitor.

13.3   CORPORATE IMAGE

Every firm has its own culture, either by design or by accident, and therefore each firm has its own corporate image or corporate identity. Corporate identity is concerned with how the firm is perceived by its existing and prospective clients, its staff, competing firms and the public. Perception will be based on experience of the service provided by the firm, the firm's culture and the manner in which it presents itself through marketing activities; it goes much deeper than the firm's logo. It is an area often taken for granted by architectural firms, yet the consistent communication of a corporate image is one way of distinguishing the firm from others offering similar services. The face needs putting to the name.

Graphic communication is the trademark of the architectural firm and both its culture and corporate image are reflected in letters, reports, presentation drawings, detail drawings and contract documentation as well as the specifically designed marketing material. As part of the corporate image the standard of graphic communication should be high but, more importantly, consistent. Many firms are aware of the importance of corporate identity through their graphic communication and operate a 'house style'. Other firms are less fussy and have an inconsistent amateur approach to the material they produce: they put out a confusing message, one that is often perceived by clients as representative of a poorly managed firm. Corporate identity should link all a firm's activities into one easily identifiable and memorable image (RIAS 1990). The establishment of a corporate identity takes time and will inevitably change as the firm itself responds to changes in the market. Once a corporate image has been designed and agreed a variety of promotional tools can be employed to raise awareness of the firm among existing and prospective clients.

13.4   PROMOTIONAL TOOLS

A number of tried and tested marketing tools are available, ranging from the corporate brochure to newsletters and direct mail campaigns. Promotional tools help to bring the attention of the firm to potential clients and also to reinforce its image with existing clients. Bringing about and raising awareness is particularly important, since if a client is unaware of the firm or the firm's range of service provision it will not be considered.

Paper literature costs money to produce, although with advances in printing technology a modest-sized brochure or newsletter need not take up a significant part of the marketing budget. Electronic newsletters, or web pages, provide another outlet for promoting the firm, although similar rules apply in terms of their accessibility and relevance. The strategies listed below rely on the prospective client becoming aware of the literature, taking note of it and deciding to make contact with the architectural firm: they rely on a certain amount of luck – landing on the client's desk at the right moment, or being easily accessible on the world wide web. Whatever strategies are used the corporate image must be consistent. The firm's name and any corporate logos should be included on both the front and the rear of any literature together with the firm's address and telephone number. The quality of the literature sent out will influence whether it is read or not and will also influence the reader's perception of the firm. Literature is a part of the firm's ongoing communication effort and needs careful consideration since it is widely accepted that it has less than ten seconds to convey a message. This literature should also be sent to the local architectural branch for inclusion in the Client Advisory Service's (CAS) database.

13.4.1   Brochures

The firm's brochure is the most important promotional tool used by architects with many firms relying on the brochure as their first point of contact with potential clients (RIAS 1990). Because of this it is essential that the brochure is well designed and carefully targeted at prospective clients. Brochures should include a brief history of the firm, why and how it started, significant projects and the services offered. A statement on design philosophy and possibly the firm's mission statement, sometimes combined, should also be included here. The text should be kept clear and short because the target audience will be bombarded by promotional literature every day and the tendency is to ignore lengthy articles. The firm's competitive advantage (to the client) should be clearly identified: what makes *it* different from the competition?

13.4.2 Newsletters and direct mail

Cheaper to produce than brochures, newsletters also need careful consideration about the content of the news and their target audience. Newsletters work best when they are focused and interesting: the mistake many firms make is to try to say too much to too wide an audience. For example, is the purpose of the newsletter to keep existing clients informed of developments within the firm or is it intended to raise awareness with new clients? It is an important question because the content will need to be different for each, quite different, purpose. Once implemented, it is important to maintain the frequency so that clients know the firm is still in existence.

Direct mail is a promotional tool targeted to a specific audience. Examples are sales letters – the use of which may be questionable for the professional service firm – and the newsletter. They work best when followed up by telephone calls. Their use is to achieve the all-important 'foot through the door' to deliver a client presentation.

Printed directories may help raise awareness and more recently a new marketing tool has been provided by the internet. There are two possible avenues here: electronic directories and the firm's own web site, which should be designed with the same care and dedication as the rest of the firm's material. Again, like the printed information, the firm relies on a potential client or client's agent searching for information and therefore it is critical to get the keywords right. You don't want to miss out simply because a search engine cannot find your details.

13.4.3 Client presentations

Client presentations need to be conducted professionally and should reinforce the corporate image promoted by the firm's marketing and advertising material. Emphasis should be on what the firm can do for the client. They should be open and honest representations of the firm based on its collective experience and qualifications. From the client's perspective they will be looking for a firm, or often a point of contact within the firm, with whom they feel comfortable dealing, so again the interpersonal skills of those doing the presentation will be under scrutiny.

13.5 MANAGING THE MARKETING ACTIVITY

Consistent with the philosophy of this book, marketing is an activity that needs to be managed. As such it should be planned, adequately resourced, monitored, systematically evaluated and maintained. Time must be found to consider, agree and implement suitable activities, set realistic budgets and achievable timescales, then monitor, evaluate and adjust as required. This can only be carried out once the purpose of the firm has been clearly defined.

13.5.1   Planning

As noted above, different strategies are required for marketing to existing clients than those employed to attract new clients. The firm's marketing activities should consider:

- Identification of new markets and opportunities
- Identification and awareness of shrinking markets and reduced opportunities
- Retention of existing clients
- Promotion to potential clients
- Client (rather than job) profitability.

The firm's marketing strategy needs to consider the services to be promoted and should identify and promote its competitive advantage to clients. Bringing the services of the firm to the attention of potential clients can be looked at as passive and active strategies. Passive strategies rely on potential clients approaching the firm after they have received information from a third party, for example a recommendation from an existing client, consultant or the client's advisory board, from information on completed jobs featured in magazines, or from the architect's signboard erected on a building site. Active strategies rely on the firm courting and nurturing clients, for example sending company promotional material to carefully selected clients and doing client presentations. The active strategy is more expensive in terms of resources than a passive approach. A well–designed *and* well-managed promotional strategy will leave the firm time to concentrate on its business. The promotional activity must be adequately resourced and monitored.

13.5.2   Resourcing the marketing activity

Marketing, promotion – whatever you wish to call the activity – is important to provide adequate resources to do the job properly. That means setting a realistic marketing budget and allocating sufficient time to manage the activity. In small firms it is very tempting to cut the number of hours allocated to marketing when additional work pressures increase and to 'borrow' from the marketing budget in tough times. Such tendencies must be resisted, since the modern pofessional service firm depends on effective marketing. Indeed, many are becoming marketing-led.

A marketing budget is required to cover:

- The design and distribution of publicity material
- Corporate entertaining and presentations
- Design competitions
- Training.

Depending on the size of the firm, the budget may be concentrated on one of these areas. For example, some small firms may spend most of their budget on interpersonal means of promotion, using corporate entertaining and presentations. Others may rely heavily on the distribution of publicity material, through advertising, direct mail and the design and maintenance of active web sites. Whatever a firm's individual strategy it is important to remember the importance of training and continual updating so that the firm's promotional strategies retain their currency.

13.5.3 Monitoring and evaluation

Management of the marketing activity is based around monitoring and evaluation. All leads generated from promotional activities should be monitored and followed up as part of a planned, systematic system. All leads, whether they lead to a commission or not, should be evaluated to see how they were generated. This provides valuable feedback about the effectiveness of certain promotional strategies and helps with the planning and targeting of future resources.

13.5.4 Maintaining the marketing activity

It is one thing to set up and monitor the firm's promotional strategies, quite another to keep the momentum going. It is of little use embarking on a promotional campaign and then, for whatever reason, ceasing to maintain it: it can do a lot of damage to the firm's reputation with clients. Consider the example of the architectural firm that embarked on a rather extravagant campaign that relied heavily on the posting of a regular newsletter. After a period of three years a decision was taken to stop the newsletter to save money; clients associated the lack of newsletter with difficulties within the firm, reported during a monitoring and feedback exercise, and the firm's presence in the marketplace was affected.

   Clients will expect the professional firm to deliver what it promises, so the promotional campaign must match the service delivered. To deliver less than an excellent service every time can cause a lot of damage, regardless of the effectiveness of the promotional activities. Retaining and enhancing reputation is critical to the success of a professional service firm and is at the heart of the promotional effort.

13.5.5 Managing change

A well-designed and planned promotional campaign will consider the impact of change on the firm, the service provision and the manner in which it is communicated to clients. As a general rule it is better to keep clients informed of intended changes before they are implemented so that clients are prepared. For example, the implementation of quality assurance will initially place additional burdens on the firm until its members are comfortable with the system, and the marketing of the service must consider this. Most clients will be understanding, especially if they know that they should get a better service from the firm in the long term. Therefore, it is important to involve the client and to keep them informed at all times through a suitable communication medium; such a strategy also helps to generate client input and feedback, in line with the philosophy of ownership and partnering.

13.6   CRISIS MANAGEMENT

A chapter dedicated to promotion of the firm's services may not be the obvious place to address problems. No matter how well managed the firm, there will be occasions when problems arise, however ordinary the building or familiar the client and consultants. The fact that every site and hence every job is unique means that unexpected events may happen, often more frequently than anticipated. Earlier in the book the use of quality management was advocated as an effective means of reducing, if not eliminating, mistakes on drawings and documents before they are issued: an essential risk management tool. It would, however, be unrealistic to expect things to run smoothly all the time because clients may change their minds, other consultants may make mistakes and builders may get things wrong. The firm's ability to deal with unexpected events quickly and effectively is an essential element of an architectural firm, and it should be part of a comprehensive public relations package. Public relations can be used to avoid or at least minimise damage to the firm's reputation in a crisis, an activity usually known as crisis management. Damage to the firm's reputation and loss of confidence in the organisation by its clients may harm the long-term viability of the business. Time spent on litigation would be better spent on more creative and rewarding endeavours. Timely, careful and sensitive public relations efforts should be used to respond to crisis situations (Kreps 1990). Just as it is essential to keep the client informed of progress, it is also important to keep the client informed of any unexpected events. A well-designed and implemented quality management system provides the framework in which to do this.

13.7   CHALLENGE OF THE NEW

Some of the ideas discussed earlier in the book are not part of the standard architectural service. Not only may they be unfamiliar to architectural firms, they may also be unfamiliar to clients. Clients, experienced or otherwise, will have their own perception of what it is an architectural firm does, just as they will have a perception of what the structural engineer or general contractor does. For many the word architecture is synonymous with design. The architectural firm offering a diverse range of services, either as a one-stop shop or as discrete packages, may find that selling its services to clients meets with some resistance, mainly because the service is unfamiliar. Other players in the marketplace will be promoting *their* own services to clients, at the same time playing down the influence of the competition. The challenge of promoting a firm's service provision is hard work and requires constant effort.

Allinson (1993) has made the point that clients, especially those with no or little experience of building, are often fazed by the complexity of procurement routes and the large number of professionals all offering their services. The clients interviewed for the purposes of this book expressed a strong desire for a professional firm that could offer a full service, that was not contractor-led, a single point of communication and full responsibility for design, cost and delivery. They were concerned about the quality and cost of both the building and the service. The demand appears to be there. The challenge for the design-led professional service firm is to raise the awareness of the client to its service provision through the use of a well-managed promotion strategy.

CHAPTER 14

EPILOGUE

Given the approach taken in this book a conclusion would be inappropriate, but an epilogue serves as a useful device to discuss future developments. Within the book an attempt has been made to explain a number of theoretical constructs, supported in part by examples drawn from practice, intended as signposts to developing and maintaining a competitive design-orientated professional service firm. Such firms need to keep up-to-date with both current management thinking and practice if they are to be in a strong position to face the future. It is only through the effective application of architectural management techniques and tools that creative design can flourish. It is well recognised that the design quality of our built environment needs to be improved and that a more environmentally responsible approach needs to be adopted. Whether such improvements will come through a purely management-orientated approach is questionable. However, the design-orientated professionals must position themselves in responsible positions where standards can be maintained and improved; architectural management is a tool that may go some way to achieving this end.

14.1.1 So what of the future?

Denis Harper's philosophy was the continuum of process and product. In his own epilogue, Harper (1978:409) concluded, somewhat optimistically, that 'a long way ahead, perhaps designers, constructors and commissioners will one day be proud to call themselves "Builders".' The recent trend has been to call just about everyone connected with building a 'manager' and builders are no exception to this trend; the integration sought by Harper appears to be even further away than it was 20 years ago. The balance in the UK construction industry has shifted too far in the direction of fragmented project teams at the expense of the finished product and consequently the environment at large. Reports by Latham (1994) and Egan (1998), both highly critical of the industry and its managers, urge the integration of design and construction with the use of partnering as one way of solving some of the industry's ills. Clearly a fundamental reassessment and change in approach to building procurement is required if the imbalance is to be redressed. But the education system is orientated to creating individuals – architects or construction managers, individuals who tend to stick to traditionally defined roles that are reinforced by their professional institutions, themselves at odds with one another over their members' respective roles in the order of things. It is not surprising, therefore, that professionals rarely work together as part of a 'real' team but are brought together as consultants for one-off projects, often with conflicting values and goals and to the detriment of the product.

We need to return to a simpler synergistic relationship from which all could benefit and which may provide the opportunity for building to catch up with other industries. True realisation of TQM combined with a lowering of corporate and professional barriers is achievable and could be helped by a return to less complex relationships and simpler procurement methods. Future changes will be determined by market forces *and* the design-orientated professional service firm's willingness to take centre stage, since it is through such action that environmentally responsible approaches to building may be widely adopted.

14.1.2 The battle within

Architectural management is a tool, an ordered way of thinking, in which design is allowed the space to flourish. But complex management systems with mountains of paperwork and many form-filling exercises at best only detract from the firm's core business: design. At their worst, such systems can alienate the members of the firm and lead to a downturn in productivity. In effect unwieldy management systems are not appropriate to most architectural firms. The simpler the system the easier it is to adopt and maintain and the philosophy advocated in this book has been to keep it simple. Good management is about delegation, responsibility, ownership and vision. It is about common sense and a consistent approach to decision-making and problem-solving within a creative environment. All the principles described here are meant to be used as 'guidelines' in line with soft systems thinking, so that design excellence can be promoted and sustained from inception to completion, reuse and eventual disposal of the building.

The culture of the firm, the manner in which it deals with individual jobs, staff and clients, will be unique to that firm and whether the design-orientated professional service firm primarily comprises architects, architectural technologists or building surveyors in many respects is not important. The important point is to *design* the firm's culture, a process that demands as much care and skill as any building design; the firm must be capable of learning and adapting to changing circumstances and thus its management structure must also be adaptive. The case studies have shown that competitive advantage can be achieved and maintained through diversity, but that achieving such a model requires a great deal of effort from the firm's directors and employees as well as support and input from their clients. But for many firms it may not be an easy transition to make, given that the traditional model of an architect is still promoted in the schools of architecture. Thus ingrained beliefs and attitudes may need to be both challenged and adjusted if change is to come about. The main battle is not with the externalities of the firm's milieu, but from within. The issue is concerned with people, communication and management: the human factor.

14.1.3   An unresolved issue

Within the book the term architectural management has been used as an umbrella to cover a variety of management tools and techniques employed by architectural practices in their pursuit of competitive advantage (see Figure 14.1). Following this argument, it would be difficult for one individual to become an architectural manager *per se*. However, recent trends have seen the rise of a number of 'new' managerial disciplines, so perhaps it is inevitable that architectural managers will enter the marketplace soon, hopefully in an integrating role. The concept of an individual being educated and working as an architectural manager needs to be addressed and the Society for the Advancement of Architectural Management (SAAM) has started to do just that. At the time of writing there are no undergraduate courses in architectural management, although the architectural technology degree, with its strong management content and the three core themes of design, technology and management, is perhaps the closest in philosophy. Applicants to the degree perceived education in all three areas as a strong foundation for employment in the building industry (Emmitt 1997). Although difficult to quantify, there is clearly demand for architectural management from school-leavers, although whether the building industry is ready for yet another professional discipline, that may further add to the fragmentary agenda, is questionable.

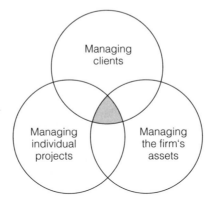

Fig. 14.1   Attributes of the architectural manager

14.1.4   And so . . .

Design-orientated professionals need to be better equipped with business skills, better communication skills and the ability to operate in a shifting market. In short, they must have an appreciation of, and the ability to apply, architectural management. Such a statement naturally leads to a reappraisal of architectural education and a reappraisal and redefinition of architectural practice. For some time now, especially within the ranks of the CIB's working group W96 Architectural Management, it has been suggested that architecture as we know it is dead. Some have, somewhat mischievously, formed an unofficial 'dead architects society' claiming that the ruptured ideology of design needs urgent medical attention.

The idea that architectural practice requires redefinition and considerable expansion has been voiced on several occasions (e.g. Fisher 1994; Jackson 1995). To a certain extent change will be forced on architectural practices. For example, the increased competition from other players in the market, combined with the dissemination of professional knowledge through information technology, will have a major say in shaping the future of many architectural firms. Other drivers, such as the reports by Latham (1994) and Egan (1998) place additional pressures on professional service firms by making clients more aware of areas for improvement and hence more demanding.

Design has been, and continues to be, overemphasised at the expense of commerce and management. This has resulted in a detachment from the realities of building both within the professional institution and in architectural education. Architectural firms must adopt architectural management tools in order to develop and retain competitive advantage. For some, this will involve a modest readjustment of staff skills; for others a major redefinition of their business. What is clear is that future change, at least in the short term, is likely to come from some of the architectural firms as they strive for the competitive edge, not from the professional institution nor from the educational establishments.

The challenge is to get the message across to those firms who are struggling. In this regard comparisons can be drawn between health promotion literature and architectural management literature. Until recently the medical profession was primarily concerned with cure. This shifted to prevention and cure, and now to the promotion of healthy living, witnessed by the rapidly increasing volume of health promotion literature. For many architects professional practice literature is concerned with the prevention and cure of contractual problems, not the promotion of effective professional management. This book has attempted to pull together professional service firm management with professional job management with the aim of promoting healthy architectural firms through the adoption of architectural management.

Clients' needs, the marketplace for professional services and the players competing in it will continue to change. This book has provided a holistic view of the architectural management discipline, rather than be prescriptive, primarily because management concepts and techniques that work today may be inappropriate in the future. A successful business not only seeks to consolidate its position in the market, but should be constantly looking for opportunities to increase market share and expand into different areas of business. The successful design-orientated professional service firms will be those that are capable of change and able to predict future trends. Architectural management as a tool, and ordered way of thinking, can provide a vehicle for the journey ahead. It is more than a specialist interest: it is a culture vital to the development of an effective business.

REFERENCES

Allee, V. 1997 *The knowledge evolution: expanding organizational intelligence.* Butterworth-Heinemann.

Allinson, K. 1993 *The wild card of design: a perspective on architecture in a project management environment.* Butterworth-Heinemann.

Arup, O. 1970 The education of architects. *Architectural Research Quarterly,* Autumn 1996, 1, Vol. 2, pp. 38–43.

Ayas, K. 1996 Professional project management: a shift towards learning and a knowledge creating structure. *International Journal of Project Management,* 14:3, June, pp. 131–6.

Baden Hellard, R. 1994 Team working through project partnering: a TQM approach for architects. *International Journal of Architectural Management, Practice and Research,* pp. 104–9.

Baden Hellard, R. 1995 *Project partnering: principle and practice.* Thomas Telford.

Ball, M. 1988 *Rebuilding construction: economic change in the British construction industry.* Routledge.

Barbour Report 1993 *The changing face of specification in the UK construction industry,* Barbour Index.

Bardin, S.; Blachere, G.; Davidson, C.H. 1993 *Are research results used in practice?* CIB.

Bennett, P.H.P. 1981 *Architectural practice and procedure: from appointment to final account for architects, surveyors and the building industry.* Batsford Academic and Educational.

Blau, J. 1984 *Architects and firms: a sociological perspective on architectural practice.* MIT Press.

Boisot, M.H. 1987 *Information and organisations: the manager as anthropologist.* Fontana/Collins.

Boisot, M.H. 1998 *Knowledge assets: securing competitive advantage in the information economy.* Oxford University Press.

Boissevain, G.W.O.; Prins, M. 1993 Some thoughts about modelling the field of architectural management, *International Journal of Architectural Management, Practice and Research,* 6, pp. 73–9.

Brandenburger, J. 1995 Managing briefing and design, *Architects' Journal,* 1 June, pp. 39–40.

Broadbent, G. 1973 (1988 revised reprint) *Design in architecture: architecture and the human sciences.* David Fulton.

Brunton, J.; Baden Hellard, R.; Boobyer, E.H. 1964 *Management applied to architectural practice,* George Godwin for The Builder.

Burston, O. 1995 *Careers in architecture,* (fourth edition). Kogan Page.

Carolin, P. 1992 Expectation vs reality in architectural education, *Strategic Study of the Profession, Phase 1.* RIBA Publications.

Carson, R. 1962 *Silent spring.* Hamish Hamilton.

Caulkin, S. 1997 The knowledge within, *Management Today,* August, pp. 28–32.

Cheetham, D.; Lewis, J.; Jones, S.T. 1995 The effect of stage payments on contractors' cash flow: some possible consequences, *International Journal of Architectural Management, Practice and Research*, **10**, pp. 1–21.

Christie, B. 1981 *Face to file communication: a psychological approach to information systems.* John Wiley.

Cole, R.; Cooper, I. 1988 British architects: accommodating science and technical information, *Journal of Architectural and Planning Research*, **5**:2, Summer, pp. 110–28.

Cohen, M.D.; March, J.G; Olson, J.P. 1972 A garbage can model of organisational choice, *Administrative Science Quarterly*, **17**, pp. 1–25.

Construction Industry Research and Information Association 1983 *Buildability: an assessment*, Special Publication 26. CIRIA Publications.

Cornick, T. 1991 *Quality management for building design.* Butterworth-Heinemann.

Coxe, W. 1980 *Managing architectural and engineering practice.* John Wiley.

Coxe, W.; Hartung, N.F.; Hochberg, H.H.; Lewis, B.J.; Maister, D.H.; Mattox, R.F.; Piven, P.A. 1987 *Success strategies for design professionals.* McGraw-Hill.

Crinson, M.; Lubbock, J. 1994 *Architecture – art or profession?: three hundred years of architectural education in Britain.* Manchester University Press.

Cuff, D. 1991 *Architecture: the story of practice.* The MIT Press.

Daniels, C.N. 1994 *Information technology: the management challenge.* Addison-Wesley.

Deal, T.E.; Kennedy, A.A. 1982 *Corporate cultures: the rites and rituals of corporate life.* Addison-Wesley.

Dewey, J. 1933 *How we think*, Heath.

Dicke, D.W. 1995 Environmental protection in construction and the role of the architect, *International Journal of Architectural Management, Practice and Research*, **9**, pp. 163–73.

Douglas, C. 1995 Project management by architects: a Belgian case study, *International Journal of Architectural Management, Practice and Research*, **10**, pp. 74–96.

Druker, P.F. 1995 *Managing in a time of great change.* Truman Talley Books/Dutton.

Duffy, F. 1993 *Agenda for change. Strategic Study of the Profession, Phase 2: clients and architects*, pp. 1–6. RIBA Publications.

Eclipse Research Consultants 1996 *Environmental initiatives in the UK construction industry: 1995 survey of current practices.* Eclipse Research Consultants.

Edmonds, G. 1996 Trade literature and technical information, V.J. Nurcombe (ed.) *Information sources in architecture and construction* (second edition). Bowker Saur.

Egan, J. 1998 *Rethinking construction*, HMSO.

Eggleston, A.S. 1955 *The practising architect.* Melbourne University Press.

Ellis, R.; Cuff, D. eds 1989 *Architects people.* Oxford University Press.

Emmitt, S. 1994 Keeper of the gate, *International Journal of Architectural Management, Practice and Research*, **8**, pp. 23–6.

Emmitt, S. 1995 Project management: a divine right for architects?, *International Journal of Architectural Management, Practice and Research*, **10**, pp. 67–73.

Emmitt, S. 1996a Building quality through architectural management systems: a case study, *International Journal of Architectural Management, Practice and Research*, **11**, pp. 69–77.

Emmitt, S. 1996b Architectural management: in search of an advocate, *International Journal of Architectural Management, Practice and Research*, **12**, pp. 49–56.

Emmitt, S. 1997a *The diffusion of innovations in the building industry*, PhD thesis, University of Manchester.

Emmitt, S. 1997b The diffusion of environmentally responsible ideas and practices, Gray, M. ed. *Evolving environmental ideals: changing ways of life, values and design practices*, Stockholm Royal Institute of Technology.

Emmitt, S.; Neary, S. 1995 The change agent: a role for CPD in a competitive environment, *International Journal of Architectural Management, Practice and Research*, **9**, pp. 91–8.

Emmitt, S.; Wyatt, D.P. 1998 The products milieu: towards an effective information domain to deliver sustainable building, *Construction and the environment*, CIB, pp. 577–84.

Esher, L.; Davies, R.L. 1968 The architect in 1988, *RIBA Journal*, October, **75**:10, pp. 448–55.

Fisher, T. 1994 Can this profession be saved?, *Progressive Architecture*, February, pp. 45–9.

Fisher, N.; Yin, S.L. 1992 *Information management in a contractor: a model of the flow of project data*. Thomas Telford.

Franks, J. 1995 *Building contract administration and practice*. BT Batsford.

Freling, W.V.J. 1995 Architectural management: a profession or a specialist interest?, *International Journal of Architectural Management, Practice and Research*, **9**, pp. 11–20.

Friedman, M. 1962 *Capitalism and freedom*. University of Chicago Press.

George, C.S. Jr. 1972 *The history of management thought*. Prentice-Hall.

Gray, C.; Hughes, W.; Bennett, J. 1994 *The successful management of design – a handbook of building design management*. University of Reading.

Green, R. 1962 *The architect's guide to running a job*. The Architectural Press.

Gutman, R. 1988 *Architectural practice: a critical view*. Princeton Architectural Press.

Harper, D.R. 1978 *Building: the process and the product*. The Construction Press.

Harrigan, J.E.; Neel, P.R. 1996 *The executive architect: transforming designers into leaders*. John Wiley.

Hartley, P. 1997 *Group communication*. Routledge.

Harvey, R.C.; Ashworth, A. 1993 *The construction industry of Great Britain*. Butterworth-Heinemann.

Haugen, T. 1994 Total build: an integrated approach to facilities management, *International Journal of Architectural Management, Practice and Research*, **8**, pp. 90–101.

Heath, T. 1984 *Method in architecture*. John Wiley.

Herriot, P.; Pemberton, C. 1995 *Competitive advantage through diversity: organisational learning from difference*. Sage Publications.

Hertzberg, F. 1966 *Work and the nature of man*. Collins.

Higgin, G.; Jessop, N. 1965 *Communications in the building industry: the report of a pilot study*. Tavistock Publications.

Hubbard, B. Jr. 1995 *A Theory for practice: architecture in three discourses*. The MIT Press.

Jackson, A. 1995 *Reconstructing architecture for the twenty-first century: an inquiry into the architect's world*. University of Toronto Press.

Journal of Architectural and Planning Research 1996 Special Edition 'Management and Architecture', **13**:1, Spring.

Kaderlan, N. 1991 *Designing your practice: a principal's guide to creating and managing a design practice'*. McGraw-Hill.

Katzenbach, J.R.; Smith, D.K. 1993 *The wisdom of teams: creating the high-performance organisation*. Harvard School Press.

Kaye, B. 1960 *The development of the architectural profession in Britain: a sociological study*. Allan & Unwin.

Kolb, D. 1984 *Experiential learning: experience as the source of learning and development*. Prentice-Hall.

Kreps, G.L. 1990 *Organisational communication: theory and practice* (second edition). Longman.

Kruse, L. 1997 Evolving the concept of sustainability, Gray, M. (ed.) *Evolving environmental ideals: changing ways of life, values and design practices*. Stockholm Royal Institute of Technology.

Lapidus, M. 1967 *Architecture: a profession and a business.* Reinhold Publishing.

Latham, M. 1994 *Constructing the team.* HMSO.

Lewin, K. 1947 Frontiers in group dynamics II: channels of group life; social planning and action research, *Human Relations*, **1**, pp. 143–53.

Li, H. 1996 The role of IT manager in construction process re-engineering, *Building Research and Information*, **24**:2, pp. 124–7.

Lock, D. 1993 *Project management* (fifth edition). Gower.

Lohmann, W. 1993 Specifications: information sources, *Progressive Architecture*, May, p. 64.

Lucas, J. 1995 Business strategy for architects, *Architect's Journal*, 20 July, pp. 40–1.

Lyall, S. 1980 *The state of British architecture.* The Architectural Press.

Macdonald, J.; Piggott, J. 1990 *Global quality: the new management culture.* Mercury Books.

MacEwen, M. 1974 *Crisis in architecture.* RIBA.

Mackinder, M. 1980 *The selection and specification of building materials and components*, Research Paper 17, University of York.

Maister, D.H. 1989 *Professional service firm management* (fourth edition). Maister Associates.

Maister, D.H. 1993 *Managing the professional service firm.* The Free Press.

Marks, P.L. 1907 *The Principles of Architectural Design.* Swan Sonnenschein.

Maslow, A.H. 1954 *Motivation and personality.* Harper & Row.

Maver, T. W. 1970 Appraisal in the building design process, G.T. Moore (ed.) *Emerging methods in environmental design and planning.* MIT Press.

McBride, N. 1997 The rise and fall of an executive information system: a case study, *Information Systems Journal*, October, Vol. 17:4, pp. 277–87

McGeorge, D.; Palmer, A. 1997 *Construction management: new directions.* Blackwell Science.

McGregor, D. 1960 *The human side of enterprise.* McGraw-Hill.

Mintzberg, H. 1989 *Mintzberg on management – inside our storage world of organizations.* Free Press.

Neary, S.; Symes, M. 1993 *Urban regeneration in the United Kingdom: a commentry accompanied by three case studies.* Occasional Paper, University of Manchester.

New Scientist 1997 The concrete jungle overheats, 19 July, 2091, p. 14.

Newton, T.; Harte, G. 1997 Green business: technicist kitch, *Journal of Management Studies*, **34**, 1 January, pp. 75–98.

Nicholson, M.P (ed.) 1992 *Architectural management.* E & F.N. Spon.

Nicholson, M.P. 1995 Architectural management: towards a definition, *International Journal of Architectural Management, Practice and Research*, **9**, pp. 1–10.

Ottaway, R. N. 1982 Defining the change agent, B. Evans *et al.* (eds) *Changing design.* John Wiley.

Parry, R. 1991 *People businesses: making professional firms profitable.* Business Books.

Paterson, J. 1977 *Information methods: for design and construction.* John Wiley.

Pawley, M. 1990 *Theory and design in the second machine age.* Basil Blackwell.

Peters, T.J.; Waterman, R.H. 1982 *In search of excellence: lessons from America's best-run companies.* Harper & Row.

Popovich, I.S. 1995 *Managing consultants: how to choose and work with consultants.* Century.

Porter, M.E. 1985 *Competitive advantage: creating and sustaining superior performance.* The Free Press.

Porter-Theodore, M. 1994 Information, power and the view from nowhere, Lisa Bud-Frierman (ed.) *Information acumen: the understanding and use of knowledge in modern business.* Routledge, pp. 217–30.

Powell, C. 1997 Responding to marginalisation, *Architectural Research Quarterly*, Spring, **7**, pp. 84–9.

Prak, N.L. 1984 *Architects: the noted and the ignored*. John Wiley.

RIBA Journal 1997 August, **104**, 8 p. 52.

Richardson, B. 1996 *Marketing for architects and engineers: a new approach*. E & F.N. Spon.

Rogers, E.M. 1986 *Communication technology: the new media in society*. The Free Press.

Rogers, E.M. 1995 *Diffusion of innovations* (fourth edition). The Free Press.

Rogers, L. 1995 Generation X, *RIBA Journal*, July, pp. 6–9

Rogers, E.M.; Kincaid, D.L. 1981 *Communication networks: toward a new paradigm for research*. The Free Press.

Roodman, H.; Roodman, Z. 1973 *Management by communication*. Methuen.

Rougvie, A. 1995 *Project evaluation and development*. B.T. Batsford.

Rowe, P.G. 1987 *Design thinking*. The MIT Press.

Rowntree, D. 1994 *Buildings face the future: is there perhaps more to architecture than you think?*. Architype.

Royal Incorporation of Architects in Scotland 1990 *The marchitect*. RIAS.

Royal Institute of British Architects 1964 *Plan of Work*. RIBA.

Royal Institute of British Architects 1964 *Handbook of architectural practice and management*. RIBA.

Royal Institute of British Architects 1991 *Architect's handbook of practice management* (5th edition) edited by Cox, S.; Hamilton, A. RIBA.

Royal Institute of British Architects 1962 *The architect and his office*. RIBA.

Royal Institute of British Architects 1992 *Strategic study of the profession, phase 1: strategic overview*. RIBA.

Royal Institute of British Architects 1993 *Strategic study of the profession, phase 2: clients and architects*. RIBA.

Royal Institute of British Architects 1995 *Architect's job book* (sixth edition). RIBA.

Ryness, L.C. 1992 *Marketing and communication techniques for Architects*. Longman.

Saint, A. 1983 *The image of the architect*. Yale University Press.

Salisbury, F. 1990 *Architect's handbook for client briefing*. Butterworth Architecture.

Saunders, W.S. (ed.) 1996 *Reflections on architectural practices in the nineties*. Princeton Architectural Press.

Schneider, E. 1992 Segmenting a diverse profession, *Strategic study of the profession; phase 1*. RIBA.

Schneider, E.; Davies, H. 1995 Breaking out of the mould, *Architect's Journal*, 6 April, pp. 52–3.

Schon, D.A. 1983 *The reflective practitioner: how professionals think in action*. Basic Books.

Sharp, D. 1986 *The business of architectural practice*. Collins.

Sharp, D. 1991 *The business of architectural practice* (second edition). BSP Professional Books.

Shoemaker, P.J. 1991 *Gatekeeping*. Sage Publications.

Simister, S. J.; Green, S.D. 1997 Recurring themes in value management, *Engineering, Construction and Architectural Management*, June, 4:2, pp. 113–125.

Slavid, R. 1996 Getting to grips with quality, *Architect's Journal*, 25 January, pp. 50–6.

Smith, G.; Morris, T. 1992 Exploiting shifting boundaries, *Strategic study of the profession, phase 1*. RIBA.

Spence, W.R. 1994 *Innovation: the communication of change in ideas, practices and products*. Chapman & Hall.

Stamper, R. 1973 *Information: in business and administrative systems*. B.T. Batsford.

Stebbing, L. 1990 *Quality assurance: the route to efficiency and competitiveness* (second edition). Ellis Horwood.

Symes, M.; Eley, J.; Seidel, A.D. 1995 *Architects and their practices: a changing profession*. Butterworth Architecture.

Taylor, M.E. 1956 *Private architectural practice*. Leonard Hill.

Taylor, M.; Hosker, H.H. 1992 *Quality assurance for building design*. Longman Scientific & Technical.

Taylor, W.J.; Watling, T.F. 1970 *Successful project management*. Business Books.

Thornley D. G. 1963 Design method in architectural education, Jones, C.; Thornley, D.G. (eds.) *Conference on design methods*. Pergamon.

Tomkinson, M.; Gillard, M. 1980 *Nothing to declare: the political corruptions of John Poulson*. John Calder.

Turner, H.H. 1925 *Practice and procedure*. B.T. Batsford.

Turner, H.H. 1950 *Architectural practice and procedure* (fourth edition). B.T. Batsford.

Vale, R. 1994 Sustainable building: what does this really mean?, *The International Journal of Architectural Management, Practice and Research*, 8, pp. 77–81.

Walker, A. 1996 *Project management in construction* (third edition). Blackwell Science.

Weick, K. 1979, *The social psychology of organizing* (second edition). Addison-Wesley.

Westley, B.H.; MacLean, M.S. Jr. 1957 A conceptual model for communications research. *Journalism Quarterly*, 34, pp. 31–8.

White, D.M. 1950 The 'Gate keeper': a case study in the selection of news. *Journalism Quarterly*, 27, pp. 383–90.

Willis, A.J.; George, W.N.B. 1952 *The architect in practice*. Crosby Lockwood.

Wills, R.B. 1941 *This business of architecture*. Reinhold.

Winch, G.; Schneider, E. 1993 Managing the knowledge-based organisation: the case of architectural practice, *Journal of Management Studies*, 30:6, November, pp. 923–37.

World Commission on Environment and Development 1987 *Our common future (The Brundlandt Report)*. Oxford University Press.

Wulz, F. 1986. The concept of participation, *Design Studies*, 7:3, pp. 153–62.

Wyatt, D.P. 1995 Project and product management: the role of the architect, *International Journal of Architectural Management, Practice and Research*, 10, pp. 151–60.

Wyatt, D.P.; Emmitt, S. 1996 The product quality chain: myth or reality?, *International Journal of Architectural Management, Practice and Research*, 11, pp. 14–22.

Wyatt, D.P.; Emmitt, S. 1997 The products information network impediment, *International Journal of Architectural Management, Practice and Research*, 13, pp. 30–8.

Yoram, R. 1996 Varieties and issues of participation and design, *Design Studies*, 17, pp. 165–80.

INDEX